Braving a New World

1962-1988

Veronica's Adventures – Book II

VERONICA ESAGUI

Copyright © 2024 Veronica Esagui, DC

All rights reserved. No part of this book may be reproduced or transmitted in any form or by any means, electronic or mechanical, including photocopying, recording, or by any information storage and retrieval system, without permission in writing from the copyright owner. No patent liability is assumed with respect to the use of the information contained herein. Although every precaution has been taken in the preparation of this book, the publisher and author assume no responsibility for errors or omissions. Neither is any liability assumed for damages resulting from the use of the information contained herein.

Library of Congress Control Number: 2023924730

ISBN 978-0-9826484-9-0
Second Edition

Book Cover Design by James M. McCracken
Graphic Design by James M. McCracken

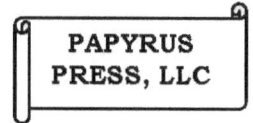

PAPYRUS
PRESS, LLC

West Linn, OR 97068

To order additional copies of this book
www.veronicaesagui.com
Printed in the United States of America.

*To Al and our sons, Ralph and Steve,
without whom, there would be no journey.*

Author's notes

The people and the stories portrayed in this book are all true as to my recollection when I began writing my diary in Portuguese, Saturday, April 26, 1986 in Howell, New Jersey. Upon translating my diary to English I have kept it as it was written, but I have changed some individuals' names to protect their privacy.

~Veronica Esagui

*Memories are the essence of existence,
and the gift of yesterday's choices.*

~ Veronica Esagui

CONTENTS

Chapter One	The American Way	1
Chapter Two	Ralph	32
Chapter Three	Steve	50
Chapter Four	Growing Up With My Sons	67
Chapter Five	Joining the Work Force	97
Chapter Six	At the Edge of Darkness	121
Chapter Seven	Mama	134
Chapter Eight	Papa	150
Chapter Nine	My Sons Are My World!	161
Chapter Ten	Valley Forge, No More	195
Chapter Eleven	The Pursuit of Happiness	208
Chapter Twelve	Music Business	264
Chapter Thirteen	The Journalist	293
Chapter Fourteen	The Producer	329

~ *Chapter One* ~

THE AMERICAN WAY

1962

Jamaica, Long Island
New York, USA

Spring of 1962

May 7th was my eighteenth birthday. On May 24th, I was married to Al, my cousin from America. On June 3rd, I hugged my parents and family for the last time, boarded the plane with my new husband, and saw Portugal, the country where I was born, fade away between the clouds below. The next day Al and I landed at the New York International Airport. Our pre-arranged marriage set up by his mother, Nelly, and my mother, Nelly's sister, had gone according to plan and everybody, including myself, was happy with the outcome. Luckily my plan to run away before he had arrived had failed. In the week we had been married I had learned to love him. He was handsome, kind, and very affectionate, and even though he was eleven years older than me, he did not look more than twenty-five.

    I was a little nervous yet eager to meet my North American family. Al's brother Joe, his fiancée Virginia, his sister Ruth, and Kim, her three-year-old daughter, waved

when they saw us coming into the terminal.
   Joe was a tad shorter than Al and had a body builder's look. When Joe was younger, he had won the title of second runner up in the Mr. America muscle competition. I never cared for muscle-bound men like Aunt Heydee's favorite Greek hero, Hercules. Joe was only three years older than Al, but his dark hair was thinning out, making him look a lot older. He spoke English slowly, and he made me laugh. I liked him.
   Virginia wore her curly reddish hair shoulder length and her face was covered with freckles, the reason I knew she was a true redhead. Virginia was very skinny and flat chested. I was surprised because I thought all North American women had big breasts. I imagined that when Virginia got older she would look like Rosa, the upstairs neighbor who lived on the second floor of our apartment in Lisbon, Portugal. Rosa was very skinny and had a dried-up look, probably because she was always in pain until the day the doctors took out her kidney stones which were as big as boiled chickpeas. I never saw the stones, but everybody else who knew Rosa spoke of their size. She proudly showed them to everyone but me, most likely because at that time I was only a child.
   Virginia had a strong nasal accent, the kind of North American accent my brothers and I used to have fun imitating by not moving our lips and letting the words come out slurred.
   Cousin Ruth's long, curly, dark brown hair complimented the bluest blue eyes I had ever seen. She was a lot prettier than her pictures and it amazed me to see how the mother of two children could have such a small waist. I had some difficulty understanding her because she spoke so softly, but her smile was enough to make me feel welcome. Al lifted Kim up in the air before hugging her and called her his little "baby doll."
   While in Portugal, Al had told me about Kim and how

beautiful she was—long blonde hair, a cute little button nose, and big blue eyes like her mom. He also told me how adorable Kim looked when she would fall asleep with her head on his shoulder whenever he was babysitting her for the evening. I attempted a few times falling asleep with my head on Al's shoulder when lying next to him but it gave me a stiff neck. Before I left Portugal, Mama warned me several times, "Watch out that nobody, not even a child, takes your place in your husband's heart." But I was not afraid of a baby stealing Al from me. Mama lived in Portugal and I was in North America. I was finally far, far away from her, and I looked forward to starting to live my own life, trusting people, and enjoying the freedom of making my own choices.

Joe drove us home from the airport. I was disappointed when we were dropped at the front door to our apartment building. Joe and Ruth told us that they did not want to disturb our honeymoon and promised to visit us when Nelly, their mother, also my mother's sister and now my mother-in-law, returned from Portugal. I wanted to tell them just because we were newlyweds; it did not mean that Al and I were having sex twenty-four hours a day without stopping.

Our address was 95-41 Stuphin Boulevard, Jamaica, New York. It was Nelly's one bedroom apartment and we would be living with her. Al told me that in the past, Nelly and Ralph, his father, used to sleep in the bedroom. Ruth and Mercedes, Ralph's mother, had slept in the adjacent room, which was part of the living room. But a thick, double-layer, wall-to-wall curtain gave them complete privacy from Al and Joe, who had slept on the other side of the thick curtain, where the television was and two couches opened into beds, one for each brother. I was amazed that one bedroom apartment was so well organized for five people at one time.

Joe no longer lived there, as he had his own place. Ruth, who had been married for four years, lived with her husband Bernie and their two children across town. Mercedes had died from colon cancer about seven years prior to my arrival. Ralph tried everything he knew as a pharmacist to save his mother. He even gave her daily shots of gold trying to induce the colon to get rid of the cancer, but it did not work, she died anyway. This was all very sad because Ralph died from pancreatic cancer two months before Kim, his first grandchild, was born.

When Nelly returned from Portugal, she would be sleeping in the room next to our bedroom. The thick curtain, which served as a wall from the other side of the living room, would continue to offer her the privacy of a "real" bedroom, but like Al said, I would have to tiptoe across her room if I wanted to go to the bathroom during the night.

I loved Nelly's kitchen. It wasn't very big but it was very modern, with a small, square, green, Formica-topped table set up against the wall, and four matching, green, metal chairs covered with see-through plastic seat covers. After eating, it was literally a step away to wash the dishes. I loved the idea that I did not have maids, like in Portugal. I was my own boss doing my own housework.

Al went to work at five in the morning. He was a nuclear engineer for the Bendix Cooperation in the state of New Jersey, where he inspected rockets before they went into space. When he got home at five in the afternoon, I had dinner ready. I tried to impress him with my culinary abilities but he did not eat much. For my first meal, I used the largest stew-pot I found under the kitchen sink and filled it with tomatoes, green peppers, and potatoes stuffed with ground beef. I could not believe the meat sold at the supermarket was already ground. It was delightful that I did not have to grind it like I used to do at home. Sometimes the grinder would get stuck with gristle and it had to be pulled apart and cleaned before finishing the rest of the meat. It was always a big mess.

Al came home and after we kissed he said, "Wow! What's that delicious smell coming from?" He walked to the stove and picked up the lid on the pot. "You made enough food to feed an army."

"Sorry, but I don't have much experience with measuring food just for two people."

"Don't worry, when Nelly comes back from Portugal, she'll teach you to cook for the three of us, and also to cook the food I like."

"What kind of food do you like?" Using a ladle, I served him a stuffed green pepper, a stuffed tomato, a stuffed potato and covered it with sauce and a few extra small pieces of potato, just in case he really liked it. I put on my plate a stuffed potato and a stuffed tomato, and sat across from him. I found it odd that he called his mother by her first name. Americans were so free of formalities, if I called my mother by her first name it would be considered very disrespectful.

"Nelly is a great cook," he said. "She does all kinds of stews with liver, kidneys, heart, and my favorite, tripe."

"Really?" I took a piece of potato and used the fork to mash it down into the sauce. It was delicious.

"Oh yes, and she also makes the best spaghetti in the world, with meatballs and tomato sauce."

The idea of tomato sauce and meatballs on top of spaghetti made it as repugnant as cooking with animal guts. The recollection of Mama boiling spaghetti with chunks of meat made me queasy.

I was disappointed when he barely finished the stuffed potato and said he was full. I did not finish the food on my plate either. I didn't want him to think I was a hog.

One Saturday night, Al took me to downtown Jamaica, to the famous Lowe's Valencia movie theatre where actors used to perform vaudeville-type entertainment before they went on to become famous in Hollywood.

It smelled like mold inside the theatre. I had a sneezing fit. My shoes were sticking to the floor as I walked between the seats. Trying not to step on the popcorn and sticky soda covering the floors was a challenge. In Portugal, if anybody threw their trash on the floor, the usher would call the police and the slob would be given a fine after being expelled from the theatre, while being booed by the audience. I did admire the exquisite architecture inside the theatre; it reminded me of an old Moorish castle beaten up by the hands of time.

We watched Disney's *101 Dalmatians*. It was my first North American movie without Portuguese subtitles and I did pretty good understanding what they were saying. After the movie, we went to an ice cream parlor and it was a good thing that Al advised me to pick only three flavors. He said seven balls of ice cream would be impossible for me to eat.

In North America, they did not make one scoop out of all the flavors you liked; it was one huge scoop for each flavor. Al ordered an American treat for me: a banana split! I was very excited, until I tried it. "It tastes like ladybugs." I spit the cherry into the paper napkin.

"I never heard anything like that. How do you know what ladybugs taste like?" he said.

"When I was a child I used to play with them in my backyard. One day I put my fingers in my mouth after holding a few in my hands." I lowered my voice. "I used to bite my nails. That's how I know what they taste like, it's a horrible taste." To Al's dismay, I only ate the banana, and the walnuts.

The main street in Jamaica had a train track that ran above our heads. When the train was running, the fumes and dirt made me sneeze, and the small particles of dirt got into my eyes; one of the reasons I was glad to use eyeglasses, not only to see better, but also for protection.

Mama and Aunt Heydee, Mama's older sister would have been disturbed to know that I wore my eyeglasses since I had arrived to North America. It didn't matter to them that I was married, if anything they believed my marriage was in jeopardy because wearing glasses made me defective and no man was turned on by a defective wife. Luckily Al liked me in eyeglasses and took me to an optometrist to buy an extra pair. I tried several frames and posed with my head cocked to the side whenever possible. "You look sexy in glasses." He kissed me. Our frames clicked against each other. We laughed.

Jamaica was a dirty city. People threw their garbage all over the sidewalks. Not at all like in Lisbon where everyone was proud to keep the streets clean.

I missed the bright colors of Lisbon's houses and the sight of flowers hanging on the windowsills along with the singing crickets in their little wooden cages. Crickets brought good luck to their owners and their chirping made everyone sleep better at night during the summer months. A lot of the houses in Jamaica were made with bricks and had a dark, heavy appearance. I asked Al why they did not paint the bricks. He said, "Brick houses are very expensive, and using bricks to build your house is a sign of wealth. It would be dumb to cover them with paint after paying a fortune for them."

I also learned I should not say that I lived in North America. Al said, "Only ignorant foreigners talk like that. You live in America."

"Oh, okay. From now on I say America."

Being an American and having lived all his life in America didn't make him an expert in geography. I had been taught in school that there two Americas, North and South America. Mama had told me many times, "Never correct your husband, if you want to be happy."

Every day I prided myself in making something new for dinner. One day I made empadão, and Al said that in America it was called "Shepherd's Pie." He said he liked it, but barely ate any of it. Later in the evening he ate a half a gallon of vanilla ice cream while we watched television.

He only enjoyed eating ice cream, cake, candy, and five or six slices of white bread with chunks of margarine in between each layer.

I tried the American white bread, but it stuck to the roof of my mouth; and besides, it had no taste! I missed my Portuguese bread, crunchy on the outside and soft on the inside. Neither butter nor margarine was required to enrich the delicious taste.

One Sunday, Al made peanut butter sandwiches for lunch. I refused to even try it. Butter made from peanuts, glued down on American white bread! I had never heard of anything so gross! I said, "In Portugal you eat peanuts right from the shell—that's the way we do it over there. I also ate them at the zoo. I enjoyed sharing them with the little monkeys who slipped between the metal railings of their cages and came up to passersby to beg for their treats. They were so adorable."

"In America the monkeys in the zoo are kept in their cages, where they belong."

"That's horrible. What kind of a zoo is that?"

"I didn't know you liked zoos. I'll take you to the Bronx Zoo one of these days. That's the best zoo in the world."

I did not ask if the monkeys were free to roam around; I already knew the answer and had no desire to go.

While Al was at work I watched cartoons on television when not ironing, cooking, or cleaning the apartment. My favorites were the Roadrunner and Bugs Bunny. I loved it when Bugs Bunny would come out of the hole in the ground chewing on a carrot and say, "What's up, Doc?" I immediately knew that he was up to mischief.

Braving A New World

Al only liked to watch police stories.

Some of the stores in America were called department stores—probably because they had lots and lots of departments. The main street in Jamaica had lots of department stores.

The grocery stores were so humongous they were called *super*markets. They had everything one could wish for, and not just one of a kind. Aunt Simy, who lived in Portugal, would have fainted if she saw how many different jams were available at our local supermarket. I also found a large variety of vegetables inside metal cans, already cooked. In America an electric can opener was an essential kitchen appliance.

Al bought several jars of grape jam and grape jelly so I could taste the difference. But when it came to grapes, I only liked them fresh.

My favorite American foods were steaks, hot dogs, and hamburgers. Al did not like fish, which was a great relief for me. Our staple food while growing up in Portugal had been bacalhau, a dried, salty codfish that needed to soak in cold water for twenty-four hours and the water had to be changed at least five to six times before the codfish could be used for cooking. There were at least a hundred Portuguese recipes on how to cook bacalhau and I had them all. Thank God that Al was a meat-and-potatoes man.

My lunch, when Al was at work, was Campbell's chicken noodle soup. With the help of an electric can opener, zip zap and there it was—tasty, yummy canned soup. It even beat Papa's favorite, German asparagus instant powder soup.

Al took me to the famous Macy's department store in Jamaica. I could not get over that instead of elevators or steps; they had escalators taking people up and down to different floors. Al let me take the escalator all the way to the top floor. Each level was full of all kinds of house commodities and clothing, and lots and lots of things to buy. Going from one floor to another was a lot of fun.

He promised that someday he would take me to Macy's in New York City, which was a lot bigger.

Before I left Portugal, Mama said, "In North America everybody is blond, and you will be a minority as a white girl with dark hair. Al will have to watch out; every man is going to fall in love with your exotic look." I wrote, "Mama, you're not going to believe this, not everybody is blonde and where I live, the majority of Americans are black. It's like being in Africa. It's very exciting. You know the stupid Portuguese belief that seeing a black person in the street brings good luck? Well, if that's true, I'll have good luck for thousands of years to come."

I wouldn't be able to read her response to my news report for at least a week and a half, that's how long it took for the mail to get overseas and back. Sometimes it even got lost, like the time I sent some homemade cookies from Portugal to America and Al got them five months later. He threw them out.

One morning Al told me to look inside the closet in our bedroom. A golden mink stole was hanging from a coat hanger. I did not want to hurt his feelings by telling him that I did not like fur. It reminded me of Aunt Simy who lived inside a mink coat, hibernating like a bear during the winter months.

I covered my disappointment with a polite smile and said, "That's nice. Thank you." I closed the closet.

"Well, aren't you even going to try it?"

I modeled it around the bedroom and hoped he would not ask me to wear it again.

Every few days Al gave me money. But I had everything I could possibly wish for. I put the money in the bottom dresser drawer and decided to wait until it was full, and then give him the money back as a present. Mama would never approve of that. In her opinion a woman should keep as much money as possible hidden from the husband in case she became destitute.

One morning, I took two hundred dollars from my stash and ventured out of our apartment all by myself. I was worried that I would get lost, so I paid careful attention to the street names and made myself a little map by writing where I had crossed. Not too far from where we lived I found a men's clothing store. A beautiful, cream-colored cotton shirt with an embroidered front pocket and embroidered design around the buttons caught my eye.

Al eagerly opened the wrapped gift box. He pulled the shirt out and frowned. "Only Puerto Ricans wear this kind of shirt."

"Is that bad?"

"I'm not Puerto Rican."

I was very surprised when the store exchanged the shirt. In Portugal there was no such thing as returning merchandise. Once you bought it, it was yours.

"I wish I could try a bubble bath just like Doris Day in the movie *Pillow Talk*," I said to Al one Saturday morning. We went to the supermarket and he bought a bottle of bubble soap. After we got home, he poured some of the soap in the tub and opened the water faucet. Mounds of foam started to form almost instantly. I slid into the warm fragrant lavender foam and waited, hoping to see a stream of dancers enter the bathroom dancing and singing around the tub, just like in the Hollywood movies.

Al brought me a glass of cherry soda to sip on. "I'm sorry, but I really don't like soda. Can I have water instead?" He brought me a glass of water with ice. Al had remarked several times that I was strange since I did not like ice in my drinks. I felt it was better not to say anything about the ice and forced myself to drink almost half a glass.

Al did not like bubble baths; he preferred to take showers. He waited until I had enough of the bubble bath and then we took a shower together. Afterward we sat on the floor in front of the television and played like children, tickling each other and laughing about nothing. I could not have been happier with my life.

The next morning I woke up with cramps; my period had started. I put one of the small towels I had brought from Portugal for that purpose, inside my underwear, but by the time Al came home from work, I needed to change it. I felt a little embarrassed but had to ask. "I need a metal bucket. Can we go to the supermarket to get one?"

"Metal bucket?"

I muttered, "It's that time of the month." I couldn't look straight at him, I said a little louder, "I need one."

"For what?"

"You know...so I can soak the towels in cold water to get the blood out."

"The blood? Oh, you mean you're menstruating. So why a bucket? Don't tell me that you wash them."

"Yes, how else can I use them again?" I couldn't understand his difficulty.

He shook his head in disbelief. "Are you kidding me?"

"Yes...I mean no, not kidding. That's how it's done in Portugal. I brought twelve small towels with me and..."

"I never heard of anything so barbaric. Here in America women use Kotex pads. After using them they get thrown into the trash. Let's go to the supermarket immediately."

No more walking around with heavy bulky towels held with safety pins like a diaper inside my underwear, and best of all, no more washing them! Kotex pads! They were the most incredible invention since chewing gum.

Nelly was due to arrive from Portugal on Monday. I could not wait to see her. I had learned a lot about America and how to be an American, but the days were long and lonely while Al was at work. I was afraid to go out by myself. Al had me scared on account of being unable to defend myself if I got attacked by criminals on the street.

Summer of 1962

It was wonderful to have a friend and Nelly and I had a lot to talk about, mostly in Portuguese and Spanish. My English was not as good as I thought when I lived in Portugal. But Al did not mind the way I spoke; he said it was cute. Nelly began teaching me how to cook her way, which was the way Al was used to eating since he was a child. She also showed me how to properly clean the kitchen floor. Before she arrived, I had been mixing wax with detergent to clean the kitchen and bathroom floor. No wonder it was so slippery. Nelly was very patient with me. She was also fun and very affectionate. She was a very beautiful lady for her age, I never saw her without make-up and her hair was always perfectly combed. She took very good care of herself.

We went out every day, shopping for groceries and clothes. She had gained weight while in Portugal and she gave me some of her silky underwear. I was very grateful for that but when I told Al about it, he said I should not be wearing his mother's old underwear and he took me shopping.

I could not believe my luck. Al bought me a dozen pieces of the silky, movie star type of underwear in different colors. He also bought me perfumed body powder to use after I took a shower. The first time I used it I put it all over my body, including my face and hands. Nelly laughed when I came out of the bathroom. "You're not supposed to use the body powder all over your face like that," she said. "You only use it under your breasts and a little down there." She pointed to between her legs.

Little by little I was learning to be a real American. Al explained that in America, "Ronnie," the nickname for Verónica, was a lot more appropriate because it was shorter and easier to say.

I wrote to Mama about my new name. I got a letter from Papa, "Daughter, I'm very sad and hurt. I want to know what possessed you to change your name Veronica to a horrible name like Ronnie, which has the same sound as *ranhosa*, snotty nose, in Portuguese. Are you ashamed of your name? I want to know why you are ashamed of the name my mother gave you at birth."

I wrote back explaining that in America nobody was called by the name they were born with, especially if it was too long, like mine. Nicknames were used a lot because everybody was in a hurry, and using extra-long words was a waste of everybody's time. Al and Nelly also told me that I had to make my name shorter because it was a pain in the neck to wait until I was finished signing my whole name. When I became an American citizen I would have the opportunity to change from Verónica Leah Toledano Ezaguy Wartenberg Esagui to a more sensible name like Veronica Esagui. I was not going to tell that to my parents. Without Wartenberg in my name, they would most likely freak out; principally Papa.

Gradually I got to know more people in our building. As I did, it became very hard to get used to waking up in the middle of the night hearing Sasha, the neighbor's daughter, crying out as she was getting beaten by her date in the hallway downstairs. Her mother, Mrs. Romanoff, was either sleeping or she was deaf because we could hear Sasha's body being thrown into the walls as she yelled, "But I love you, but I love you. Stop hitting me. I love you."

The first time it happened, I told Al we should go downstairs and rescue her or call the police. But Al said,

"Don't pay attention. It's her choice to date men that beat her. She must like it."

I did not agree. If Sasha liked it, she would be saying, "More! Hit me more!"

I was no psychologist but nobody likes to get beaten. The poor thing, she was nothing but a victim of love and he was a bad man. If I was a man I would go downstairs and beat him just to see how he liked the same treatment. Of course, I did not share those thoughts with Al. He was my husband and it would be disrespectful to contradict his opinion; besides, he was older than me and he knew more about life than I did. When we went out I always looked at the downstairs walls and was surprised not to see any bloodstains, possibly from Sasha's head.

I had seen Sasha a few times in the hallway as she waved goodbye to her mother. Mrs. Romanoff was a bit heavy which made it hard for her to stand for too long; she used a cane for support. Sasha was almost as hefty as her mom, probably the reason why it was so noisy when she got punched against the walls downstairs. Both women were very polite and they always said hello when we saw each other in the hallway.

Nelly told me they were low-class Russian Jews and we were not to socialize with them. I felt sorry for Sasha. She could not be much older than me. I would have loved to have had a friend my own age.

Nelly reminded me several times, "You are very fortunate to have me as your mother-in-law." She had not been as lucky as me when she came to America. It did not matter how nice she was to Mercedes, her mother-in-law liked to argue and was a very demanding woman. Nothing was ever good enough. Nelly never complained to her husband about the daily sacrifices she had to make while putting up with his mother who lived with them for thirty long years. "When Mercedes got sick with terminal cancer, I took care of her," she said. "I didn't have the heart to tell my husband to put his mother in a home. I treated her as if she was my own mother. At the end of her life, I used to carry her on my back to the bathroom, because she was too weak to walk and every day I gave her sponge baths in bed. I took care of her day and night until she passed away peacefully in this apartment." I was impressed with the sacrifices she had made toward someone so mean. I hugged her and gave her a kiss on the cheek and said with admiration "You are truly an angel of kindness.

Al's brother Joe and Ginny tied the knot the following month. Her name was Virginia but everyone called her Ginny. It was a great nickname, it sounded like genie. Before the wedding Nelly told me she was not completely happy with Joe's choice because Ginny was not only older than him, but she also had a nine-year-old daughter from a previous marriage. But at the wedding, Nelly admitted that Ginny would be a good influence on Joe. Ginny's parents were German, so consequently Ginny was very clean and an exceptionally good cook.

"Ginny will be a good homemaker and keep Joe straight," she said. "He used to be a wild young man. He ran around a lot but he was also very smart. He fooled around only with married women so he would not catch a venereal disease. He even had an affair with an Indian Chief's wife Her husband came home one day just as Joe was leaving the back-way." She laughed.

"He was lucky he didn't get caught," I laughed. "He could have wound up with a tomahawk in his head."

"I know." She got a serious look on her face "My husband Ralph was a very good father and never hit his children except once when he slapped Joe after catching him playing dice with some street boys. Only derelicts play dice in the streets." She made a deep, audible sigh. "Joe was always in trouble. He was a troublemaker, but Al and Ruth were my perfect children."

I got a feeling that Joe was her least favorite child.

One morning while having our breakfast in the kitchen Nelly showed me a picture of Lorraine, Al's girlfriend before he asked me to marry him. I wondered why she had kept the picture and why was she showing it to me. I covered my feelings of jealously by saying, "She's so beautiful. Why didn't he marry her? What happened?"

"She was gorgeous," Nelly said. "But she was also a slut, trying to seduce him every time they went out. Of course he got tired of her being all over him. I told him if she did it with him, she most likely was doing the same with all the other men she dated. Thank God he listened to me. I knew you were the one for him. I used to have one of your baby pictures on my bedroom wall and every morning when I got up, your smile made my day."

I was so lucky to have smiled in that picture. I was also lucky to be living in America. I had not seen any cowboys or Indians or movie stars yet, but I did not mind— living with Nelly and Al was all I needed to be happy.

I did not know anything about driving, but I could tell that Al was not a good driver because he swerved all over the road. He got a lot of traffic tickets, mostly for driving at night without the headlights on or for not driving straight on the road. One day he made a turn too quickly and had to jam on the breaks and Kim, who was sitting on my lap in the passenger seat, went flying into the windshield and bruised her forehead. But I didn't care how bad Al drove, because I was happy. I even cried from happiness one evening when we went out for a drive. He asked me if I was crying because I missed my family in Portugal. I lied by saying yes, but I rapidly added the truth by telling him that I was also crying with happiness from being in America with him and Nelly. Then I thought to myself, *and because I'm no longer treated like a child.*

Over the weekend we had a family get together in our apartment. Al was sitting next to me on the couch and as always, very lovingly holding my hands, when suddenly he whispered in my ear to follow him. He took me to our bedroom and locked the door. He wanted sex!

I tried reasoning with him, "We have company; this is not the right time." I tried pushing him gently away from me and pleaded, "They'll know what we're doing."

But he would not listen to me. He was my husband and as such I had no rights to say no. I did not enjoy it, that's for sure. When we came out of the bedroom, they were all gone.

"My goodness that was so rude!" said Nelly. "They were here visiting you and Ronnie. They were your guests, and you both got up and went into your bedroom like rabbits!" Nelly was right to be upset.

Al shrugged. "If they don't like it, it's their problem."

I could have died of shame.

Al kept his promise that we would have a second honeymoon because the one we had in Portugal had been too short. Before we went to the Pocono Mountains Resort, Al asked me if I minded Nelly coming with us. He was concerned with her heart and leaving her home alone for the weekend. I agreed to take her with us whole-heartedly; besides, she would have her own room. I knew it would be fun; the three of us together like the three Musketeers.

I found out on the first night at the Pocono Mountains Resort that all those times I went to dancehalls with Aunt Heydee had been a waste of time. I still could not dance the Cha-cha. I stepped all over Al's feet and felt spastic. I did a lot better dancing free-style to rock and roll music, and the newest dance, the Twist. I used to have a hula-hoop when I was living in Portugal and was very accomplished with torso twisting.

For breakfast I had pancakes for the first time. Al

showed me how to eat them; one pancake, lots of butter and syrup, another pancake on top, and another layer of butter and syrup. I did not like the American breakfast. So much butter and syrup made me sick to my stomach. I never did well with grease, oil, or fats, or in this case, flat cakes covered with butter and syrup.

That evening Al did not want to participate in the square dancing and encouraged me to dance on my own. It was fun following the directions where to go, changing partners, and soon I found myself dancing with a boy about my age. He asked my name and if I wanted to go outside to talk.

I told him, "Sorry, but I can't. I'm with my husband on our honeymoon."

He laughed. I pointed to Al sitting next to Nelly. "That's him, over there next to his mother." Al waved back at us and the boy got red in the face and I quickly lost sight of him in the crowd. When I sat next to Al, I did not know how to explain how I felt, except that for a fleeting moment I was conscious of my young age and having missed a time in my life where I should have had the opportunity to date a boy like the one I had just met. Instead, I had gone from my parents' nest to being a married woman. But I pushed aside any further thoughts, because I loved Al, I loved Nelly, and I loved everything about America.

It was a wonderful weekend of honeymooning, kissing, hugging, sex, swimming, horseback riding, eating, laughing, and having a good time; like cowboys at the big ranch in the Pocono Mountains of New York.

When Al told me that he was going to teach me to drive I was very excited and happy. But my joy was soon gone when we got into his car and he said, "Go ahead, drive."

"I never drove a car before, what do I do?"

"It's easy, just turn the key and keep your right foot on the brakes." He pointed to a pedal.

"Okay, I think I got it. Then what?"

"Then put your left foot on the other pedal when you want to change gears, and use the right hand to move the stick shift."

I had no idea what he was talking about. I turned the key and prayed for the best.

He raised his voice, "Use the brakes to stop! What's the matter with you?"

He yelled at me every time I put the car into the wrong gear. He called me stupid, over and over again. It was hard to turn the wheel. He called me a weakling. I started to cry and he said, "It's for your own good. If I don't yell, you'll never learn to drive."

I refused to talk to him afterward. He kept asking me what was wrong and why I was angry with him. I had no intention of telling him. He should know that he hurt my feelings and apologize without me telling him why, otherwise he would say he was sorry only to make me happy.

Autumn of 1962

Al had to take me to the dentist because I had a toothache. The dentist gave me an injection in my jaw and said the shot would help control the pain during the drilling. Not only did the shot hurt, but my heart sped up and I could not breathe. I thought I was going to die.

The dentist said I was allergic to the anesthetic and I should only have Novocain from then on.

In Portugal they drilled or pull the teeth without any injections. I liked that a lot better. When I used to go to the dentist in Portugal, I would concentrate on being somewhere else more pleasant, like in space, and I was able to distract myself from the pain of drilling.

"I had a lot of practice as a kid," I told Dr. Swan. "They drilled every single tooth in my mouth for cavities when I was about 12 years old. As a matter of a fact, except for the annoying drilling sound, I felt no pain while the Portuguese dentist was drilling my teeth."

Dr. Swan laughed. "There's no way you can put pain aside while being drilled for a cavity. You're a masochist."

Cousin Ruth visited us almost every day. One morning, she caught me ironing. "Why are you ironing?" she asked.

"Everything is wrinkled..."

"That's a waste of your time. When you take the clothes out of the dryer, all you have to do is stretch them out with your hands, until they're smooth."

"Veronica is being a good wife," Nelly said. "Don't go teaching her bad habits. You're putting the wrong ideas into her head."

"Mom, this is ridiculous. She can be a good wife without being a slave. No one irons bedsheets, towels, or socks anymore. Those days are gone forever." She winked at me. "Veronica, the next time I go to the laundromat I'm taking you with me." She sat at the kitchen table, looked at me almost apologetically, and said, "I've been meaning to tell you that parting your hair to the side has gone out with the days of Veronica Lake. Would you like me to try and make your hair style a little more up-to-date?"

"Yes, please," I begged.

She asked Nelly for a pair of scissors and had me sit on a chair in the kitchen. She cut a few loose bangs on my forehead and then teased and puffed my hair up like a hill, high on top of my head, and she sprayed it with a glue type of spray that made me cough when I inhaled the fumes. It was called hairspray and she carried it in her large purse. I was very happy when I looked in the bathroom mirror—I looked very American. Before she left, she gave me her personal can of hairspray as a present.

The more food we bought, the more S&H stamps they gave us at the supermarket, and the more choices we had from the merchandise catalog. All we had to do was buy their groceries which we were going to buy anyway. The whole thing was amazing—something unheard of in my country.

It was hard to believe that American storeowners were so rich they could afford to give away such expensive gifts. It was difficult to decide which we needed the most; a hamper for dirty laundry, a scale so we could weigh ourselves every morning in the bathroom, or a modern, hanging lamp for the living room. We settled for the hanging lamp, a green round glass ball with chains that could be used to hang from the ceiling above the couch in the living room.

Ruth took me out shopping for makeup. She showed me how to use eyeliner and eye shadow, and said I should use an overall facial cream and a touch of pink powder on my pale cheeks. I did not want to hurt her feelings, so I did not tell her that I did not like makeup, only lipstick. Ruth was doing her best to make me Americanized. Ruth was the sister I had always wished for. She was ten years older than me but she was young at heart.

Nelly and I were seated alone in the kitchen having tuna sandwiches for lunch when she poured her aching heart out to me. "Ruth is married to a good-for-nothing alcoholic. When she was eight months pregnant with Kim, he would stay home drinking while she went shopping for groceries, and when she would ask for help carrying the groceries up the stairs to their apartment on the third floor, he would yell down at her, 'What are you, an invalid? Bring them up yourself. I'm busy.' And he would sit in front of the television watching a game and drinking beer. I cried the day my daughter married that bum."

On the first trip to the laundromat, Ruth confided that getting married to Bernie had been the only way to get out of her parents' house. "They were very strict and everyone I chose to go out with on a date was scrutinized," she said. "Finally I gave up, and when Bernie asked me to marry him, it was my way to freedom." Cousin Ruth was not happily married and that made me sad.

Whenever we went out, Al's head turned like a spinning wheel every time a girl walked by. That was very confusing to me. Did he love me or not? If I ever started looking at other men it would mean I did not love him anymore. I was no movie star or model, but I was nice to look at and had been compared to Sophia Loren several times. I tried to come to terms with my feelings, and after analyzing my situation calmly for a couple of days, I decided to recall Grandma Rica's famous words of wisdom, "The day my husband stops looking at other women is the day he'll not appreciate female beauty, and in that case, I'll be the one to lose."

When Grandma Rica went out with Grandpa Leão and a beautiful woman walked by, she would say, "Leão, my love. Did you notice that woman's gorgeous eyes?" or "Have you ever seen anything so magnificent as her hair?"

Grandpa Leão would always turn to his wife with loving eyes and say, "Yes, she's beautiful, but Rica you're the most beautiful to me."

True or not, it reinforced that he appreciated her more than anyone else. I could not wait to test Grandma Rica's wisdom the next time we went out.

Nelly was cooking tripe one afternoon and Al had to take me out of the apartment for a breath of fresh air because I felt like I was going to throw up from the smell.

When we got back she said, "I bet your wife is pregnant. You better take her to see Dr. Smart."

"I can't be pregnant!" I cried out with a mixture of disbelief and unexplainable fear. "That's impossible." Yes, we were having sex and Al had used a rubber once for birth control but then he said it was a pain in the neck and besides he was looking forward to having children. I wanted a baby too but didn't expect it to happen so fast, just like that. I was hoping Nelly was wrong.

Dr. Smart said I was definitely pregnant! He was the one who delivered Ruth's children and according to her, Dr. Smart was a very good doctor. I could only hope he would live up to his name and be able to make the birth process as easy as possible. I didn't ask any questions. He was a man, and I was too embarrassed to speak my mind. Nelly was ecstatic about becoming a grandmother again and she couldn't stop kissing and hugging me. When we took the bus home, we sat next to each other and she held my hands. "Veronica," she was glowing with happiness. "I want my grandson to be named Ralph, after my husband." She kissed me on both cheeks.

"How do you know it's going to be a boy?"

"Of course it's going to be a boy. Both Al and I expect it."

I was more concerned with other aspects of the pregnancy. "How is the baby going to grow in here," I pointed to my belly. "And then come out of my vagina? The head is going to get stuck and we'll both die." I was not joking.

"You're being silly," she laughed. "I had three children. It's no big deal." Of course it wasn't a big deal for her; she had a round large belly perfect for growing babies. When Ruth came over that afternoon I made the same question.

She said, "It's amazing that's all I can say, Ronnie. Your belly will stretch out to make room for the baby. Here, let me show you what happens to the skin." She lowered her jeans just enough to show me the stretch marks. It was an ugly sight. Then she said, "And when it comes to the vagina, don't worry, it will expand big enough to allow the baby to come out." She brought the palms of her hands together as if she was going to pray and then keeping her finger tips touching she moved the palms away slowly creating an unmistaken vagina opening up.

"Oh my God!" I cringed and tightened my jaw in despair. The whole thing sounded brutally inhuman. "Does it ever go back to its normal size?" I repeated, "Does it?"

"Oh yeah, right after the baby slides out, it closes again."

"It must hurt like hell when it's opening."

"The pain you'll feel doesn't come from down there it comes from the contractions that are helping the baby to come out."

"What shall I do to get prepared for giving birth?"

"Except for taking vitamins and eating healthy," she said. "There's no real preparation. Every woman has a slightly different experience. Kim was a joy, after the first contraction she was out in half an hour, but with Tom it took me four intensive hours of labor."

"Labor? I don't understand the word."

"Yes, I know the English language is not perfect but when it comes to describing the pre-delivery time it is the perfect word for it. Later on when you hold your baby in your arms, you'll forget what you went through. I promise."

Al was thrilled with the news of becoming a father, and like Nelly couldn't stop kissing and hugging me. I was very happy too, scared but happy.

Ruth was my best friend, a sister of the heart, and every time she came over I had plenty of questions. She took away my fears, and I began to enjoy the prospect of being a mother.

Once a month I visited Dr. Smart. He used a stethoscope against my belly to listen for signs of life and I was always told that everything was going along fine.

On weekends when Al was off work, the three of us traveled to New Jersey to look for a house to buy. Al felt our apartment was too small and we needed a real home since we were going to have many little monkeys, as he called our future children. "New Jersey is our best bet," he said. "We will live in the countryside where it's safer and the air is not polluted. And I'll be close to Bendix, where I work."

Al asked me if I minded taking Nelly to live with us. He had to be kidding; of course she was welcome to be with us; I loved Nelly. She was his mother, my aunt, and my very best friend besides Ruth.

It was late one Sunday and we were heading back to Long Island after looking all day for a house in New Jersey, when a miracle happened. I noticed a large sign on the road, "New homes for sale, $17,500 each." There it was, our dream house; a brand new, split-level model home in the Winnfield Development in Freehold, New Jersey. We walked through one of the model homes and agreed that it was the most attractive modern style house we had ever seen and the price was not too high. Right then and there Nelly lent Al $500 for the deposit. We chose a corner lot where our home was to be built. They told us it would be ready April of next year.

I learned that Al would be paying the bank a fixed monthly fee for many, many years. It was called a mortgage. The banks lent the money to buy things, and then we paid the bank back through monthly payments with interest added every month. With a bank loan almost anybody could buy what their heart desired; like cars, houses, appliances, clothes, and so on. "It's the American way. Everybody does it," Al said. "There's no reason to wait to own anything when we have good credit." I told them I would never buy anything on credit. They laughed and said what I was saying made no sense.

Winter ending 1962

Nelly had boxes and boxes of beautiful Christmas ornaments in storage. A tall green plastic tree was placed in the corner of the living room between the two couches, and we covered the whole tree with silvery tinsel, colorful bright lights, and all kinds of unique ornaments. I had never done anything like that in my life and I found it very entertaining to make a tree so festive Nelly covered the floor underneath the tree with a red mantle cloth.

I could not let my parents know we celebrated Christmas! One of the reasons Mama had arranged for my marriage to Al was so that my children would grow up in a Jewish home celebrating the traditional Jewish holidays.

Al and Nelly explained that Christmas and Easter were too much fun to miss and had nothing to do with their religious beliefs. They did not follow any specific religion. On the other hand, once a year they did enjoy celebrating Passover at home, a traditional and festive Jewish holiday. But that was as far as they went. They preferred to keep our faith a secret, because in America there was a lot of discrimination.

"When you go to the hospital to have our baby," Al said. "They are going to ask your religion."

"Yeah," Nelly interrupted him, and added quickly. "You tell them you are Protestant."

"Why, do I have to lie?"

"You'll be safer that way, that's why." It did not take much to convince me. I still remembered how I felt as a child when I was told I had killed Christ and was persecuted by my schoolmates. When Nelly's husband could not get a job as a pharmacist they become aware of prejudice. Al said, "Dad had to lie on his application. He wrote he was Protestant and got hired immediately." Then there was the story of Al being in Korea, and Gisela the neighbor next door. Gisela, who was their closest friend for twenty years—used to send Al a care package every two months until one day Nelly made the unfortunate mistake of telling her they were Jewish. Gisela stopped talking to them. "Our neighbor is German, so what do you expect? She obviously sympathized with Hitler," reaffirmed Nelly.

I didn't say anything, but my feeling was that the woman was angry with them because they had lied to her all those years.

For Christmas dinner, Nelly prepared a turkey stuffed with chestnuts, baked potatoes, and all kinds of delicious salads. I was used to eating plain, roasted chestnuts in Portugal and the idea of putting them inside a turkey was very unappealing to me. But I changed my mind when she gave me a spoon filled with the delicious stuffing. I was very happy that I no longer felt nauseous at the sight or smell of food. I still could not eat animal guts but Christmas dinner was a gastronomic experience for me and most likely my baby enjoyed it too. I was told that babies received their nourishment from what their mommies ate. I was sure my baby was very happy with my dinner.

Christmas was a very peculiar holiday in America. It was all about exchanging expensive gifts. There was no religious feeling as in Portugal where one celebrated the birth of Christ with the Nativity under the Christmas tree, and the presents were mostly handmade items like a wool scarf or hat, and some goodies like candy, which got hidden inside the shoes left by the Christmas tree. The children in Portugal got toys or special gifts, not the adults. In America it was more like everybody was celebrating their own birthday but I could not complain about it. I saw a lot of wrapped gifts under the tree and my name was on many of them. It was also a lot of fun shopping with Nelly for Christmas gifts for the whole family.

After Christmas, Nelly still wanted to go out every day. She loved to shop at department stores. I carried a large purse full of fresh fruit. They were my breakfast, lunch, and snacks until dinnertime when I had a fresh salad and more fruit. Nelly told me that pregnancy was known to cause weird cravings. Some women like pickles with ice cream, and others went as far as craving odd things, like dirt. Nelly said my cravings were normal to have. But I did not believe I was having a pregnancy craving. The reason I enjoyed eating fruit and vegetables was that I had always loved them. Pregnancy was just an excuse to enjoy those treats wholeheartedly. While growing up, I did not have such lavish expensive food items at home. We could not afford them.

Winter of 1963

Al bought me a maternity outfit. It was very expensive and I only wore it when we went out. It was made of soft cotton and it was dark blue. The skirt had a stretchy material on the belly area. I would be able to use it even when I became huge at nine months. I chose that outfit because it had a white collar and white cuffs. When I wore it, I felt like a pregnant Audrey Hepburn, my favorite actress.

My lower back was hurting a lot when I walked, and I had to sit often. Sometimes I did not go inside the stores with Nelly. I sat cross-legged on the sidewalk and watched the people going by. When Nelly came out of the store I had to have help getting up. She loved shopping. I went with her for the pleasure of her company and because I did not want to stay home alone.

Al and I switched rooms with Nelly so I could get to the bathroom faster during the night. The baby was getting bigger every day and most likely sitting on top of my bladder.

There was nothing worse than being pregnant and suffering with a cold. It was snowing and I had been left at home. Al had taken Nelly to our favorite supermarket to buy food for the week, which meant more S&H stamps. I took it upon myself to call Dr. Smart's office, and the nurse said nothing could be done about my cold and I was to remain indoors and keep warm. I felt horrible. It did not feel like the common cold. I was sure that I was suffering from some rare disease from Africa. Besides, my belly button was sticking out and the belly could not stretch any more. I was afraid I was going to burst every time I sneezed.

To celebrate my recovery from the cold, they took me to a Chinese restaurant. That was my first experience eating Chinese food. I didn't care for the shrimp and vegetables in the gummy sauce, the fluffy fried rice was very tasty but the long smooth noodles on the side smelled burned. The Chinese people serving us dinner were very petite. Inside the restaurant it was dark and smelled like old wood fried in oil, most likely the way it was in their country. Someday I would visit China, where Marco Polo once traveled. In Portugal, everybody was Portuguese except for a few foreign tourists during the summer months. In America, everybody was foreign, everything was new and exciting. I loved America!

Dr. Smart was appalled at my fruit eating. He said it was too much fruit and I was going to get fat if I kept gorging myself. I was too embarrassed to explain that I did not eat all the fruit myself. When Nelly and I went out, I took double of everything because Nelly also liked fruit, so she ate half of the fruit I carried. Then to top it off, Dr. Smart said I was not allowed to eat sweets. More than once Al had told me, "I'm worried that after the baby is born, you'll keep gaining weight and get as big as your mother." He must have shared his fears with Dr. Smart.

But I could not resist sweets and during the night when I

went to the bathroom, I made a clandestine stop in the kitchen. I got a knife and carefully sliced the bottom of whatever cake was in the refrigerator that Nelly had bought for Al. I was extra careful not to take too much of the cake or they would notice the cake was losing its height. After the baby was born, I would confess my crime.

~ Chapter Two ~

RALPH

1963

Spring of 1963

It made me smile to think that someday I would teach my future daughter or daughter-in law how to cook Moroccan style, just like Nelly had learned from Mercedes, her mother-in-law. I had not met Mercedes but her recipes would live on as they passed from generation to generation in our family. Besides stuffed turkey with chestnut filling, I also loved Italian food. Nelly made the best spaghetti with meatballs I had ever had.

It was only the beginning of March, but the baby was getting ready to come out because it had been kicking pretty hard. I liked it when he kicked; I knew he was alive and well. I had a feeling it was going to be a boy because I dreamed about him when I was still living in Portugal. He looked like Al, with dark, thick, curly hair and dark-rimmed eyeglasses.

Nelly and Ruth were able to go out together a lot more since I did not mind staying home and babysitting Kim and Tom, her little baby brother. He drank milk from a bottle and I fed him pre-made baby food from a little glass jar, bought at the supermarket.

Kim was very finicky about food. She only liked Campbell's chicken noodle soup from the can, and after three or four spoonful she would say she had enough. I would eat a whole can of chicken noodle soup and then her leftovers.

Babysitting gave me a lot of experience with children, and I enjoyed watching cartoons with them.

One evening, Ginny and Joe came over to visit us and they brought along Ginny's mother who was 80 years old. She was shorter than me and her round body and round face, matched her little round black hat sitting gracefully on her white short hair. She extended her hand to me and after saying, "Nice to meet you," she poked one of her fingers into my hair. "Is that real?" She stood transfixed at the door way.

I nodded my head.

"How do you keep it up so high?" She tried to poke at it again.

I quickly backed away from her probing finger and said, "With hairspray!" She didn't know about hairspray? It was all over the commercials on television! Ginny and Joe helped her in and sat her in the living room couch. There was no place else for me to sit but next to her.

She turned toward me and said, "I bet you're having culture shock,"

"Thank you. Yes, and it's wonderful!"

She looked puzzled.

It was only the beginning of April and I wasn't supposed to have the baby until May, but after we had dinner, I had a feeling the baby was getting ready to come out because he was kicking up a storm. It really didn't hurt, but since I never had a baby before, I did not want to take any chances that he might just come out.

Al drove me to Dr. Smart's office. He listened to my belly with a stethoscope and agreed that I should go to the hospital. He would meet us there later.

When I got to the hospital, they gave me a hospital gown to wear and put me in a metal framed bed. I fell asleep. Later on, they woke me up to give me a shot. They said it was going to help me relax, which sounded funny to me since I had already been sleeping. Sometime later, what felt like the middle of the night, they tried to wake me up, but I could not move or open my eyes. It felt eerie, as if I were trapped in a dark tunnel of the Twilight Zone. I could hear people talking, but I could not understand what they were saying or doing. Everything became a heavy blur in my mind, and when I woke up, I was in a cold room surrounded by Dr. Smart, a nurse, Al, and Nelly. They were all speaking to me at the same time. I tried to open my eyes but my head felt like it was being sucked up in a vacuum and everything was spinning. I could not think straight. Dr. Smart put something wrapped in a blanket on top of my stomach and said it was my baby. I wanted to ask, what baby, but I couldn't move my lips. Al stroked my forehead with his hand, which felt like a crushing weight on my brain. "It's a boy, honey!"

I pushed Al's hand away and then pushed away the bundle. I needed to go back into the dark comfort of the silent space from where they had pulled me out.

I woke up later screaming in pain, "Help! The baby is coming out! Somebody help me, this is it!"

A nurse appeared next to my bed. "You already had your baby, now be quiet." Her strident voice was less than comforting.

"No, it is impossible! It hurts horribly. I can feel the baby trying to come out; it's pushing hard to come out!" I was shaking as my heart was pounding fast and my head was going to blow up and my insides were being ripped open in pain. I was pushing and pushing. That was the pain of birth! She came back, told me to turn over, and gave me a shot. I kept crying and I was given another shot. Another nurse came in and said, "What you need is company. There's a Portuguese woman who gave birth two days ago, and her room is just across the hallway. I'll bring her over."

Madalena had the gift of gab. Portuguese gab no less. Her voice scraped and undulated in waves like someone running their nails on a chalkboard. I begged in Portuguese, "Madalena, your voice hurts my head, please come back another day."

She would not go away, so I covered my ears with both hands and yelled in English, "Stop talking! Go away, and don't come back."

The next morning I woke up feeling weak, but the pain was gone. I touched my belly and it was flat. That meant the baby had come out, after all. I was confused, I had missed the whole event. I took a look around to evaluate my surroundings. A woman was lying in a bed like mine, closer to the window. "Hello?" I said. "Are you having a baby too?"

"I'm done with it and so are you. What a racket you can make. You have been crying and moaning for the last two days. You have been experiencing postpartum pain." She went on to explain that my uterus was not aware of the baby coming out, and was going into contractions automatically. She knew what she was saying because that was her third child. "What's the name of your baby, a boy, right?"

I said, "Yes, it's a boy and his name is Ralph after my husband's father's name."

"Mine is David and he's having his circumcision this morning."

"Wow, you're Jewish!" I was ecstatic. I was ready to share with her that I was also Jewish but before I could say anything else, she cut me off.

"No, I'm not. Everybody nowadays has their boy

circumcised. It's done for health reasons."

"Then why did you give your baby a Jewish name?"

"Because I like the name, that's why." She turned her back on me.

Nelly and Al came to visit later that morning and after hugging me, she said, "We just came from the nursery and saw your baby. I'm disappointed with his looks. I hate to say this but Ralph is an ugly baby." I looked up at Al waiting to hear his report. He said, "I'm not worried, Ronnie. All babies are ugly when they're born. He'll change when he gets older." He handed me a three-inch porcelain baby doll. "Ruth said I should give you this gift because it will be a lasting memory of our son's birth."

I was disappointed with the doll and very sad to hear our baby was ugly.

After they left, a nurse helped me sit up in bed and propped some pillows behind my back while another nurse came in and handed me a small bundle wrapped in a blue blanket. "Here he is," she said joyfully. "Enjoy your baby." They both left.

It was our first encounter as mother and child. I uncovered his face cautiously even though I had prepared myself to love him no matter how hideous he looked. His face was round, his skin was pink, two big, round blue eyes opened and closed as if checking me out, and he had the most adorable button nose. His perfectly round head was covered by a slight fuzz of blond hair. I kissed his forehead very softly. He was adorable. Nelly and Al must have looked at a different baby because Ralph was beautiful. He had five fingers in each hand and ten little toes. He was perfect! He was also very heavy and it wasn't too long before my arms got tired and I had to ring for the nurse to come and get him.

That afternoon a lady from the office personnel at the hospital came to my room and asked what Al's profession was. Since he worked with missiles I assumed his engineering degree was nuclear of some kind.

Early the next morning a nurse came to take me for a walk to the bathroom. It took me by surprise that when I got up from the bed, my knees gave in. I would have fallen if Nurse Francis had not been holding my arm. She took me down the hallway and helped me to sit on the toilet. "You need to move your bowels. I'll wait out here until you go."

I squeezed and pushed as hard as I could and finally gave up. I called out from behind the closed metal door, "It's not coming out. I can't do it. I'm sorry."

"Bend backward as if lying down and stretch your legs out. It'll come out."

I did as she told me. "It worked!" I announced with jubilation. But the worst was yet to come; I could not reach backward to wipe myself. I felt like an old lady falling apart at the seams. I was dying of shame but I had to tell her. She held me up like a rag doll and, after looking back making sure we had no witnesses, she whispered, "Don't tell anyone I did this for you. I'm not supposed to wipe you."

Later on I told Nelly about it and she said, "Most likely she was hoping you would give her some money."

What a heartless thing to say about a nurse with a heart. Nelly was a nice person but she could be very crude at times.

Ralph and I went home two days later. Nelly was still making remarks about his looks. It was as if she enjoyed hurting me. No mother wants to hear that her child is ugly when it's not even true. His name was Ralph, like her husband. I could only hope she would learn to love him.

Later, Al and Nelly laughed at me because on Ralph's birth certificate it said his father was a nuclear engineer.

"That's okay, honey," Al said. "Just so you know, I'm an electric engineer."

It did not make me feel any better. When they asked my religion I had told them I was Protestant like they had me instructed to do. My son's birth certificate was full of lies. During the first week at home I kept waking up crying every night from the same nightmare. I was the queen bee and I was stuck in a cocoon in the bee hospital, giving birth to bees. All around me were cocoons with bees buzzing around and women like me with big bellies covered in white gauze like mummies waiting to give birth.

When Ralph cried during the night I felt disconnected, strange. I did not feel qualified to take care of him. How could a bee take care of a real baby? What if I dropped him, or gave him too much milk? What if I hurt him? I told Nelly about my night fears and she started getting up to change his diapers and give him his milk bottle. I asked God to bless her for helping me out.

Al and Nelly said breast-feeding was not as good as formula. I always thought that mother's milk was the best for babies, but they said it was a thing of the past. Nelly gave me special pads to use inside my bra to help soak up the milk from staining my shirts. Out of curiosity Al sucked a little of my breast milk to see what it tasted like and said it wasn't bad, but not his cup of tea.

At my first check up with Dr. Smart, he asked if I remembered what I said in Portuguese, when he put Ralph on my tummy after he was born.

"No, I don't remember anything, except feeling horrible."

He smiled and said it was probably better that way.

I wish I knew what I said to him, it might explain why I felt inadequate as a mother. Dr. Smart also said that Ralph had been premature and was not supposed to be born until the end of May.

When we left his office Nelly said, "How can an eight pound baby have been born premature?" She laughed heartily. "He already looks like a blimp. Another month and you would have to have a cesarean to get him out."

I got a letter from Mama reminding me to make sure I got a birthday cake with nineteen candles. She always had something sweet for my birthday, even if it was a cup of rice pudding or a cupcake; a candle was always there to be blown. I did not intend to remind Al and Nelly about my birthday. It would be the same as asking for a present. Besides, I had everything I wanted: a healthy baby boy, a wonderful husband, and a sweet mother-in-law who fed Ralph during the night.

They remembered my birthday. Al gave me a delicate silver necklace with a pearl attached to a small diamond. Nelly bought a beautiful yellow birthday cake decorated with little pink and blue flowers made of vanilla frosting and a gold shoe charm with Ralph's name, to add to my charm bracelet, a Christmas gift from Al, last year. Ruth took me out shopping for my very first pair of jeans. She confided on me when Nelly was not around "My husband Bernie spends most of his paycheck at the bars. A year ago I was invited to a friend's wedding but I couldn't afford a formal dress. So, I went to an expensive store and bought a very stylish black dress and kept the ticket on the inside of the dress and wore it to the wedding." She giggled as she added, "The next day I took the dress back to the store and got a full refund." She was proud of her accomplishment and I was impressed with her courage to participate in such an outrageous scheme. I could not believe that in America you could return anything back to the store, especially used. I would be too embarrassed to do such thing.

My birthday was a very joyful day because I was surrounded by the people I loved—my American family and my little baby sleeping quietly in the other room. I also met Marcus, Nelly's brother-in-law. Marcus brought us a New York cheesecake and a box of doughnuts. In his younger days Marcus was the most handsome man Nelly had ever seen, as she had told me more than once. Now he was bald, fat, and a nervous wreck because of all the suffering he went through while married to a woman who had little if any brain and three kids who, as they would say in Portugal, were like curses on his back. His dark destiny started when he drank too much one night and got his future wife pregnant. He had to do what any man with morals should do—he married her. According to Nelly, the kids were born slightly retarded like their mother. Marcus lived in Brooklyn with his family, the worst place in the world anyone could live, unless you were trying to commit suicide, because crime ran rampant in Brooklyn. One daughter had been born mentally slow. The other daughter was normal until the day she was playing on the beach and someone pushed her head under the water for so long that when she came up, something snapped in her brain and she became mentally affected by the trauma. Marcus's only son was a drug addict and the police were always knocking at his front door looking for the boy.

Marcus spoke loud and fast as if racing for the last word. He reminded me of Aunt Ligia, Mama's younger sister, who had been diagnosed with a hysterical personality. My own life was so happy, it was sad to know the story of Marcus's life and that Nelly and Al didn't want anything to do with him or his family.

Summer of 1963

You had to travel on a long stretch of dirt road to reach Freehold in New Jersey; most likely what the pioneers had encountered when they first crossed America. There was absolutely nothing around where we would be living. Freehold could not be any farther from civilization. I told Al, "Perhaps we're making a mistake moving to New Jersey."

"What do you expect," he said. "It's the countryside."

Nelly offered to take care of Ralph while Al and I spent

Braving A New World

one day getting our new home ready for us to move in by the end of the month. Al washed the windows while I washed the dusty wooden floors with water and vinegar, to revive the wood back to life. Then I waxed all the wood floors in each room to make them shiny.

While checking the air vents in the house, Al found a bunch of empty beer cans inside one of them. He said in the winter the cans would have blocked the heat from coming into that room. Except for one of the burner grate missing from the top of our kitchen stove, the house was ready for us to move in. I called the company that built our house and their secretary promised to send us a new grate.

Our new address was 71 Koenig Lane, Freehold, New Jersey. Our house was a split-level. There were three bedrooms upstairs. Our bedroom was connected to the bathroom, which had another door to the hallway. The other bedroom, next to us, was Nelly's, and the one next to her, across from our bedroom, was Ralph's. On the floor below us were the kitchen, living room, and dining room. In the next floor below were the playroom, den, the extra bathroom, and the laundry room. We had a quarter of an acre of land on a corner lot.

The outside became Nelly's domain. She said, "You already have enough to keep you busy inside the house." I didn't mind her offer. She liked to garden and kept her days busy watering the clay-like ground, patiently waiting for the grass to grow. She gave me free reign over the cooking. I did all the housework and took care of Ralph.

I enjoyed being a housewife and making bread, and at least once or twice a week I experimented with a new recipe from Nelly's old cookbooks. Ralph was easy to take care of. As long as he had his milk and his diapers were changed, he was a smiling, beautiful baby. On weekends, Al took us shopping for food and things for the house. Where we lived there were no stores except for Shop Rite, an old supermarket on Route 9. I carried Ralph on my hip and every time we went out, people would say to me, "What a beautiful baby! Is that your little brother?" I took that as a double compliment.

At the driving testing center in Eatontown, Al had to take the test twice in order to be licensed in New Jersey. We all agreed that I should go to a different testing center. Al took me to the one in Toms River. It turned out the examiner was more interested in knowing me personally than my driving skills. He did not ask me to make a U-turn or parallel park. He asked me to drive out of the parking lot and take my time on one of the country roads. He asked me a lot of personal questions like where I was from, what hobbies I had, and said he liked listening to my charming accent.

On the way back to the motor vehicle building he asked for my phone number and I told him he would have to ask my husband for it, because I did not remember the number offhand. When we got out of the car, Al was waiting for us in the parking lot. "Your wife is a good driver," said the examiner. He did not ask Al for my phone number.

I had to use all my muscle power to turn the wheel in Al's car and I also had to press really hard with my foot on the brakes to make the car stop. Mama was right when she told me time and time again while I was growing up that I was a weakling. I looked strong but it was only appearances.

As a kid I had a lot of trouble helping the maid with stretching the bed sheets after being outside to dry. There was one particular maid who got a lot of pleasure pulling me across the room with a strong tug. No matter how hard I tried pushing back and holding myself in place, she always sent me flying across the sunroom. I always laughed along, but inside I was feeling disheartened for not having muscles like her and everybody else. I kept hoping when I was an adult that I would become stronger but it didn't seem to be happening yet.

New York City was my favorite place to drive to. I parked the car at Port Authority, and then Nelly and I took turns pushing Ralph in the baby carriage. We walked fast through 42nd street, the most sinful street in New York City, which according to Nelly was where the pimps, prostitutes, and drug dealers hung out, but we always took our time walking on Broadway. I kept my eyes open, hoping to see a movie star go by. Once in a while we went as far as Fifth Avenue and did some window shopping.

Al's dinner was always ready to be served when he got home from work. Nelly had taught me not to bother Al with anything trivial until he was done eating because he was a very nervous man and needed peace and quiet after working hard all day. I followed her advice and made sure Ralph had been fed and put away for the night in his crib. After we were done eating dinner in the kitchen, the three of us sat in the playroom to watched television. Al got paid well for his work but we still could not afford to buy a dining room set.

Nelly bought three TV trays and we started having dinner in the playroom while we watched our favorite television shows like *Bonanza*, (Al's favorite) *I Love Lucy* (my favorite), *The Beverly Hillbillies*, (we all liked it) and Nelly's favorite, *The Ed Sullivan Show*. Ralph went to sleep at 8 o'clock and Al at 9 at the latest since he had to get up at 5 in the morning to go to work. I hated going to bed at 9 in the evening. I dreamed about going out dancing in nightclubs and meeting other people my age and having a good time with friends. I did not mind the daytime because I was busy all day but the nights were boring, lying awake in bed listening to the silence outside. I knew there was life out there somewhere. Sometimes I cried.

Thank God Nelly did not like to watch television alone

so when Al wanted me to go to bed with him she would say something like, "Ronnie will be in bed after we finish seeing this program. It's almost over." But after the program was over we watched another. Then by the time I got into bed, Al would be sleeping so I'd get in bed carefully so as not to wake him up.

One day I had no choice but to go to the dentist because of a toothache. Al informed the dentist that I could only have Novocain, but the dentist said he had something better, Xylocaine. The dentist never got a chance to drill into my tooth, because as soon as he injected the Xylocaine into my jaw I had a similar reaction as when I saw the other dentist in Jamaica, Long Island. My heart started racing and it was difficult to breathe. I felt like I was going to pass out. The dentist insisted I leave immediately and go home and then go to a different dentist since he could not work on my tooth. He was probably scared I was going to die in his office.

Al had to hold me up as we walked the main street in Freehold hoping to find a doctor to help me. He pointed to a house with a sign on the front lawn, Dr. Freedman, MD.

"Freedman sounds like a Jewish name," Al said. "I bet he'll be able to help you."

Thank God, Dr. Freedman was able to see me right away. He shook his head up and down and said, "It looks like you're having a reaction to some medication, huh?" He gave me a shot in the arm and I was fine within a few minutes. He encouraged me to always carry Benadryl in my purse and if I ever had a reaction again, I should take a Benadryl immediately.

Dr. Freedman recommended Dr. Wise, a dentist and a friend of his. I went to see Dr. Wise but he was a dental surgeon, he only pulled teeth. Al encouraged me to have the darn tooth pulled since it was all the way in the back and had given me nothing but trouble since I had arrived in

America. I was given a shot that knocked me out. But I did not have a reaction except for feeling a little nauseous afterward.

Al's rubber broke during intercourse one night. I ran into the bathroom to wash myself as fast as I could, but he said, "Forget it. It's a done deal. Most likely you're pregnant. There's no reason to use any more rubbers from now on. They're nothing but a pain in the neck."
    He seemed to be glad about the incident and it crossed my mind that he had sabotaged the whole thing. The idea of another painful birth experience brought back the queen bee nightmares.

I was cleaning the hallway steps when I felt slightly dizzy and nauseous. Nelly was not home; she was spending two weeks in Long Island with Ruth and Joe. I got worried that I might faint, so I took Ralph out of the playpen and with him in my arms, I went to visit Susan, our next-door neighbor, who in the past had waved back at me while we were both in our backyards.
    Susan's yard reminded me of my own in Portugal—dried up and unkempt. Two broken-down cars in her driveway had not moved since they had moved in. One was held in place by pieces of wood behind each flat tire. The other, an old pickup, had no wheels so it was safe to say it did not need anything to prevent it from rolling backward on the tilted driveway.
    I knocked at her door. "Excuse me. I don't feel too good. Do you mind if I stay with you for a little while until I feel better?"
    Susan was toothless, skinny, pale, and pregnant. She was wearing a pink cotton robe over her matching pajamas. She smoked and offered me some coffee while we talked at her kitchen table. I told her that coffee made me jittery and I would rather have plain water.

Susan stared at me for a bit while inhaling what seemed an endlessly deep puff from her cigarette, and then as the smoke came out of her nostrils she said bluntly, "You're pregnant."

"No, it's impossible." Then I reconsidered my words. "Do you really think so?"

"Honey, this is my fifth time. I'm an expert on pregnancy."

"How come you have so many children?" I asked perplexed, realizing she was not in the best of finances.

"We're Catholic!" she said. "Besides, when we have sex it happens while I'm asleep. He gets on top of me, does his thing, and then turns over and goes back to sleep."

I was horrified with the description of her sex life. Al always made sure that I was wide awake. I could not even imagine anyone sleeping through it.

Autumn of 1963

Trying to establish our roots in New Jersey, we started inquiring about local doctors. Marilyn, the neighbor across the street, was a nurse. "I bet she knows a good doctor to deliver your baby." Nelly encouraged me to pay her a visit. I agreed. It was kind of crazy to drive all the way to Long Island to see Dr. Smart or Nelly's heart specialist when there were so many doctors in New Jersey.

Marilyn seemed annoyed when I knocked at her front door. She stood in her doorway as if guarding an angry dragon inside and did not invite me in. I thought she was very rude, especially since it was raining. "Wait there." She closed the door. She returned and handed me a piece of paper. "I don't know Dr. Adler personally, but I heard he's an old doctor with a lot of experience." She paused. "I don't mind that you came over to get a referral from me, but that doesn't mean we're going to be buddies. I'm a very busy person and unless it's something quick we need from

Braving A New World

each other, I would rather we stay in our own places."

Wow, I could never speak my mind like that to anyone. But she had the right to have no friends, if that's what she wanted. We did not have any friends either.

Al drove me to Dr. Adler. He was a bigwig at the Red Bank Hospital, which was conveniently located forty-five minutes from where we lived. He paid close attention when I told him, "It's very important to me to see the birth of my child. I want to be part of it, to be present." He promised not to give me drugs to put me to sleep like Dr. Smart had done. Instead he would give me a special shot at the appropriate moment and I would be able to stay awake to see and even help with the birth process. I could not be happier.

My blood test results came back; I was anemic. Dr. Adler said it happened to a lot of women when they got pregnant. He prescribed special prenatal vitamins for me to take every day. Nelly said I needed to eat liver three times a week! I hated liver. Mama used to force me to eat fried beef liver and she would lie to me by saying it was steak. We were too poor to afford steak. I was a kid, but I was not dumb; steak had a completely different texture and taste.

Al insisted on cooking the liver. He said it had to be nearly raw in order to work. He covered the almost raw calf liver with lots of onions and for the baby's sake I ate it, against my will.

November 22nd President Kennedy was shot and killed on television! They showed everything on the news, from beginning to end. I felt sorry for the way he died, with his wife right next to him. What a terrible way to die. Nelly and I wondered what was going to happen to America while they looked for another president. Al said the rule was for the vice president to take over, and the country was perfectly safe from turmoil.

The whole thing looked very peculiar to me. As soon as the police caught the murderer; someone else killed him, as if to shut him up. I did not dare share my political views with Al or Nelly. They already had accused me of being weird whenever I expressed an opinion.

Winter ending 1963

Neither Nelly nor Al put much thought into the new baby's name. Nelly said, "It's going to be a girl, we already have a boy." They picked the name Linda. I did not want to be pushy about what I liked, but Linda in Portuguese meant beautiful, and that was a lot to carry on one's shoulders. What if she was not beautiful and just average like me? If it was up to me to name my baby girl I would have picked Audrey or Susan instead. I told them just in case I had another boy I would like to be prepared. I chose the name Steve.

Winter of 1964

Doing his best to avoid another car that had lost control on an icy road, Al drove into a metal fence. He totaled the car but did not get hurt. He took the accident as a sign that he needed another car since it was in dying need of engine repair. He bought another used car at a dealership and since we didn't have the money to buy it, he took a loan.

It was utterly boring living in the country. The only thing saving my sanity during the day was playing with Ralph and listening to the radio. I sang along and danced while doing housework. Nelly liked the same music that Al liked—slow, boring old music from days gone by. She even liked the Fado, the Portuguese blues, which was the most depressing music I had ever heard!

If Nelly and I wanted to go anywhere, I had to drive Al

Braving A New World

to Sayreville where he met with his carpool buddies at 5:30 am, and then I had to go back to Sayreville to pick him up at 4:30. That meant having to go to bed at 9 in order to be able to get up at 4:30. But I could not fall asleep so early; I stayed awake in bed for who-knows-how-long. Less than eight hours of sleep made me tired all day. I could only hope Al would feel sorry for me someday and surprise me with a car.

I was pushing Ralph in the baby carriage, walking with Nelly in Britts, a brand new department store within walking distance from where we lived, when we heard an announcement over the store intercom. The Beatles had just arrived in America.

Along with their British music, they introduced the latest hairstyle for boys—long hair. Parents were not happy about it, but I did and made the mistake of sharing that with Al who said, "That's because you are a hippy, if I had not married you, you would be living with the hippies in Greenwich Village, New York." I did not dare tell him I also found the Beatles ugly and their music unexciting. I felt the Beatles were selling their adolescent music because of their provocative hairstyle. Credence Clearwater Revival and The Animals were groups who made my kind of music! I had no idea what they looked like and I did not care if they had long hair or not. They were really good musicians and that's what mattered when I listened to the radio.

~ *Chapter Three* ~

STEVE

1964

Spring of 1964

I was coming down the steps with a load of clothes to wash when I slipped on the fifth step from the bottom and fell on my lower back. Nelly called the ambulance. Dr. Adler kept me in the hospital for two days because he was worried I might have a miscarriage. He was also afraid I had hit the back of my head when I fell and even though I told him I did not, he ordered an x-ray, anyway. It showed my head and my brain were normal, I didn't say anything but I was glad to know the brain was working well.

Al had a really eerie experience. He was driving on Route 9 on the way home when he started feeling tired so he decided to stop at his favorite diner. The very second he pulled off the road, the car behind him got into a head-on collision with another car coming the wrong way. If he had stayed on the road, he would have been killed instantly. He definitely had an angel on his shoulder when he drove that day.

Mama asked me to write to my brother Max-Leão, who

lived in London, regarding how I felt about his choice of girlfriend. She wrote, "Your brother wants to marry Patricia, a non-Jewish woman, and that's an unforgivable sin. He must break up with her immediately! You must write to him and put some sense into his head."

I did not agree with Mama; it was his life and his choice, not ours. Max-Leão and Patricia were my friends and what Mama was asking me to do was very difficult for me.

But because I did not have the guts to express my feelings I hid behind the excuse that I could not do it because I did not know what to write to Max-Leão.

Mama wrote back with the exact words to send to Max-Leão. Her overbearing pressure and the idea of not obeying my mother's wishes was too much for me to handle I was a nervous wreck with her unreasonable request and prayed to God she would forget all about it. I was prepared to say her letter must have gotten lost.

April 6 was Ralph's birthday. I could not believe that he was already one year old! I had him seated in his high chair, and I put the vanilla birthday cake in front of him so I could take a picture of the occasion. In less than a second he literally dove his face into it. I took a picture of his "cake face," and his glorious smile.

Joe, Ginny, and their daughter Laura came over to help celebrate Ralph's birthday. I was hoping that Ruth could have come with them, but she could not make it. I would love it if we could all reside closer to each other. It was a long trip to Long Island where they lived. We did not visit each other in the winter, only for Christmas because it was a special time of the year—gifts!

After receiving two letters from Mama inquiring if I sent the "letter" to Max-Leão, I finally broke down and wrote exactly what she wanted me to say. Upon putting the letter in the mailbox, I felt I was making the biggest mistake of my life, but I sent it anyway.

Al was sleeping next to me when I felt a kick followed by a contraction that woke me up. It was almost the end of April; to be precise it was April 27 and about ten at night. I was confident it was time to go to the hospital.

I nudged Al out of his sleep. "This is it, Al. I need you to drive me to the hospital. The baby is ready to come out."

"You're imagining." He turned over.

"No, I'm not imagining, I'm telling you this is it."

"Let's wait awhile to make sure." He went back to sleep.

I got jolted by another contraction. I started to panic and pondered what to do next. I grabbed Al's hand and took a little bite, just hard enough to wake him up and get his attention.

He yelled, "Are you nuts?"

"I'm telling you I have to go to the hospital, now!" I proceeded to cry just in case he wanted to bite me back in revenge.

Poor guy, he had to get up at 4:30 every morning to go to work and there I was being selfish and waking him up when he had fallen asleep an hour before. But it was his fault that we lived so far from his work. Just because our house was in New Jersey, did not mean his job was right across the street. He assumed there would be a train from Freehold to Bendix in Teterboro, North Jersey, but after we bought the house, he found out it had been a pipe dream. The trains passing the so-called train station in Freehold didn't even stop. They were cargo trains. The station's ticket booth was used only for purchasing tickets for the buses going north to New York City or south to Atlantic City.

Luckily we got to the hospital just in time. The contractions were getting closer, and Dr. Adler was already at the hospital waiting for me, having received our call before we left the house. I thought it was dumb when they had me lying down on my back; it felt more natural if I could squat and curl up instead. I was crying because the pain was taking its toll on my endurance. One nurse got irritated and said to me, "Stop crying, it's not that bad."

I hated her for being so insensitive, and decided to cry as loud as I wanted since it seemed to help me at least on an emotional level. I thought to myself, *What is she going to do, throw me out of the hospital?*

Dr. Adler took a peek between my legs and called out, "I can see the baby's head. She needs the epidural, right now." He had someone turn me on my side, and they gave me a spinal injection on the lower back and then pushed my bed into another room looking like a lit up round stage. It was the delivery room.

There I was, lying on my back with both legs up in stirrups, looking at the white ceiling with a huge light above my bed, and without any pain. I was smiling, waiting for the baby to pop out. I figured this was going to be easier than I had thought. I could have a dozen kids this way.

I was surprised when they started to yell at me, "Push! Push!"

"Push, how? I don't feel anything from my waist down!"

"Push, anyway. Just concentrate. You can do it."

It was totally ridiculous, how could I push when I did not sense anything? The shot had made me numb from the waist down! Didn't they understand that? They could have cut my legs off and I would've still been smiling.

I was terrified by the thought that my baby might die by choking to death, stuck with his head halfway between my vagina and the outside world. Everybody was yelling and getting frantic and one doctor kept repeating over and over again, "Push! Push, darn it! You need to help us, now push!"

I pushed and pushed inside my head and in my imagination, since half my body was not working.

Then, I heard Dr. Adler's announcement, "It's a boy.

Look!" He was holding Steve upside down by his feet. He was a slimy beauty!

I yelled out happily, "Yahoo!" And then I started to sing, "La, la, la, di, la, da, la, la, la, la." I was singing for the new baby's life, singing for joy, singing for being a witness to my own son's birth.

"What's the matter with her? Is she crazy, singing at a time like this?" said the nurse next to me.

"Don't pay attention; she's obviously having a reaction to the meds." Dr. Adler responded with a know-it-all tone.

Stupid morons, they couldn't comprehend that I was overwhelmed by happiness as I heard Steve crying for the first time. I had just witnessed my son's birth! It was not a drug reaction! It was a life reaction! *Sing with me, you morons*, I thought to myself. *Look at my beautiful baby boy, with Japanese eyes and long dark hair, just like a rock star!*

Summer of 1964

Nelly and Al did not recover well from having another baby boy. They wanted a girl and acted as if it was my fault I did not produce one. Their plans did not include a Steve, only a Linda. Suddenly one evening Nelly realized a serious dilemma which she brought to our attention. "Al, you and Ronnie are very lucky to have two normal children. Having another one could be a serious problem considering you are first cousins. You can't have any more babies, do you hear me?" I did not know about the dangers of cousins getting married, and even if I had known about it, I still would not have been able to stop Mama and Nelly from planning my marriage to Al. The subject of being married to my cousin and producing defected babies was very difficult for me to handle. I called Dr. Adler's office and was told the latest in contraceptives for women was a special rubber diaphragm I could insert before intercourse which was guaranteed to work a lot better than condoms. I immediately made an appointment to see him.

Max-Leão and Patricia stopped writing after receiving "my" letter. I had lost them forever. They got married anyway and most likely never forgive me. I did not blame them; I did not forgive myself either. Meanwhile, my parents cut all relations with Max-Leão and wore black as a sign of mourning.

I was not allowed to socialize with our neighbors because they might want to come over. Nelly and Al did not like to have company unless it was family. They said our home was private and it was nobody's business what we had and did not have. I did not agree with their way of thinking, but I could not do anything about it. Nelly said, "We don't have enough furniture to invite neighbors over. It will be all over the neighborhood that we don't even have dining room furniture and just an old couch in the playroom, with the corner piece of the same couch in the living room."

Laurie, our next-door neighbor, was my age, and she had a little baby girl the same age as Ralph. Nelly felt that Laurie was a stuck-up snob and I was forbidden to invite her over to our house. When Laurie and I saw each other we always go together and had girl talks over our fence. She wanted to know how I kept my hair so shiny and my skin so clear and she told me about her new kitchen curtains and what she was cooking for dinner. It was fun to talk to her. But Nelly would always show up to call me in to do something inside the house which could not wait another minute.

Nelly bought two colorful small birds. Their cage was kept in the den downstairs. Nelly insisted that I had to clean their cage when she forgot to do it, which was quite often. I really did not want to take care of her birds. While growing up, I never had a pet. Maybe because of that or maybe because Mama always said animals inside the house created an unhealthy environment, I had not developed into a pet lover. Papa did not agree with Mama. He had a dog when he lived in the Island of Azores and he was heartbroken when he went to live in Portugal and had to leave his dog behind.

I think what helped Al change his mind concerning having more children was the fact that Ralph and Steve were in competition when they cried at night because of wet diapers, or because they had gas, or simply because they couldn't sleep anymore—probably a combination of all three plus the lurking possibility of giving birth to a mentally retarded baby on account of us being cousins, put a serious damper in our sexual relationship. Rarely a night went by where Al or I slept straight through. Al said two children were more than enough. When we got married, he had told me he could not wait to have one dozen cute little monkeys running around the house. But that was before we had children and Nelly's statement that another one and it might come out mentally retarded.

Autumn of 1964

Early one morning, Nelly took the bus to New York City. She returned later that day after walking home from the bus stop at Shop Rite. She found me ironing in the playroom.

"Did you have fun in New York?" I couldn't wait to hear about it.

"You sound like you have a chip on your shoulder," was her nasty response.

"Why do you say that?" Worried I had offended her I stopped ironing Al's shirt and gave her a hug. But she didn't hug me back. "I'm just wondering if you had a good day." I said again.

She looked at me as if my words were tinted with poison. "You're obviously jealous because you couldn't go with me."

"That's not true. Nelly, I swear I'm not jealous. Why are you saying stuff like that?"

"Don't lie to me. I knew you were upset the moment I walked in the door."

"You're mistaken; it's fine with me if you go out. Please go out again. I like it when you go out."

I meant what I was saying, but she did not believe me and all she wanted was for me to argue back. But I couldn't. I hated arguing and confrontation. She did a bad job at reading my mind, and to top it off, she was wrong. It was our first argument. She did not stop until she made me cry. I did not know what came over her. The loving feeling between us seemed to be disappearing and I wasn't quite sure why except that since Steve was born she had been acting strange and angry with me for no reason.

Winter ending 1964

Nelly's two birds died within two days from each other, and she wanted me to take her out shopping for more birds. But Ralph had been running a high fever and I did not want to take him out of the house.

Christmas came and went. Al and her put the tree up but with Ralph being sick I was far from a holiday mood.

I was very concerned about Ralph, and kept wondering why he did not get better. I took him back and forth to his pediatrician in Freehold, but the antibiotics I gave Ralph every day were not helping at all. Dr. Thompson said Ralph had the flu. Just in case it was contagious, I moved Steve's crib into our bedroom.

Winter of 1965

It was January and Ralph was far from improving. He had lost his appetite, and the fever ran day and night, sometimes going up to 103 degrees. I had heard high fever could produce brain seizures and I was scared. He rocked inside his crib, knocking his head into the wood railings so hard that the crib kept moving away from the wall. Nelly did not go into his bedroom because she did not want to take a chance, with her weak heart, and catch whatever it was making Ralph sick. I did not blame her.

I spent most of my time with Ralph trying to keep him busy enough so he would not knock his head against the crib's railing. I began teaching him the alphabet and even though he was not quite two years old, he was learning it fast.

Dr. Thompson prescribed a new antibiotic but the next morning Ralph's temperature was 104 degrees. His fever had always been lower in the morning, and that meant it was going to get a lot higher later in the day. I immediately called Dr. Thompson and he told me to take Ralph to Fitkins Hospital for observation. He was put in the children's ward with other sick children. I stayed day and night with him. The hospital must have been understaffed because they had me, instead of a nurse, wrapping Ralph with ice. He cried and tried to push the ice cubes away from his body. When I protested to the nurse in charge, I was told that if I did not ice him, he might go into convulsions and die. I cried along with Ralph as I put the ice against his tiny body and kept saying, "I'm sorry Ralph, I'm sorry, please forgive me, but I want you to live."

After a week in the children's ward, Dr. Thompson made arrangements for Ralph to have a spinal test. Al, Nelly, and I met with the specialist who performed the spinal test on Ralph. His diagnosis was spinal meningitis. The doctor said, "If your son doesn't die, you still need to be prepared for the worst. There's a good chance the meningitis might affect his brain and mental abilities in the future.

"Spinal meningitis? Where did he catch that from?" Al asked him.

"Hard to say; sometimes contact with infected birds can do it."

"Our two birds died not too long before Ralph got sick," I said.

"That's a possibility. Some birds carry meningitis."

I ran into the bathroom, locked myself inside, and screamed and cried and hit the wall with my hands as hard as I could. I remembered Mama pulling at her hair and crying over losing the bathtub because we needed to sell it in order to get some money to buy food. I was just a child then but I never forgot the pain she had experienced. To her it was the end of her world. I now understood how she felt. I cried out, "It's the end of my world! I'm going to lose my son!" I got on my knees and putting my hands together, I prayed, "Please dear God don't let my son die, he's just a baby."

From Aunt Heydee I had learned that we all had our moments of uncontrollable agony and despair. She used to tell me, "Each and every one of us some time or another will carry our own cross." She was referring to Jesus Christ and how no one was immune from suffering.

The parents who had their children in the same ward as Ralph were very angry that the hospital had waited weeks to transfer Ralph to a private room. On his door there was a sign, "CONTAGIOUS — DO NOT ENTER."

I bought a pack of cigarettes from the cigarette machine in the waiting room at the hospital and decided to start smoking when Ralph was sleeping. Someone had told me that smoking helped with tension. Misery liked company and I liked the prospect of talking to other unfortunate parents.

Puffing away on my cigarette, I sat between a man and a woman who were also smoking in the smoking room in the hospital. But she stood and left when I sat down. Peter, the man, was conveniently talkative and I took my role of a smoking mother in despair very seriously. His three-year-old daughter was very sick and neither he nor his wife had been told what was wrong with their child. He was also having marital problems and felt like his whole life was falling apart. On Friday he did not show up. I asked another mother with her baby in the children's ward, "Have you ever seen Peter's wife?"

"Yes, she's a beautiful young lady and he doesn't deserve her."

I walked away feeling awkward, I had no business chatting to a married man, who complained about personal issues with his marriage when the truth was that his wife was beautiful and he didn't deserve her. I was guilty of trying to act grown up by smoking and being friendly with Peter and the people in the waiting room. I was just a novelty. Everyone asked me the same questions, "Where is your accent from? What brought you to America? How long have you been here?"

I stopped hanging out in the waiting room, smoking and talking to strangers. When Ralph slept, I began doing the same; I sat in the armchair in his room and closed my eyes.

Dr. Thompson prescribed me sulfur medicine so I wouldn't catch meningitis. I was the only one allowed in Ralph's room. A nurse came by the door once in a while to ask me how things were going and to pass me his medicine, the thermometer, the bed sheets, a cup of Jell-O, and some soup broth for Ralph. I took my meals in the cafeteria. Ralph was still not eating. His blond hair had fallen off and he was skin and bones.

I was sitting next to his bed, patting him on the back, when I felt strange; my heart started to speed up and I was shaking uncontrollably. Lucky for me, Al showed up at the door just then. He called the floor nurse and they took me to the emergency room downstairs. We were afraid I had caught meningitis from Ralph. By the time they put me in a bed, I realized I was experiencing a reaction to the sulfur I was taking. I told the doctor in the emergency room about it, and asked to be released so I could go back to Ralph's room and get my purse where I kept the Benadryl. The doctor wanted to know if I was taking drugs, and if I was having a problem with my boyfriend. Al was standing next to me. "This is my wife you're talking to and she has no boyfriends! The only drug she is taking is the sulfur the doctor prescribed for her."

They would not listen to him or me. One of the doctors started to inspect my arms and Al said, "What the heck are you looking for?"

"I'm looking for tracks." said the young doctor overseeing my care.

"The only tracks she has are in your head, mister! I already told you, my wife doesn't do drugs. Why don't you listen to what she's telling you? She's having a reaction to the sulfur!"

"We're only doing our job," he said apologetically.

"Al," I said turning toward him. "Please go upstairs and just get the Benadryl capsules from my purse. It's on the table next to Ralph's bed."

"Oh no, you can't take anything unless I authorize it," said the same doctor.

Al left anyway, and came back with the Benadryl and handed it to the doctor. He looked at the container and said, "Oh, okay, I guess you're allergic to the sulfur. You better take two of those capsules."

Good thing we had Blue Cross Blue Shield Insurance to cover all our medical expenses. I was put on penicillin.

Monday night I went home to take a bath and change my

clothes. "Ralph is dying!" I bellowed out like a mother bear about to have her cub taken away. Nelly and Al were sitting at the kitchen table having dinner and the look on my face made them both stand. Al tried to comfort me but I pushed him away and yelled out again, "No, I don't want hugs I want Ralph to come home!"

Nelly had a crazy look in her eyes. "This morning I broke into a million pieces the lobster-shaped ceramic dish you and Al brought from Portugal. It had a malevolent look about it. It was probably made in one of those prisons where the criminals make pottery while putting curses on the work they create. That dish was evil and most likely cursed."

I never liked that dish, but to blame an inanimate object for someone being sick was pretty odd. And they called me weird? I felt she had no right to break anything that was mine unless she asked me first. But the serving dish was gone, and there was no point in crying over spilt milk.

As Mama said many times when something broke or got stolen, "Que se vaia capará por todos nós." In other words, "May the thing that got destroyed or damaged take our place as an offering of goodwill to the evil gods so they are appeased and take their minds off of us!" It was something she had learned from her mother who was from Morocco where they had all kinds of superstitions.

"We need to do something immediately." I dared to speak up. "We need to change his doctor." I was afraid they would think I was crazy, but they agreed with me.

Nelly recalled the name of a doctor in New York that her husband had known and regarded with great respect. It had been a long time ago, but we kept our fingers crossed, he might still be alive. We got his number from the telephone operator.

Not only was Dr. Mitchell still alive and practicing, he immediately got in touch with a specialist, and arrangements were made at the New York Hospital to receive Ralph within twenty-four hours.

I called Dr. Thompson to get consent to take Ralph out of the hospital. His response was, "No, I'm his doctor and I'm not allowing that. He stays under my care!"

Al and I rented an ambulance that same evening and we paid an extra bonus to the ambulance driver so he would be cooperative with our plan and willing to drive the same night to New York City. It was snowing heavily. I took a blanket with me, and Al and I snuck in, in the middle of the night to the hospital. The staff was nowhere in sight. We had picked the perfect time to enter the hospital, most likely the doctors and nurses were resting somewhere after a long hard day's work. Ralph was sitting and looked at us as if he had been expecting us. I put a finger to my mouth and said, "Shhhh, mommy and daddy are taking you out of here, but you need to be very quiet, okay?" He smiled. Al grabbed Ralph and covered him with the blanket, and we ran out of the hospital carrying Ralph, like thieves in the night, and into the ambulance waiting outside for us.

Josh, the ambulance driver, said, "Don't worry about the snowstorm. With God on our side, nothing is going to stop us. I promise to get your son safely to the hospital."

Josh kept the ambulance's red light flickering as he drove past all traffic until we finally reached the emergency room entrance at the New York Hospital. We were told to go home and left Ralph in God's hands and Dr. Mitchell's Josh drove us back to New Jersey but he refused to accept any money. He was just as concerned as we were and asked us to call him as soon as we heard the results from New York.

The next morning, I called the hospital. "I know you are worried, but don't call us. We'll call you when we know something," said Dr. Mitchell's associate.

At home we hardly spoke to each other. We knew Ralph was close to dying when we left him in New York. We were all afraid to pick up the phone every time it rang. No phone call meant he was still alive and there was hope.

Three days later we received a call directly from Dr. Mitchell. "Come and get your little boy, he's fine and ready to go home."

"What happened to his meningitis?" I asked. "He's completely cured?"

"He was suffering from Otitis Media. Whatever he may have had prior to coming here, we know nothing about it."

"Thank you doctor, thank you so much." I was crying and laughing from joy.

"Ralph is okay? He's okay?" Nelly said.

"Yes, we can go and get him; as soon as Al gets home. We'll drive to New York and bring him home." We hugged exuberantly and then I picked Steve up from his playpen and twirling with him in my arms I sand my own joyful tune, "Your brother is coming home. Oh, happy days are here again. Your brother is coming home." He was just a baby but he smiled back at me as if he understood.

Dr. Thompson never called back to find out what happened to Ralph.

Nelly took over Ralph like a ferocious tiger defending her newborn. I have lost my son to her. She bathed him; hand fed him, and anything he wanted he got. Nelly also took over the household. She got angry if I re-touched something she supposedly already cleaned. "What are you cleaning the kitchen sink for? I already did that. Go wash the windows!" Nelly ordered me around like a slave saying, "Go wax the living room floors. Go clean the kitchen floor. We are having this and that for supper."

If I wanted to play with Ralph, she would say, "Ralph is mine, and Steve is yours." It was like a nightmare, but I did not have the courage to speak up. I wanted to tell her they were both my children, and why could we not share them. But I did not want her to get upset at me.

I began buying and then reading love novels and felt like

I was back in Portugal under my parents' control. In Nelly's mind, Ralph had taken the place of her husband, whose name was also Ralph. I was just a servant, receiving orders, and I had nothing to say about anything.

Since Steve was born, I only knew life with Nelly had changed and after almost losing Ralph, it had gotten worst. I shared my feelings with Al but he said nothing could be done about it. Nelly was his mother and she had a heart condition to boot. He couldn't take a chance at getting her upset.

Then out of the blue, Nelly began nagging me about how to take care of Al. "You should be getting up every morning at five with your husband and make him breakfast and you should get his car started so it's warm when he gets into it to drive to work. That is what a good wife is supposed to do for her husband."

When I told Al about it that night, he laughed. "She's nuts. It makes no sense for you to get up so early since I never eat breakfast and the car doesn't take long to get warm."

Later the next morning Nelly said, "Well, did you take care of your husband this morning like you're supposed to do?" I shook my head. "You could learn a lot from Ginny," Nelly continued. "She's a good wife. She always gets up with Joe, makes him breakfast, and in the winter she goes into their cold, freezing garage to turn the engine on so Joe's car is nice and warm when he gets into it."

In my opinion Ginny was an insomniac, and that's why she did not mind. But feeling guilty, I got up the next morning with Al to do my wifely duties. I turned his car on and then asked what he wanted for breakfast. He said, "I told you I don't eat breakfast." I stood half-asleep against the kitchen wall and, after kissing Al goodbye, I went back to bed but could not fall asleep.

Al and his carpool buddies had made a pact when they first started driving together, if they ever got into an accident they would never sue each other. Then one day, on the way home from work, Al rear-ended another car. Nobody got hurt except one of his buddies got a little bump on his forehead.

"Nothing to worry about," he told Al. The next day however, his friend changed his mind and was suing.

"So much for making a promise. Now you know why I don't trust friends—they're all out to screw you."

I did not agree with Al. I would have loved to have had friends.

We heard some disturbing news about Dr. Thompson. He quit pediatrics and went back to medical school to become a heart specialist.

"I wonder how many kids died under his care when he was their doctor," Nelly said.

"What scares me even more," I said. "Is what kind of heart surgeon he will be, when he can't even help little children."

"He probably wasn't making enough money as a pediatrician," Al's statement made the most sense.

~ *Chapter Four* ~

GROWING UP WITH MY SONS

1965-1969

Spring of 1965

Aunt Coty sent back from Portugal the see-through baby doll lingerie pajamas I had sent to her for her birthday. I thought the gift was very original and sexy, and since Aunt Coty was very skinny, I thought the pajamas would look nice on her. Mama said Aunt Coty was offended because it was not the kind of outfit a lady wears to bed. Obviously she was a very conservative, old-fashioned person. Here in America, married people like me wore sexy pajamas to bed so we could please our husbands. Love, passion, and sex went together. I felt sorry for Uncle Augusto, most likely Aunt Coty wore a long flannel nightgown to bed.

I was bathing Steve when I noticed a round bump in the middle of his left collarbone. His right shoulder was also higher than the other. I immediately looked up the name of a bone doctor in the Yellow Pages.

Dr. Lehman was an orthopedic surgeon and he had Steve's shoulder x-rayed. The bump was calcification; the result of an old fracture. Steve needed surgery to fix his shoulder, but we would have to wait a few more years because he was too young. Nelly told me that Steve's collarbone probably broke when I fell down the steps while I was pregnant.

Only I knew the truth. When Steve was about three months old, I was changing his diapers on the bed downstairs in the den, and left him unattended while I ran upstairs to get the talcum powder. When I returned, I found him on the floor. Even though he was not crying, he probably broke the collarbone when he rolled off the bed.

Summer of 1965

What a wonderful surprise, Al bought me a really nice, used, red, automatic car. I no longer had to get up at five in the morning to borrow Al's car for the day.

Nelly did not drive. She did not believe she could ever learn. Besides, we were always together, so she depended on me to take her to Jamaica, New York to see her heart doctor, eye doctor, and foot doctor. She did not feel comfortable with anyone else to treat her. She had been their patient for years and years. She only trusted them. I loved driving, so I did not mind taking her wherever she wanted to go.

Autumn of 1965

Time stood still when taking baths with Ralph and Steve. They were just babies, so I could get away with getting naked into the tub; it also made it a lot easier to wash them. I made paper sail boats and put them in the tub for them to play with, but the paper boats did not last too long once they got soaked. Ralph and Steve liked to watch the paper boats sink. The rubber ducks were a lot more practical, but not as much fun.

Winter ending 1965

Al and Nelly liked ground beef molded into the shape of a loaf; to me it was nothing but a super-giant boring hamburger. By accident I discovered how to make a chicken loaf! While waiting for a chicken to defrost, I was amazed to notice how easy it was to remove the chicken's skin in one piece. I ground the raw chicken and mixed it with bread, raw eggs, fresh parsley, and some herbs. Then I stuffed it back into the skin. The result was a boneless chicken that came out of the oven looking like a full roasted chicken. Everybody loved it; even Al was impressed and asked me to make it at least once a month.

Winter of 1966

It broke my heart to witness Steve looked upon as a freak. Nelly and Al were constantly pushing him out of their way, and neither one of them showed him any affection. "He gives me the willies," said Al. "He reminds me of the hunchback of Notre Dame," said Nelly. The fact was that since he was born neither one liked him. To them there could only be one boy, Ralph.

Spring of 1966

I knew that Al loved me, but sometimes he wanted sex at the oddest of times. He got horny one morning after seeing two young girls hanging around our neighbor's yard across the street. He was cutting the grass outside and I noticed him looking at them in their tight little shorts, and not too long afterward he grabbed my hand and took me into the bathroom downstairs.

    First of all, it should be a mandatory law that anyone having oral sex should take a shower first, and I felt revolted that my feelings were not accounted for. Sex to me meant being in someone's arms and feeling passionate about each other, not about someone else. Maybe I should not have been so prejudiced since most of the time I fantasized being in love with someone else when I was having sex with Al. I had an eerie feeling that because he was my cousin it was no different from having sex with my own brother or something like that. I could not recall when I started thinking that way, but sometimes I felt like I really should be having sex with a stranger, not a family member. That afternoon I didn't have time to put on my fantasy thinking cap and hated the whole situation with Al. He smelled of sweat and grass.

I had a most humiliating experience when Joe and Ginny came from Long Island to visit us one day. Thank God there were no witnesses around when Joe thought it was funny to greet me in the hallway of our house by poking hard at my bellybutton with one of his fingers as he said each word, "Hi-how-are-you?" As he pressed my stomach for each word, a fart came out. That was a total of four farts!

He continued to tease me by poking me again and saying, "What-was-that?"

Three more farts came out. I promised myself never again look straight at Joe's face, never ever in my life. I hoped and prayed Joe would get amnesia.

Summer of 1966

It was almost the end of the summer. The days went by as if time stood still. Most of the time I felt disheartened with Nelly's attitude, but it did no good to complain about something that did not have a solution, so I wrote about each incident on a piece of paper and then flushed it down the toilet. It was my way of dealing with the situation after Al told me that he called Joe and Ruth, asking them if they could keep Nelly for half the year so we could have some peace at home. They refused. It sounded like Nelly was going to live with us forever and I had no other choice but to accept it.

I had lost all my respect for Nelly. I did not like her anymore either and I could not be happier than when she was in Long Island visiting Ruth and Joe. They both lived in the same town of Brentwood, Long Island. Life was a lot better and without the hassles when Nelly was away for three wonderful weeks out of the year. Sometimes she was away only for two weeks, but beggars could not be choosers. Each time she went away, I dreamed and hoped she would stay away a few extra weeks, or better than that, she would never come back.

Autumn of 1966

I was proud of myself for being slimmer than when I got married, except for my breasts which used to be a size A, but after having two children were now a size bigger. I asked Al if he was happy with my breasts or would he like me to have bigger ones like the movie stars and he said, "I love their size. Anything more than a mouthful would be a waste."

I liked his answer.

When Ruth came over to spend the weekend with us, I noticed I had reached my goal to be as skinny as her. We all went to the nearby town of Red Bank with the kids, and when it was lunchtime I ate half of my hotdog and threw the other half away. I was maintaining 117 pounds since Steve was born. My secret was not to eat too much and to only weigh myself once in a blue moon. Mama had taught me that. "Look in the mirror. If you don't like what you see, do something about it, but if you like it, keep it that way."

I always had breakfast with the kids and Nelly. On

weekends I enjoyed making pancakes and sausages on the grill and scrambled eggs or eggs sunny-side up. During the week it was usually Cream of Wheat or oatmeal in the winter and cold cereals in the summer. Then for lunch we had a sandwich, a salad, and a piece of fruit. That was it until dinnertime when Al came home. I drank lots and lots of water because I loved water. But I missed the water in Portugal. It tasted so much better than the water in America.

I was sure that being a housewife kept me fit because I did the housework as if I were a professional dancer; every move was planned to the sound of the music on the radio. If I had been born in America and was single, I would have been a go-go-dancer. My deepest secret desire was to be a go-go dancer someday.

Winter ending 1966

I left Ralph and Steve seated in their training plastic potty seats in the bathroom upstairs while I ran downstairs to fold a few clothes from the dryer. When I got back, they were finger painting the bathroom walls with poop. I could not leave them alone, not even for one minute.

I heard Al and Nelly having a disagreement downstairs one morning. They argued constantly with each other about petty stuff, and it just went on and on every day. When that happened, I made believe I had something to do in another part of the house and stayed away from them.

Al came upstairs to our bedroom where I was keeping busy dusting and gave me a big hug and kissed me in the lips saying, "She wants me to stop kissing you because you had tuberculosis when you were a baby, but I love you and I'll kiss you any time I want. She's not going to tell me how to live my life."

She knew I no longer had tuberculosis. It was true I had

it when I was one or two years old, but that had been more than twenty years ago. She was no longer my loving aunt and friend, she had become a crazy mother-in-law.

I got a "personal woman-to-woman letter" from Mama. "Never, never let your marriage go without sex for more than one week."
   I did not answer.

I took one of my summer dresses back to the store where I bought it to exchange it for a winter dress. I figured if Ruth could do it, I could too. I didn't know what to expect and I was very nervous. I didn't even have proof of purchase. The saleslady asked me if I had worn it.
   Getting red in the face I said, "No, I never used it."
   She lifted the dress up to look at it in more detail. What was she looking for? I wondered.
   Then slowly like the start of landslide loose granular sand began falling out of the hem and spreading like salt over her glass counter. "There's sand coming out of the seams!" her shrilled tone pierced my ears like an ice pick into my chest. I stopped breathing as she added with disdain. "Are you telling me that you didn't use it to go to the beach?"
   I looked in the direction of the exit, but if I ran out I would be admitting guilt. A sticky, dry feeling in my mouth and throat cut out the sound to my vocal cords An unique guttural sound came out as I said barely audible, "Maybe someone else that owned this dress before me returned it to your store after she went to the beach." She stared at me momentarily, shook her head and said, "I'm going to call the manager."
   That's it, I was going to prison. I would never see my children again, Nelly would take over the household on a more permanent basis but at least Al would marry an honest woman.

The manager, a young man with long dark hair smiled at me and then said to her, "Just give her store credit." And he walked away nonchalantly.

I had successfully returned a used clothing item to a department store and gotten away with it. I couldn't wait to call Ruth. She was going to be proud of me.

I was at Shop Rite buying some groceries and Ralph was seated inside the carriage playing with a box of animal cookies and Steve was seated on the top seat when he grabbed my hand and took a bite. I immediately grabbed his hand and took a bite back. Of course he started crying and the only reason I didn't cry too was because I was an adult.

A woman was watching and said, "Oh my God, she bit the child's hand!"

"Yeah, and I bet you he won't do it again!" I said.

I was a great believer in parental example.

Winter of 1967

When Al and I saw the movie *Dr. Zhivago*, he was moved to tears. I thought the movie was too long and boring. Joe said he liked it a lot too. I guess it was a man's type of movie. I preferred exciting adventures or comedies. My favorite comedy movie that year was *The Russians Are Coming, the Russians Are Coming*.

Miniskirts became the latest fashion, and they were causing a lot of controversy in the news. I bought myself a pair of brown imitation leather boots and a light brown leatherlike vest to wear over one of my silk brown blouses and an imitation leather miniskirt to match the vest. Al liked it a lot, and every time we went out he asked me to wear my "sexy outfit" as he called it. I enjoyed getting compliments from Al. It was nice to know that after being married for four whole years my husband still found me attractive.

Uncle Augusto, who was a doctor in Portugal, had diagnosed me with juvenile rheumatoid arthritis, when I used to suffer from bone pain in my legs as a child. I still experienced the same pain on and off. When it hit me it was excruciatingly deep, like knives stabbing my legs. I thought about going to a doctor, but since the pain, only lasted a few days I just waited for it to go away.

Mama and Papa were heart broken. Max-Leão had told them he was an arms dealer and sold guns and ammunitions to whatever country wanted them. I wondered why Max-Leão even told them such nonsense, unless he wanted to get back at them for what he suffered when they disowned him for marrying Patricia. If that was his intention, he had succeeded.

Spring of 1967

Al got home from work at five in the afternoon. We all had dinner and then watched television before going to sleep. On weekends he cut the grass, we went shopping for food and we had more of a family gathering at meal times. To an outsider it would seem we had a relatively normal and calm household, but it was far from the truth. Steve's mere existence continued to annoy Nelly and Al. A day didn't go by that Steve was not maltreated with verbal abuse, slapped or pushed out of their way. "Steve is only three years old, how can you do that to him?" I had told Al several times. To which he would respond, "He's always in my way. Nelly told me she has the same problem. He gets what he deserves." On the other hand, Ralph was treated as if he was the only one with human rights. I didn't know if it was because of the special way he was treated, but Ralph was hardheaded and if he didn't get his way he threw a fit until he got what he wanted. He was learning to be selfish. When I tried to get Al to put a stop to it he would say, "You're right about Nelly, spoiling Ralph but she's my mother and she has a bad heart, I can't get her upset."

I began making plans to run away with my sons. I had to save them from their grandmother and their father. Going away was the only solution for the problem that I could think of at the time.

I found the perfect travel box and hid it under my bed. I painted it with flowers so it didn't look like luggage. I began putting a few children's clothes into it. I wasn't sure where we were going, but I knew it had to be to another state far away from New Jersey so no one could find us.

On the way home from work, Al got into a car accident. It was a bright sunny day, so maybe the sun got into his eyes. His car and another car sideswiped each other as they both lost control of their vehicles on Route 9. Al said the woman wasn't driving straight. Nobody got hurt, but both cars were towed. Al was smart; he only bought used cars. What was the use of buying a new car if it was only going to last one or two years?

Summer of 1967

Nelly, the kids, and I went to spend a lazy afternoon at the beach in Asbury Park and I was putting down our blanket by the water when Nelly said, "Did you turn off the kitchen stove before we left?" I couldn't remember, and she didn't remember either. It felt as if we were being afflicted by amnesia. We immediately gathered everything together and ran with the kids back into the car and I drove home as fast as I could while Nelly kept giving me a visual description of our house burning to the ground.

When we got home, the stove was off. One of us had turned it off on the way out, but we would never know who did it.

I was glad to be home on such a hot day. I was experiencing a pounding headache and felt like I was having a heatstroke. I had been spared from dying that day and it opened my eyes to stay away from the beach until the sun went down. The heat didn't bother Nelly—she loved it.

Al was a missiles inspector at Bendix, but he didn't have much say when the company wanted to pass something that was not safe to use. Al complained a lot about it when he got home. If the parts were not ready by a certain date the company could lose their next government contract. His boss was under constant stress and pushed the inspectors to give their seal of approval even when they knew things were not up to par. If Al didn't go along with his boss he could lose his job. That type of procedure went against his better judgment and it ate him up. Al came home frazzled and Nelly was worried about his health. One afternoon, Al came home laughing. "It was funny today to watch an engineer at work who lost his marbles. He was taken away to the nut house after standing on top of a chair flapping his arms up and down as if they were wings while making loud chirping sounds like a bird." I didn't see anything funny about it. It made me sad for days, thinking about the poor man and Al's lack of concern toward his co-worker.

Autumn of 1967

Al couldn't wait to retire and that was all he talked about. The word retirement to me meant stopping, dying, or not being productive. I didn't like the idea of Al retiring, because it would mean I had to sit down and watch television all day with him. That thought drove me crazy. He liked it when we sat together to watch television, but I was not allowed to do anything else—no crochet or needle point—he said only old ladies did that kind of stuff. I was not to read a book either, because it meant I was not paying attention to the police movie he watched and he wanted me to pay attention to every boring detail. I was also not allowed to talk unless it was during a commercial break, but during a commercial break he went into the kitchen to get snacks. I used to enjoy watching television, but I didn't like it anymore. I would rather do active things like hiking and camping which I had heard could also be fun to do with the family. But Al said he was too tired for any physical activities during the week and the weekends were made to rest.

The problem with Nelly staying at Joe's house more than a week or two was that Ginny went berserk when Nelly was there. Ginny blamed her increased daily alcohol intake on Nelly. Ruth was not a happy camper either. Both of them called me to complain and couldn't wait until Nelly left. "She has to go out every day to buy rye bread with seeds, and fresh fruit and vegetables. What the heck is that about?" Ruth would say to me.

"How can you live with Nelly?" Ginny asked me, several times.

Ruth would say, "I swear she's addicted to shopping. I have to stop my normal life to drive her all over the freaking place as if I don't have anything else to do."

Big deal! Buying stuff was the least of my worries, and when she bought any food she always shared it with us. I didn't mind taking Nelly shopping. I didn't understand what they had to complain about. My only gripes were the way Nelly spoiled Ralph, mistreated Steve, and treated me as if I was a nincompoop. Those things were what made me upset.

Nelly and I were thrilled when Theresa, the neighbor on the corner from us, invited us to her Tupperware party. Theresa was cross-eyed and she wore corrective eyeglasses which made her eyes look double their size. On top of that, she wore a ton of eye makeup, which made her eyes appear even more drastically unreal. I wondered what her eyes really looked like. Theresa was deaf and had a speech impediment. She spoke in guttural sounds. It was very hard for me to understand her. But Theresa was a very nice person—probably the reason why her husband had asked her to marry him.

It was the first time anyone in our neighborhood had invited us over. I hired two young girls from the neighborhood to babysit Ralph and Steve while we were away. I figured with two sitters there was a better chance they could handle them.

After an hour at Theresa's party I received a phone call to come home immediately. Ralph and Steve were giving the two sitters a hard time and they had had it with them.

Winter ending 1967

I removed my silly runaway box from under my bed and threw it away. I couldn't come up with a good idea on how to survive alone with my children. Where would I get the money to buy food and pay for a roof over our heads? I needed an education and then a good paying job to accomplish that.

I got my wish for Christmas. Al bought me a sewing machine table with a cabinet. I went shopping for patterns and material and soon started making my own clothes. I bought some flannel material to make pajamas and matching robes for the boys. I also made yellow cotton curtains for the kitchen window which made the kitchen bright and cheery. My greatest sewing achievement was reupholstering the couch downstairs. Al kept saying we needed a new couch, and I surprised him and Nell with my work. I was lucky that the couch had a simple design. It was easy to staple the thick material to it.

Winter of 1968

Al and I were waiting in line at our bank in downtown Freehold. In front of us there was a black lady talking to the teller and she had her little girl, who was about two or three years old seated on top of the marble counter, close to her.

Al said to the child, "Hi little monkey." He threw her a little kiss. "You sure look like a cute little monkey."

The woman turned around and wanted to hit Al as she shouted, "Who are you calling a monkey? How dare you call my daughter a monkey!"

Instead of apologizing, Al said, "But she's a little monkey, look how cute she is."

I grabbed Al by the arm and pushed him out the door, whispering, "Do you want to have us both killed?"

In Al's opinion the mother was a pathetic racist and obviously very ignorant. Al affectionately called me his little monkey and so were all the kids he found cute. But he didn't think before he said things like that to strangers who might find his remarks offensive.

It was snowing heavily when Al knocked at our front door. He had lost control of his car when it skidded on ice and into the farmer's fence across from Shop Rite. Once again he had walked away from his demolished car without a scratch. As always he said he was due for another car.

In Portugal people kept their cars forever unless there was a head-on collision, and in that case both cars were demolished beyond repair. Usually cars were passed on to the next member of the family as an inheritance, but like Al said, "Here in America even if people change the oil every three months, it's meant to fall apart after five years, which is about when the last car payment is due. They know what they are doing. It's all about making money."

Braving A New World

On March 4, 1968 I finally became an American citizen! I had to memorize all the presidents' names starting with George Washington and some of the laws of our government. I was a nervous wreck when I went to court, but it turned out that all we had to do was to stand in front of the judge, raise our hands, and all ten of us got sworn in as a group. I was issued a certificate of naturalization and my name was shortened from Verónica Leah Toledano Ezaguy Wartenberg Esagui to Veronica Esagui.

I wrote to my parents about my achievement, I was now an American, but I didn't share with them that I had officially dropped my middle name, and their family name. A few years back I had told my parents that in America I was called by the name of Ronnie, a nickname for Veronica and they were very upset principally Papa. I could only imagine how hurt he would feel if he found out that Wartenberg, his family name no longer existed when I used my signature.

Spring of 1968

It was just before lunch when Ralph inserted his head between the metal railings going up the steps from our front door. He was yelling, "I'm stuck! I can't pull my head out." Nelly panicked and insisted I call the Freehold First Aid Squad. They were able to pull Ralph's head out without having to cut the railing off, but as soon as they left, Steve put his head in between the railing and looked at us with a smile of accomplishment. Talk about wanting attention! It was just a question of delicately maneuvering Steve's head out from between the metal bars. The kids thought it was a joke as they showed us how easy it was for them to put their head in and out between the railing bars. Once Nelly and I walked away, they quit doing it as they realized we were no longer impressed.

Driving with Nelly and the kids had become a job in itself. "Aren't you going to do something about the way Steve picks on Ralph? How can you drive as if nothing is happening in the back seat?" she would ask me.

What did she want me to do? Stop the car in the highway, beat Steve up, and pat Ralph on the back? I bet she did. They were being children, both were being bad, both were at fault, and yes, I blocked out their carrying on or I would have had an accident.

"Look at the pink bunny! Oops, you both missed him running over there," I said, pointing to the side of the road. They always fell for it, each looking out their window and away from each other.

"Keep your eyes open to the road or you'll miss the bunnies." They were so gullible!

We always sang with gusto to their favorite tune the rest of the way. "All together now, "Ninety-nine bottles of beer on the wall, ninety-nine bottles of beer…"

Dr. DeCicco, our family doctor, felt that Ralph needed his tonsils out and recommended Dr. Stewart, an ear, nose, and throat specialist in Red Bank.

Dr. Stewart agreed but added, "He also has bad adenoids and they need to be removed." Then he pointed to Steve, who was standing next to me, and asked if Steve had his tonsils out yet.

"No. He's very healthy. He never gets sick."

"That's a big mistake in your part, not to have it done now, before he starts to have problems. Besides, the insurance will cover the surgery and it will save you the headache of returning to my office."

"I don't mind coming back if he has problems later on. I'd rather wait."

"The tonsils and adenoids are of no use to the body and I can do both kids on the same day. What do you say, mom?"

"If you think it's better, I guess so."

Braving A New World

He then grabbed my face with one hand and turned it side to side as if looking for a pimple. "I'm also a plastic surgeon," he said. "I could make your nose round and cute." Aunt Heydee had always told me that my nose was one of the most perfect noses she had ever seen throughout her career as an artist, so I decided to stay the way I was. It also bothered me when he used the word "cute." Why would I want to look cute at the cost of having my nose cut with a knife?

I was allowed to visit Ralph and Steve while they slept after their surgeries. They were very lucky to be born in a time when medicine was no longer antiquated. They didn't have to suffer like I did when I was a child and the doctor took my tonsils out by having me tied to a chair with my hands behind my back, while screaming from the top of my lungs.

In this spring of 1968 the Mafia killed Dr. Martin Luther King Jr. and then they killed Robert Kennedy. I knew the reason why some Americans killed without even blinking an eye. They had criminal minds; they were the descendants of some of the original pioneers who used to be murderers and had been sent to America hundreds of years ago as punishment for their crimes.

"When I first came to America," said Nelly. "There were a lot of gangsters in those days. They used machine guns to kill store owners refusing to pay for protection. They would drive their cars through the streets of New York City and bang, bang, bang." She accented each bang by extending her lips out and pointing her right hand to look like a gun while using her thumb up and down as if shooting someone.

"It was called the Mafia, a family of organized crime." Al added, "They never left, they are still powerful. Their children grew into the business and now they know how to handle crime in a legal manner by paying top lawyers to keep their necks out of jail and making it all look very innocent and legalized. Our country is being run by a bunch of criminals and there's nothing we can do about it."

Even though the whole thing was very depressing, they confirmed my suspicions.

Once my brother Max-Leão and his wife Patricia had their two children, my parents wanted to forget the past and open their arms to them; after all, they were their grandchildren. They seemed to be on better terms with each other, but it was too late to completely discard old memories still painful to both sides. I wrote to Max-Leão and Patricia trying to rekindle our family ties but after a month of silence, I knew they didn't intend to write back.

"The birds! The birds are coming! They're attacking the children outside!"

The cop on the phone was not impressed with my dramatic call. But it was true. It was a nice sunny day and both Ralph and Steve were playing in the front yard with two other children and the birds from one tree across the street from our house started diving toward them. The kids started running and screaming and Nelly and I had to rush Ralph and Steve inside while the other two ran home. It was happening just like in the movie *The Birds*. But the police took my phone call as if I was a nut and I was told that the children were probably playing too close to a bird's nest and I should keep them home for the rest of the day.

Aunt Heydee wrote that she was coming to America to visit us for a whole month! I couldn't wait to see her. She was going to be surprised that I could drive. I couldn't wait for her to meet my children, too.

Braving A New World

Summer of 1968

Aunt Heydee was the first one to disembark from the airplane. I was not surprised. As always, she was the first one at everything. She had not changed much, except for being a little shorter and blonder. As we drove into New Jersey she wanted me to stop in the middle of the ongoing traffic so she could look at New York City from a distance. Of course, I didn't stop the car in the middle of the highway or on the bridges—we would have gotten killed. She was moved almost to tears when she saw the row of headlights from the oncoming traffic across one of the New Jersey bridges. She pointed to it and said, "My God, this is what I call spectacular. It's a thousand times better than the Palace of Lights in France for which I paid a small fortune to see."

I had missed Aunt Heydee. She enjoyed life like a child eating an ice cream cone for the first time. Everything we took for granted she saw as if through a magic window of wonders. But Aunt Heydee didn't like Freehold. I felt the same way. After so many years of living in Freehold I still had not gotten used to the silence of the nights, and nothing, absolutely nothing to do for miles. If we were to walk all day we still couldn't get to a mall without a car. "If I didn't have my children to play with, I would have gone mad." I confided.

Aunt Heydee said, "I know how you feel. What a forsaken place. It's in the middle of nowhere. "

She and Nelly began taking the bus to New York City on a daily basis. I went with them once but it was hard on the kids, as they were still too young and got tired easily.

Aunt Heydee watched quietly as I washed the kitchen floor on my knees with Nelly supervising my cleaning as she always did. "Go back and clean more over there," Nelly said pointing to where I had missed with the sponge in hand. "And then wash over there too."

When Aunt Heydee and I were alone in the backyard she said, "If I had not seen it with my own eyes I would not have believed it. She treats you like a servant, the way she tells you what to do."

"Ordering me around is not as bad as interfering in my children's lives."

"That's no excuse for acting like a mother-in-law instead of a loving aunt to you. I'm very disappointed with her, my own sister. And you so young, your lifestyle is abominable, cleaning all day, taking care of the kids without a cultural community to be involved with. I don't know how I'm going to tell this to your mother."

Aunt Heydee was right, but culture was not that important to me. Peace at home was a lot more desirable.

Saturday morning Aunt Heydee and I left for Atlantic City. Al offered to babysit while I was out for the weekend. Before leaving, Nelly and Al stood by my car window. He said, "Promise that while in Atlantic City you will not go into any nightclubs."

"Decent women don't go into such places without a man," Nelly said.

I made it to Atlantic City in one hour's time. I wanted to show off my driving abilities but Aunt Heydee took it the way it was; a car was supposed to drive fast and she didn't even blink an eye when I drove over the speed limit.

We had a great time in Atlantic City, visiting all the shops on the boardwalk, the famous Pier and watching the horse with the girl rider jumping into the ocean, but Aunt Heydee was disappointed that we couldn't go into a strip club. I told her I couldn't disobey Al and Nelly's orders. She said, "I admire you for keeping your promise to them. Let's explore all the beautiful hotels, then. They didn't make you swear on that."

It was a lot of fun going up on the elevators and

checking out some of the hotel roofs overlooking the ocean and we took a few peeks at the huge and beautiful staterooms where they held banquets.

We stayed overnight in a motel because Al was worried about me driving back at night. We slept late and after lunch we headed home. I took my time driving back. It felt good to have someone to talk to. "I wish I had the guts to speak up but I can't," I told Aunt Heydee. "I can't handle any kind of confrontation."

"Your mother did everything possible to groom you to be a good, obedient little girl without individual thoughts or opinions. The idea was to keep you under her control until you got married and then you would make a smooth transition to being an obedient, happy wife. The problem is that you're still without personality or any backbone." She added her own practical philosophy. "Our destiny lies in our own hands. Grow up and get on with your life. Have you forgotten that you're Napoleon Number Two?"

We laughed. She was Napoleon Number One and I was her pupil growing up in Portugal. She had taught me how to get inside the opera house, the movie theatres, and the circus without paying. Yes, she was a little Machiavellian and took lots of chances in getting caught, but she had no other choice. Her meager earnings as a French teacher were not enough to pay for her lifestyle. We talked about the old times, and how much fun we had while she educated me in the ways of life.

Al took a few days off from work, and we all went to Niagara Falls. On the way to Canada we saw a two-car accident. Both cars had turned over in the grassy median field, and some of the passengers were lying on the ground. Al didn't stop the car and kept driving.

Aunt Heydee yelled out, "Al, why aren't we stopping to help those injured people?"

"In America, if you stop to take care of someone hurt in

an accident and they die, their family can sue you."

"I never heard of anything so heartless," Aunt Heydee cried.

"Don't worry. The police and the ambulance will soon be there to take care of them," Nelly said.

I was just as much at fault for not insisting we help them. Before I got married, Mama told me over and over again, "Once you get married you will have to make the family decisions because a man no matter how smart he is depends on his wife's common sense. They think they are making the decisions, but we are the ones that control them. Remember behind every successful man there's a woman telling him exactly what needs to be done." I should have insisted that Al stop the car. He would have listened to me, just to make me happy. But I couldn't speak up; it went against my grain. I was a weakling, a coward, a non-assertive blob of "Yes ma'am, yes sir."

Al got fed up with Aunt Heydee during the trip to Canada. We were in bed when he said, "I'm sorry we brought her along. She's running us ragged trying to see everything in three days and two nights."

"If she hadn't suggested places for us to visit we would not have seen Niagara Falls on the American side." I felt proud of myself for expressing my thoughts to him. My goodness, Aunt Heydee was 68 years old. If we couldn't keep up with her at our age, there was something wrong with us.

Before Aunt Heydee got in the plane back to Portugal, she said, "Write to me every time Nelly does something that upsets you. It will help you get it off your chest and then you won't feel so sad and oppressed." I promised.

Our neighbor Susan told me she was very offended with the way Aunt Heydee had spoken to her one morning when she was hanging out her laundry. Aunt Heydee had said, "Good morning, madame."

"I'm not a madam. I'm a decent woman with seven children."

But Aunt Heydee just waved goodbye and kept walking away saying, "Nice meeting you, madame." I explained to Susan that French was our second language in Portugal, and Aunt Heydee was being nice to her because madame meant "lady" in French.

I also learned from Ralph that Aunt Heydee had told him and Steve to go and play with the toys in the neighbor's yard, even after he told her the toys were not theirs and they were in "the neighbor's yard." She had told them, "I don't see a fence. Now go and play." I had to smile, it sounded like something Aunt Heydee would say. I really, really missed her.

After listening to Nelly over and over again telling Al and me, "There's something mentally wrong with Steve," I agreed to take him to Dr. Orlando, a psychiatrist in Freehold. Nelly said to the doctor, "Steve doesn't talk much and plays with a single toy for hours. This can't be normal for a child. In my opinion, he's mentally retarded."

Dr. Orlando said to me, "You're his mother, what's your opinion?"

"I used to be the same way when I was a kid and nobody called me retarded; they said I was an introvert. I believe Steve is like me, that's all."

The psychiatrist took Steve to another room to do a few tests and when he returned half an hour later, he said, "You are right. There's nothing wrong with your little boy. What he needs is some type of social integration with children of his own age. I recommend you put him in some type of pre-kindergarten. There he will get the attention he needs."

No kidding he needed attention—how about his grandmother's and his father's love? I didn't tell the doctor that I was constantly defending Steve and trying to pick up the pieces when they mistreated him. I was satisfied with the psychiatrist's opinion. Hopefully Nelly would stop picking on Steve and leave him alone. The idea of sending him to school and away from her a few hours a day was a great idea.

Autumn of 1968

Ralph started kindergarten and Steve started pre-kindergarten. On their first day Ralph came home and there were no problems. But when Steve's school bus stopped in front of our house, Steve was not in it. Somehow during the 30-minute drive home Steve had disappeared from the bus. The driver said she had seen Steve entering the bus and sitting down. I called the school and they said he was not there. I panicked. I got in the car and drove to his school. No wonder they couldn't see him, he was playing on one of the swings in the playground behind the school building. He smiled and waved at me. He didn't understand that at the end of the day he had to come home. He had gotten onto the bus, but he must have left before the bus drove off the school's parking lot.

I got a letter from Mama. "You have hurt my feelings very deeply. You rather confide your personal tormented life with Aunt Heydee than me, your own mother?"

I sent a letter asking her to forgive me, it wasn't my intent to ignore her. The letters to Aunt Heydee were simply the result of her visit to America and asking me to write to her, which is what I did.

I stopped writing to Aunt Heydee and began opening my heart and soul to Mama, hoping to get some words of wisdom from her. But it was just a dream, a pointless, hopeless dream. Mama never gave me any comfort while growing up, why would she do it now? She lived in another world; a place where she was the only one existing. I didn't have the courage to tell her to write me a normal letter instead of poetry. She was still writing like a poetess and none of it made sense. She went on and on, page after page. I felt terrible, but sometimes I didn't read her letters until I was seated on the toilet so I didn't waste time reading so much gibberish. Mama was getting ready to publish a poetry book and it looked like she was practicing on me. I would have loved to have had a normal mother to talk to. I asked her a simple question and she answered with poetry and philosophy about things which had nothing to do with what I had written.

Winter ending 1968

Last night, Al woke up thirsty in the middle of the night and was about to go downstairs to the kitchen when he barely saw a cup of water on my nightstand. It was dark except for the moonlight coming through the bedroom window. He picked up the cup and heard a little rattle coming from inside so he assumed it was ice. He should have known better, since I didn't use ice in my water. I woke up to the sound of his shrieking voice when he drank the water and yelled out, "What the hell is this?" He turned the bedroom light on and stood by our bed holding my front tooth partial plate between two fingers as if holding a dead animal. He repeated, "What the hell is this?" He wore a horrified look.

"Oh my God, you almost swallowed my tooth." I got up as horrified as him, but for a different reason. "You could have choked to death." I took the partial from his hand and put it back in the cup, then went to the bathroom to cover it with tap water. "I've always waited until you fell asleep to put my partial in water until the morning so the plastic didn't dry up. I felt embarrassed letting you know about it."

He followed me into the bathroom "It's plain gross, that's what it is," he said. "I'm gonna be sick of my stomach." He gargled with mouthwash.

I understood how he felt but it was not as bad as he made it sound to be. The partial had been brushed with toothpaste and the water in the glass was clean. I told him about my cousin Rachel in Portugal who bragged about her French husband running after her to kiss her. He would stick his tongue into her mouth and even lick her teeth to show her how much he loved her.

Marilyn, the neighbor with an attitude, sold her house and in moved a couple with their five-year-old daughter. Barbara was very neighborly—just the opposite of Marilyn.

Nelly and Barbara got along great. Once in a while Barbara called me on the telephone and asked me to come over because she was feeling lonely. Her husband didn't pay much attention to her, and she classified the other neighbors as snobs. She told me not to tell anyone including Nelly that she used to be a call-girl and that's how she had met her husband. She showed me pictures of when she was skinny and blonde. She kept Lisa, her daughter, locked in her bedroom with lots of toys. "I don't have the patience for her; she gives me a headache." She did let Lisa out to play with Ralph and Steve.

Al loved to shop on weekends and he used his credit card as if it were free money. I did my best to dissuade him, but he would say, "That's what the card is for. By using it often, we benefit from good credit." He loved to buy gadgets because they were on sale. Bills were bills no matter how one looked at it. In the end we had to pay for them plus interest. We were far from being rich, and it did not make sense to me to waste money on junk just to get credit to buy more junk.

For Christmas, I surprised Al with an acoustic guitar. I bought it at Sears, my favorite store to buy appliances and everything else, because if not satisfied, they took the stuff back without a hassle. Barbara gave me a discount coupon she had found in the local newspaper, for one free guitar lesson at the local music store in Freehold. "I have no interest in playing guitar," Al said. "You take the guitar lesson." He took me to the music store and had me sign up for a month of private guitar lessons, starting in January of 1969.

Winter of 1969

Since Steve started school he had started to talk and was a lot more outgoing. The only problem was that Nelly liked picking on him when he got home from school. I told her, "Please to leave him alone and stop arguing and picking on him. He is just a child."

"It's not arguing, it's a debate." I called it an emotional beating since he got hit if she didn't like his answer.

There were other problems like saying things that were plain mean and hurt my feelings, like prophesizing my children's future. She kept saying over and over again, as if it were a joke of some kind, "Ralph is very intelligent just like my husband. He's going to be a doctor someday, but Steve will probably be a garbage man. That's all he's good for."

How dare she say that in front of the boys. I never thought someday I would hate Nelly, but I did. She took pleasure out of being a nasty grandmother. She constantly put the kids into competition with each other, and they were always going at each other like cats and dogs. I bought them identical outfits and even identical toys to make them feel equally loved. I hated what was going on but I didn't know what to do to stop her.

I loved playing guitar. It was like learning a new language. The concentration it took to learning to read music, took me away from daily family matters. I could only concentrate on one important thing—where to put my fingers to get a clear sound. After the first week of practicing, all my left fingers had blisters from pressing against the metal strings.

I made the mistake of showing my fingertips to Mr. Crocker, my guitar teacher, who said he felt sorry for me, and then proceeded to kiss my fingertips, one by one. "This will help to heal them," he said. The way he looked at me reminded me of my cousin Leão, the pervert and I felt very uncomfortable. I was too bashful to pull my hand away from him.

I asked Mr. Crocker to show me how to play rock and roll, but he said, "If you are going to be good at playing guitar, you need to learn classical first." As soon as I learned to play rock and roll, I planned on stopping taking lessons from him.

When Barbara came to visit us, which was at least three or four times a week, she always used our blender to prepare a drink for herself. She had tried to make us drink with her, but neither Nelly nor I drank alcoholic beverages. One day she was making her usual drink and forgot to take the metal spoon out of our blender. The glass broke, and there was brandy and cream all over the kitchen. Barbara promised to buy us a new blender. Nelly didn't care; she felt that Barbara was the best friend we had ever had. When Barbara asked me to go out with her on Friday night to the movies, I was surprised when Nelly offered to babysit. She usually just babysat once a year for a couple of hours when Al and I went out in the evening to celebrate our wedding anniversary. Al also went along with my escapade with Barbara and said it would do me good to have a girl's night out. My first time out with a friend, I was very excited.

The movie was *Bullitt* with my favorite actor Steve McQueen. Barbara talked throughout the whole movie. I made plans to see it again on my own. After the movie, she said, "Let's go and have a drink at a high-class joint."

We went to Van's Restaurant in Freehold and sat at the bar. Barbara ordered two Brandy Alexanders. I looked at her surprised. "I know you don't drink," she said reading my thoughts. "Just hold the glass and act like you do. When I'm done with my drink I'll have yours." We got to talk and found out why Nelly had offered to babysit. Barbara had convinced her to do it. She had me laughing. I told her about the incident of Al drinking from the glass with my partial and she encouraged me to see a dentist and have him build a bridge for my front tooth. She said it was a simple procedure and much easier than what she had gone through. A few years back they had implanted all her front teeth into her gums after she was involved in a car accident. There were all kinds of new dental procedures available now that I was not aware of. It gave me hope.

I was surprised when a man in his fifties, dressed in a suit and tie, came over to talk to us. Barbara introduced him as the ex-mayor of Freehold.

He got real close to my face and said, "That drink looks delicious. Do you mind if I take a sip?"

I obediently handed him the drink. "Where did you put your lips?" he asked thinking most likely that he was being seductive. "I want to drink from the same side."

"Sorry, but I haven't tried it."

His body was very close to mine. "Go ahead then, I'll wait," he said.

I took a sip and handed the glass to him, noticing his wedding band. He drank from the glass while giving me the eyes of love. "It tastes delicious, coming from your lips," he whispered in my ear.

What a jerk! Not knowing what to do next, I pushed him awkwardly away as I got up from the barstool. "Barbara, we need to get going; it's late."

"You must excuse my friend," she told him. "She's a bit

shy for her age. How about I give you my number and you call me?" She wrote her number on a napkin and he slipped it into his pocket.

As we walked out, she was laughing. "Wasn't it exciting to know that we still have it? And did you notice how much he liked you?"

"Yes, but we are married and so is he."

"So what, we were only talking, not doing anything with him. Wasn't it fun to act like we're single?"

I nodded my head up and down, but I wasn't convincing enough because she called me prudish. Then she asked me not to tell Al or Nelly about our little escapade. I had no intention of telling anyone, much less Al or Nelly. I felt out of place going out with Barbara, just like I did when I used to go out in Portugal with Morena, Mama's sister, as Morena loved men, all men.

While visiting the family in Long Island, Ginny took me aside and encouraged me to get myself a bottle of liquor and drink it throughout the day. "That's what I do when Nelly stays with us, and it works great." The way she laughed I could tell she was already tipsy.

When I got back to New Jersey I bought a bottle of vodka and hid it in my bedroom, inside the dresser's top drawer, under my sweaters.

Nelly started nagging me so I went upstairs, grabbed the vodka bottle, and was about to take a slug when I felt someone staring at me. Ralph and Steve were both standing in the bedroom's doorway. They didn't have to say anything.

I knew what I was doing was the action of a coward. I wrinkled my nose, and stuck my tongue out as if ready to throw up. "Yuck," I said. I took the bottle downstairs and put it into the bar closet in the playroom. I promised myself never to drink alcohol again to deal with life.

~ *Chapter Five* ~

JOINING THE WORK FORCE

1969

Spring of 1969

Al had been talking for over three years about the layoffs set to happen anytime soon. His biggest fear had come true. It took a couple of years of being worried and stressed out, but it finally happened. The government was no longer interested in the production of missiles. After ten years of working for the Bendix Corporation, he was officially out of work.

Two months went by and Al couldn't get hired. "You are overqualified." Was the answer he got everywhere he applied for a job. Nelly was nice enough to lend us some money to pay our bills, but she wasn't made of money. I told them I wouldn't mind working.

At first Al said no way, but as the weeks went by it began to make sense. If we were going to pay the mortgage and the monthly bills, one of us had to work.

"Don't count on me for babysitting," Nelly said.

"Ronnie, if you find a job, I'll stay at home and take care of the kids," said Al.

The next day I applied in person at the Freehold

Pharmacy and they hired me to clean the drugstore, stock merchandise, and deliver medicine to people's homes. Except for working in my father's office when I was growing up, I had no work experience. It was my first job in America and I was very excited about it.

Mama had taught me how to keep a monthly budget before I got married, and the time had arrived for me to apply my knowledge to keep us afloat. I was very gentle when I told Al that we needed to have a budget so we were aware of not spending more than I made. As long as Al didn't keep charging, we could survive temporarily with my paycheck.

My full time job at the pharmacy lasted two weeks.

Al found out I was delivering medicine to the black community. As it happened, in one of the houses where I delivered some medicine, an older lady remarked that I was taking a big risk coming into her neighborhood as a young white girl with a load of drugs in the trunk of my car. In her opinion I was asking for nothing but trouble. Of course, once I related her comment to Nelly and Al, I was jobless.

But at least Nelly got something out of the experience. At her request I asked the pharmacist, "In your opinion what is the best facial cream?"

"Vaseline is the answer! But no woman will walk around with her face covered with it. They'd rather pay a fortune for some tutu junk cream."

Nelly got rid of all her face creams and began using Vaseline. She swore by it.

I answered an ad in the local newspaper for a secretarial position at a lawyer's office on Main Street in Freehold. The lawyer was not a nice person. He made fun of my accent by trying to talk like me and then said, "We don't hire foreigners. They don't know the alphabet and can't file. For the fun of it, let's hear it."

I got scared of making a mistake and said the alphabet in Portuguese. He got up from his chair "Just like I thought."

He opened the door to his office with one hand, and used one finger to point out. "Leave, before I lose my temper."

I left his office with my flushed face down so no one in the waiting room could see the shame I felt. I had no intentions of telling Al or Nelly what had happened. We had a lot of bills to pay, and I quickly pushed aside my feelings. I was determined to get a job, any job. One of the things I had learned from Aunt Heydee was to never give up.

The next day I applied for another job and got hired as a typist at the Motor Vehicle Department. I lasted one whole day. I would still be working there if it weren't for the supervisor who caught me typing with two fingers and a little slower than everybody else. She turned me into the main office. When I got hired, they asked me if I could type more than eighty words per minute. In Portuguese I was very, very quick at typing. I told them, "Oh, probably even faster than that." They never asked me how many fingers I used.

We were in a very challenging financial situation, and since I was not working to help my family, I had to help in other ways. I sold my thirty-five-diamond, moon-shaped-pin for $500 to a woman who saw me trying to sell it in a jewelry store at the Eatontown Mall. I felt bad because when I left Portugal, I had sworn to Mama that I would never sell the pin. It had belonged to Grandma Rica. Grandpa Leão had bought it from the last Queen of Portugal when she had to flee the country.

I took all the silver plates I brought with me from Portugal, my gold bracelet with the charms I had collected through the years and the rings Al had given me when we were engaged and everything I could think of that would bring in some money, to a jewelry store on Route 9.

"They're old and have no real value," said the jeweler from behind the counter, and he paid me by the pound, which was very nice of him. He gave me $350 for everything, and I was able to put together a total of $850, which I gave to Al to help pay our bills.

I got hired at Freedman's Bakery in Freehold. I felt like a nurse in my white uniform and matching white cap.

It took me two days before I learned to reach into the showcase and take my arms and hands out without getting whipped cream all over them.

Papa rarely wrote. Usually he just added his signature at the bottom of Mama's letter. I felt horrible that my last letter to Mama, had such a bad impact on him. He wrote, "The thought that my daughter is unhappy and describes her life as being tied with her hands behind her back, drowning in the middle of the ocean, breaks my heart. I have cried every day since I read your letter."

I decided to stop writing to Mama about my problems with Nelly and face my own evils. I wrote back, "A miracle has happened. Everything is hunky-dory and I'm the happiest woman alive." Not too far from the truth, I was still working at the bakery and bringing home a paycheck.

I got an idea of how to get rid of Nelly. I was going to use voodoo. I had seen it done in movies, and it always seemed to work. I would attempt to kill her when she was outside, watering the grass.

I closed my bedroom door and got a few pins from the sewing kit with the intention of inserting them into Nelly's picture. But when it came down to actually inserting a pin into her photograph, I couldn't do it. I didn't hate her enough to kill her. I just didn't like it that she made all the decisions, running my life and my children's lives as if she were their mother. She was like a protective mother hen with Ralph, and a screwed up psychotic killer with Steve.

Still, I couldn't do the voodoo; if she died, I would have to live for the rest of my life as a wicked person.

I won the cherry cake-selling contest at the bakery! I sold six cherry cakes in one day, even though the other two girls paid for my lunch and asked me to take my time during my lunch break so they would have a better chance of selling some cherry cakes while I was away.

The owner gave me a bottle of champagne and asked me if I wanted to be the bakery's manager. It was only a title, not a raise, but Al said it was a good start. I accepted the position. At the end of the day, I was allowed to take home milk, bread, and cakes, all at half price. Ralph's favorite was the rainbow cookies, which were soft cookies with marzipan layers. They were my favorite too. Steve only wanted milk. Nelly liked the rye bread with seeds and Al liked the doughnuts. Except for the rainbow cookies, I didn't care much for sweets, probably because I worked all day in the bakery. By the end of the day, the scent of sugar and vanilla coming from the ovens stuck to my clothes, my skin and hair and entered my lungs leaving a taste in my mouth that took away the desire to indulge.

I received a letter from my parents. They were very concerned with my younger brother José. He had gone to France for the summer and worked in Paris as a dishwasher in a restaurant. Everything was going fine, and he even got engaged to a French girl. But then José started acting strange and his fiancée broke off their engagement. Mama and Papa had to go to Paris and bring José back to Portugal. The doctors didn't know what was wrong with him. The whole letter was very vague and details were missing as to what and why, etc. After José stood on the roof of my parents' apartment house and tried to jump, they had him heavily medicated.

Paul, one of the cleaning boys at the bakery, and I

became friends. He was only eighteen old but we got along great. One day we were both busy in the kitchen placing freshly baked bread loafs on large metal trays to be taken to be displayed in the front of the bakery when he whispered, "I need your advice." I was all ears. "I hitchhiked home yesterday evening and the motorist who picked me up advised me to have sex with a man before I settled with a girl. He told me that way I could decide what was best for me when it came to sex. What do you think?"

I didn't give it much thought. "Maybe he was hoping you would have sex with him." I said jokingly.

"You might be right. I had a feeling about it. You're very wise for your age."

"I'm twenty-five—not as young as you, but I'm married and I have two children, so I have some experience about life." I knew I was bragging, but it felt good to act like a mature woman. Al and Nelly would be shocked if they knew I was giving advice on matters of sex. Working at the bakery had provided me a new lease on life, I was free to express myself and talk to customers with a sense of knowledge. I admit it, it went to my head.

A man bought a loaf of bread and then asked me if I was wearing lace underwear from Frederick's of Hollywood. I had never heard of that store. I thought it was an odd question from a man and tried to be polite in case he was gay. I pulled him to the side and said, "I get my underwear from next door, Britt's department store. You can find anything you need there, and it's not as expensive as going all the way to Hollywood."

"Are you for real?" he said.

"Of course I'm real." What a dumb question. I went to take care of another customer.

When I got home I told Al what happened. He laughed. "Honey," he said. "Frederick's of Hollywood is a famous line of sexy women's lingerie. He was a pervert, and he was trying to pick you up, that's what he was doing." No wonder the guy had looked at me as if I was from out of space. I have so much to learn about life.

Paul told me he cried his eyes out when he went to see the movie *Romeo and Juliet*. "I have decided," he was still emotional about it. "If I have children the boy will be named Romeo and the girl Juliet."

My goodness he was so sensitive, and what a traumatic experience for his children to be named after two people that killed themselves. But because of what Paul told me, I felt obliged to see the movie. I already knew the story of Romeo and Juliet and nothing was going to make me cry.

But I cried and cried and cried. The harder I tried not to cry, the more I cried. I cried for lost love and for all the lovers who could never be together because of this or that. And I cried because in fifty or so years later, nobody would give a damn about it anyway. When I saw Paul the next day I confessed crying copiously. Paul hugged me and said, "Honey, we're both very sensitive."

When I left the bakery that afternoon, my lower back started to hurt for no good reason, and I couldn't sleep a wink at night because of the pain. I went to work the next morning, but I couldn't bend to reach into the showcases without hurting. By the middle of the day the sharp pain was going down my right leg and I could hardly walk.

It didn't get any better at night. Two o'clock in the morning, Al had to take me to the hospital because I couldn't even turn in bed without crying.

When I got to the hospital, they gave me a shot in the arm, for the pain. I had a really strange reaction to it. My whole body felt as if it was made of glass and I was going to fall and crack at any moment. I was convinced that I had lost my mind as I cried uncontrollably curled up in the corner of the hospital bed shaking from head to toe. A doctor and two nurses came to see me and one of the nurses tried to calm me down, but when she touched my head it was as if I had been plugged into an electric socket. I screamed, "Don't touch me, Please, don't touch me. Somebody help me, I'm gonna die. But don't touch me. Please don't touch me." Mama and Aunt Heydee would probably have described my situation, as uncontrollably hysterical. The nurses and the doctor spoke to each other and agreed, I was responding badly to the medicine they had given me and I was better off left alone until the symptoms went away. And when it did I finally fell asleep.

Dr. Lehman, the orthopedic surgeon who had x-rayed Steve's shoulder, showed up the next morning with some medical students. He was doing the medical rounds. He pointed at me and smiled as he said to the students in his heavy German accent, "This girl can't have meds for pain. She gets a nasty reaction from it. All she can have is good food and sunshine." He winked at me. "You're going home tomorrow and taking it easy. No more work for you at the bakery."

His ridiculous suggestion before I left the hospital made me smile. "You need a maid to help you with the house chores." Dr. Lehman was an old, kind, and gentle man, but he didn't understand our financial situation. Al was still unemployed and I had become an invalid. The only maid we could afford was Al. It was a good thing he was still out of work, because Nelly could only do so much housework.

Before I left the hospital, Dr. Lehman fitted me with a metal corset for back support. "You must use this corset day and night. You can't return to work at the bakery. Your back is too weak to lift trays."

I was very sad with my future prognosis. I loved my job. How were we going to pay our bills?

Al said, "Don't worry about it. Anything we need we can charge it, and then pay it off little by little until I get a job again." I didn't say anything but I had no hope for him to get a job. There weren't any missile sites where we lived.

Braving A New World

The insurance company for the bakery called later in the day. They wanted me to see Dr. Mockinson, an independent medical examiner, to evaluate my present condition.

Dr. Mockinson asked me to bend over and touch my toes. I said, "Sorry, but I can't do that."
"You're a malingerer."
"What?"
"You're faking. Your back is not that bad."
"I don't have pain now, but if I bend over I know I'll have pain afterward and that's why I'm not doing it." I had no idea why Dr. Mockinson didn't believe me. I had no intention of ever using him as my doctor.

To my surprise the insurance company paid for all the medical bills, the days I lost from work and an extra two thousand dollars for all my suffering. It was like winning the lottery.

I got a phone call from Mama. "Surprise! Guess what? Your brother José and I just arrived in New York and we're about to board a helicopter to New Jersey. Can you pick us up in Newark? I have come to take care of you."

Mama was heavier than ever. She would run out of breath when walking. She used too much makeup. Her glittery fake jewelry was an eyesore, and her beat-up wig didn't match her hair color. My brother José was no better off than Mama. I didn't even recognize him. He was obese and wore a big smile while talking to himself. I was glad my back was too sore to take them out anywhere. I was ashamed of my family and I felt guilty for being such a snob. Al and Nelly felt uncomfortable too. Ralph and Steve, even though they were very young, could tell there was something wrong with José and didn't stick around him. What happened to my brother? He was fine when I left Portugal seven years ago. Mama said, "There's nothing wrong. I brought him along so he can meet a rich, young and beautiful American girl who will fall in love with him and will want to take care of him."

Mama brought me a bottle of my cherished Portuguese water. I poured the water into a glass and sat down to savor its pure taste. I had to spit it out into the kitchen sink, it not only tasted foul, but I could actually see dirt in the glass. I had gotten out of Portugal just before the water went bad. I had been dreaming about the water in Portugal ever since I arrived in America. For seven years I kept making references in my letters to Mama as to how clean and sparkling the water was in Portugal and how much I missed it. But after tasting this Portuguese water, I preferred to drink the American water with all its chlorine and other chemicals.

However, the Portuguese pastries (pasteis de nata) Mama brought, more than made up for the dirty water. I often experienced nightmares that I was in Lisbon and going from one pastry shop to another looking for pasteis de nata but they no longer made them or they were sold out. Pasteis de nata were small, fluffy, layered pastries filled with custard, and nobody could eat just one.

Mama finally told me what happened to José. He had typhus when he was sixteen years old. (I was glad I didn't swallow the water she had brought me.) The fevers that came along with typhus were devastating and he almost died, but the doctors were able to save him by giving him medicine that made him sleep. He slept for about a year. She believed those drugs saved his life. But when he finally came about, he was no longer the same person. He started acting weird. They sent José to France in the hopes he might return to his normal self, but he never did.

Now Mama mixed José's prescription drugs into his food; otherwise he refused to take them. The drugs kept him from killing himself.

I didn't agree with Mama. This medicine, which is what

they called the narcotics José had taken for a year, was what had deteriorated his brain. Sleeping for a year! My goodness! No wonder he couldn't be normal without it—it was a drug addiction. Mama tried to convince me to take some of her "medicine" drops, telling me they would help me with my back pain. I kept saying I didn't want them and she kept saying it was good for me. I didn't want to hurt her feelings, so I started to cry. "I can't take that stuff, Mama. I'm allergic to all drugs. I almost died in the hospital due to the 'medicine' they gave me."

She didn't insist anymore, but I intended to keep an eye on her. I was afraid she would put some of her wonderful medicine into my food like she did José's. Most of the men on her side of the family, including her brother Augusto, were medical doctors. She believed they were the gods of healing and as proof of her faith; she carried a shoebox filled with prescription drugs. She took a lot of them on a daily basis, "For my nerves," she said.

José slept on the couch downstairs. Mama slept with Nelly because there was no other bed for her to use. One morning, Nelly asked me to follow her to the backyard because she had something disturbing to tell me. "I woke up with your mother slapping me hard all over the chest and arms. I asked her what she was doing, and she said she was killing the ants crawling on me. I believe your mother is having hallucinations because there were no ants. I don't feel safe with her sleeping with me. I'm going to make arrangements to go visit Joe and Ruth."

I didn't say anything but knowing Mama, she was up to something. She was weird but she wasn't completely crazy. I was right. That afternoon it was Mama's turn to take me to the backyard. "That son-of-a-bitch, I can't believe she is my own sister. I caught her beating Steve downstairs in between the washer and dryer. Steve couldn't escape from her; she had him locked between her legs as she was beating him over his head with her fists. I gave her a taste of her own medicine this morning by hitting her as hard as I could. See how she likes it. I told her she had ants crawling on her chest." Then she grabbed my hands and implored, "Veronica, you need to put your foot down and stop her from hurting my grandchild."

"I'm sorry Mama. I just can't do anything about it. I can't stand what she does to my children, but she's going to live with us until she dies and I can't make it worse than it already is between her and me."

Mama was very upset and cried. She said it was her fault. She gave me the same explanation as Aunt Heydee. "While you were growing up I did everything to keep you submissive so that you would be a good wife. I did not count on Nelly living with you."

"Don't worry Mama. Sooner or later I'll do something about the situation with Nelly. I just don't know what yet."

That same evening Joe came over from Long Island and took Nelly with him. She would return when Mama and José were gone.

The next morning Mama asked me for the one thousand dollars she had given to Al as a dowry when we got married. I asked her how she could even ask such a thing when she knew we were flat broke.

"Okay, okay, when you get out of debt maybe you can send me some money," she said. "I need to put it into a fund for José's future. If something happens to your father and me, your brother will need money to live on."

I promised her that if we got out of debt, I would try and help. Then she said, "I had a dream, and I have to make sure your future is secure. Show me the papers for this house with your name on it. If something were to happen to Al and he didn't put your name on it, you have nothing."

To prove her wrong, I ran upstairs right away to get the mortgage papers. Of course my name was on it, right along with Al's. She left me alone after that, but later she said, "Americans are just like everybody else. I'm so surprised; I

Braving A New World

thought they were all millionaires."

I could tell Mama loved Steve and Ralph, but she felt about Steve the way Nelly did about Ralph. Also, Mama was convinced that Steve had healing hands because when he hugged her, the pain she felt all over her body went away.

Mama sat staring at me one morning and said, "You would look great if your hair was jet black." To make her happy I colored my hair for the first time. She was right, I did look better with my hair darker. The price of hair coloring was a lot more affordable than in Portugal. She bought a few bottles to take with her.

I was under strict orders from Dr. Lehman not to do any housework, including washing the dishes. Al got fed up one evening after washing so many dishes by hand, and in the morning he went to Sears and bought a dishwasher with the credit card. Our house was very modern; we had a dishwasher, an electric stove, a washer and dryer, and a television. No wonder Mama thought we were millionaires. We owed a lot but we lived like kings.

Since Mama kept complaining about her heart and my back was improving enough to drive, I made an appointment for her to see Nelly's new heart specialist in Red Bank. After the exam, the doctor took me to the side. "I'm amazed about your mother's deteriorating health and being overweight as she is, I would be surprised if she lasts three more months."

We left his office but once outside, she grabbed my arm and said, "I saw the doctor talking to you and his face was not a happy one. I'm not stupid, I know something is wrong. What did he say? I want to know the truth."

"He said you have a bad heart."

"I'm not a child, Veronica. I want to know how bad."

"He said you have three months to live because your heart can't handle your weight."

"Really? Well, I'll show him what I can do. Wait and

see what your mother can accomplish."

I didn't ask what she was going to do. Mama and José went back to Portugal two days later and I was glad they were gone.

Summer of 1969

Ever since I had hurt my back I couldn't handle any lifting and I couldn't sit too long either. But Al was still jobless, so I applied at a hardware store. It was a real dumb idea since I had to pick up heavy paint cans and metal pipes, and before the end of the first day at work, my back started to hurt. I called Al on the telephone. "I'm not going to make it with this type of work. My back is starting to hurt and I'm afraid I'll wind up in the hospital again." Al told me to quit right then and there and come home.

We were all walking around the Eatontown Mall, something we did on weekends for entertainment, when I saw a hiring ad in the front window of Bonds, a men's clothing store. At first Al didn't want to go in because he was an engineer, not a salesperson, but I convinced him that he had nothing to lose by applying for the job. They hired him on the spot!

With Al working full time, life was back to normal and I again started taking half-hour guitar lessons once a week with Mr. Crocker. I couldn't wait to start playing guitar like the Rolling Stones, The Animals, or Credence Clearwater Revival.

Nelly and I were taking a walk with the kids around the neighborhood when the ice cream truck came by. I bought ice cream for all of us and as the ice cream truck took off Nelly said, "I saw you smiling flirtatiously at the ice cream boy. You're a married woman. You should be ashamed of yourself."

"That's not true. Why do you say stuff like that to hurt me?"

"If it's not true, why did you smile at him?"

"I was being polite. I always smile when I say thank you. Come on kids, let's run home." I threw my ice pop away and the kids followed me home. I was too upset to cry. By then, I should have been used to the way Nelly treated me, but I wasn't. I kept thinking of the old days when she was nice and we had so much fun together. Why she had changed into a malicious person was beyond me.

We went to the moon! I watched it on television but I couldn't believe it was true. Aunt Heydee wrote, "Veronica, I hope I don't hurt your feelings, but the whole thing was staged by the American government and Hollywood to give the American people a good cover-up for burning so much money every time they send a missile into the air." Al and Nelly said that Aunt Heydee was out of her mind. I didn't tell them I agreed with her.

Autumn of 1969

Steve's shoulder surgery was a success. He would have to wear a shoulder cast for a while until it healed, but his back was straight and his shoulder, according to Dr. Lehman, would continue to grow normally.

Nelly and Al didn't treat him any better after the surgery. When Steve was sent to bed after being pushed around and went upstairs crying, I would wait a few minutes to make an excuse like I had to go to the bathroom upstairs and I would sneak into his bedroom. "I love you Steve, remember that. I'm so sorry about all of this happening to you. Someday, as soon as I can figure out how, I'll fix the problem, I promise." I always hugged him, told him I loved him and I was sorry about what was going on.

Ralph and Steve were very different from each other, but a lot of people thought they were twins. Steve had blue eyes with long eyelashes that made him look like a deer, darker skin, and light brown, curly hair. Ralph had green eyes, like me, a round face with a small button nose, and his skin was very pink and delicate like porcelain. According to some old pictures of my father when he was a child, Ralph looked a lot like his grandfather. Papa was very happy when I told him his first grandson looked like him.

Ralph was very spoiled. When he didn't get what he wanted he would yell and go into a tantrum, stomping his feet on the floor. Whatever he wanted he got it from Nelly. When I tried to stop her, she would say, "It's okay for my Ralphie to be a little spoiled; he could have died when he had meningitis as a baby."

I bought a bunch of Avon make-up from Barbara and decided to play with it while the kids watched Batman on television. After applying black hair color to my hair and while waiting the recommended forty minutes before washing the color out, I began to apply the cosmetics on the right side of my face—eye shadow, mascara, eyeliner, and rouge. I was comparing one side of my face with makeup to the other side without when I heard Ralph crying in the playroom. He had fallen against the end table and his forehead was bleeding. I rushed him to the hospital and of course took Steve with us. I didn't want to leave him alone at home since Nelly and Al were out shopping. The three of us looked like outcasts. Steve was wearing his shoulder cast, Ralph was bleeding from his forehead, and my face was painted only on one side, with my hair dripping black hair color.

The emergency room doctor didn't say anything but from the look on his face I knew he was thinking, "What

Braving A New World

the heck happened to this woman and her kids?" Ralph didn't need stitches but they gave him a tetanus shot.

Mr. Crocker, my guitar teacher who had kissed my fingertips months ago, continued to make me feel very uncomfortable. He was now teaching me guitar in a room small enough to be a closet. He sat very close and his knee kept rubbing against my knee. When he reached over to show me how to play something on my guitar, his arm rubbed against my right breast, just ever so slightly. I moved away as soon as he reached for my guitar, but he always found a way to touch me. He acted as if it was all very natural and he didn't even say, "Excuse me." Maybe it was my imagination. Still, I felt like I should smack him, but I didn't have the courage. If I told Al, most likely there would be a fistfight for my honor, and I would never learn to play rock and roll. I decided it was in my best interest not to complain.

Al surprised me with a brand new classical Yamaha guitar. It was the best one Mr. Crocker had in stock, and it was so expensive that it came with a written lifetime guarantee. I loved my new guitar. It possessed a strong mellow tone and each note rang in the air like magic. It was also much easier to play than the junky one I had with metal strings. Soon I would be playing my kind of music—rock and roll.

After Steve was born, Dr. Adler gave me a rubber diaphragm, to be inserted into my vagina prior to having intercourse with Al. It was the latest prevention device against pregnancy.

But it was hard to know if we were having intercourse ahead of time so every night before going to bed I went into the bathroom and inserted the diaphragm. It was painful to put it in and even worst to try pulling it out with my finger, especially when it got stuck way inside. I was too embarrassed to ask Al if that night was the night, so I didn't have to go through the whole trauma for nothing.

Sex was still a mystery to me and whenever I was at a bookstore by myself I read about the subject. It was a great relief for me to read in a magazine that it was healthy to fantasize. I thought it was a form of cheating and a sin. It was wonderful to know that I was normal; I could finally relax about it.

I finished the second classical guitar book to find out there was no third book. I had rushed through number two, putting in extra hours every day for nothing. Mr. Crocker didn't know anything about teaching rock and roll! In his opinion I should be teaching guitar.

He called Al and me to his office and made us an offer we couldn't refuse. He would pay me 50 percent of the money coming in for teaching beginner classes, 65 percent for intermediate classes, 75 percent for advanced classes, and for private lessons I could keep 50 percent. The guitar classes would have at least ten students; therefore, I would be making a lot more money than teaching private students. At such pay rate, I could count on making as much money as Al when he was an engineer. I was also hired to teach adult guitar classes in the morning.

My picture, holding my acoustic guitar, was published in a full-page newspaper ad. Mr. Crocker's wife, who did the advertising for the music school, put me down as part of their professional teaching staff. Under my picture it read, "FOLK GUITAR CLASSES with Ronnie Esagui."

I had never played folk music! I didn't have a music degree and definitely had no experience teaching. Mr. Crocker said, "Don't worry, you come in as my assistant and watch how I do it. You'll feel confident to teach by yourself in no time."

He was present at the first three guitar classes, and then

Braving A New World

he stopped showing up. He was too busy running his music business. He was right. I was fine without him and couldn't believe that I was getting paid to do something I absolutely loved.

Two weeks later Mr. Crocker called me to his office. "You're doing better than I expected. I'm getting calls from parents telling me how much their kids love you as their teacher. My wife set up a student for you on Monday. He's an adult and only wants private lessons."

I was a nervous wreck when I sat next to my new student. He was my age and his name was Jorge. I tuned his guitar while praying he didn't ask me too many questions. "I want to learn to play country style music," he said.

"I'm sorry but I can only teach classical or jazz."

He put his guitar in his case and I did the same. Jorge told Mr. Crocker that he was going somewhere else since I was the only guitar teacher in his establishment. "I'm not happy with the way you handled, your new student."

"Sorry, but you have never taught me country music only classical and jazz."

He asked me to follow him to his office closed the door and handed me a red Yamaha electric guitar. "Hey, what do you think of it? A real beauty wouldn't you say?"

"Wow! It is beautiful." I had never held an electric guitar and wasn't quite sure what to make of the situation. "You know how to read music," he said handing me some books on popular music. "Now practice. And the next time you get a student who wants to play country or rock or whatever the style, you don't say you can't play it, you just teach them classical, like I taught you. And by the way, keep that guitar at home. You are never to use it in public, do you hear?"

"Why?"

"I had a robbery a while ago and lots of instruments were taken, that guitar was one of them. Do you understand?" I must have looked dumbfounded because he said, "Don't worry the insurance already paid me. You need an electric guitar and you can't afford to buy one, so be thankful I'm giving you this one. Now, go on and don't ask any more questions." He put the guitar in a hard case and handed it to me.

When I got home I showed Al my electric guitar and said, "Supposedly this guitar was stolen from Mr. Crocker's store along with other musical instruments. Mr. Crocker asked me to be quiet about it since the insurance company will be paying for all the instruments taken."

"What a crook!" Al said.

"When he told me what he was doing, I was shocked. And when he insisted I accept the guitar I felt like I was an accomplice in the robbery."

"You bet. You could go to jail for accepting stolen merchandise."

"So what do I do? Do I quit my job? He did tell me not to bring the guitar to the music store; it's only for me to practice at home so I can learn to play Rock and Roll."

"You can't go against your boss even if he's a crook. Just keep the guitar at home to practice like he said and you should be okay. I bet when his other store burned down a few years ago, he started it."

I wouldn't be surprised.

By now I was really deep into my job as a guitar teacher. In fact, one morning Al said, "Do you remember talking in your sleep last night?" He laughed.

"No. What did I say?" It scared me that I was talking in my sleep—what if I started to talk about my feelings and personal matters?

"You were saying stuff like, 'I have six guitars to tune up really fast, and I can't do it in five minutes. I need help.' And you kept saying, 'Help, help!' You were so stressed out that I said, 'Okay Ronnie, I'll help you to tune the guitars.' And you said, 'Thanks, Al,' and then you turned over and slept quietly the rest of the night."

I kept my fingers crossed that had been the last time I talked in my sleep. My goodness, what was next? Was I going to start sleepwalking, too?

What possessed me to tell Mama about my new job as a guitar teacher, I would never know. She did not say she was proud of me as I was hoping for. Instead, she wrote, "A married woman should never be alone with someone of the opposite sex without being escorted by her husband. You're asking for trouble. Make sure your husband goes with you and watches that nothing happens. He should be present at all the private guitar lessons you give, making sure you don't get sexually attacked by one of your male students."

Thank God my parents didn't live near me. They would be treating me like a stupid little girl. I wanted to write back to Mama and explain how ridiculous it would be to have Al seated next to me watching over my students' every move. Then I realized I would be wasting my energy. Mama was from a different time. She just wouldn't understand.

Winter ending 1969

Since I was a child, I loved playing with clay. I bought some at a craft store and made a bust of Al.

He almost passed out when he came home and saw his head sitting on the kitchen table. Then I made the mistake of putting it in the hot oven to dry. It dried it all right; it blew up into pieces.

But I figured that if I could make Al's head look so real, I could make others and give them away as presents for Christmas.

I bought a tape recorder and a bunch of cassette tapes, and I started teaching myself not only country music but also rock and roll. First I taped the rhythm, and then I played the lead along with the tape. I would teach classical and jazz, but I would also teach the kind of music I enjoyed. The calluses on my left-hand fingers proved how hard I practiced every day. I also enjoyed singing along with some of the more popular songs. I was delighted when one of my students asked me if I was a professional singer. I didn't tell him that when I was in high school, the choir teacher put me way in the back and asked me to move only my lips.

Mr. Crocker was shocked when I gave him his full-sized clay bust as a Christmas present. He put it on top of his bookcase and said, "I'm keeping it up there so everybody will think I'm looking at them, and work harder." I warned him not to put his head in the oven. Only time could dry it.

Winter of 1970

I was satisfied with my clay work and had no desire to pursue it any further. Later on I did a watercolor painting of a street in Lisbon, Portugal and then an oil painting of a forest reflecting on a lake. My last art endeavor involved black ink and I drew a Portuguese castle in the distance with a river on one side. I included a tall tree losing its leaves on top of a tomb that was engraved with musical notes. I copied the musical notes from one of Mama's old sheet music she had written for the piano, when she was single. It had a dark theme to it—almost psychedelic. I liked it. But once I knew I could do something, it was no longer a fun hobby. I was done with painting.

    I started assembling a small brigantine plastic model. The parts of the sailing ship were very tiny, and it was a real challenge putting the ropes through the wheels and hanging the masts onto a foot-long ship. The kids liked to sit next to me and watch. Al came home one day and said,

"You're a good example of why women get hired to work in factories. You adapt better than men at doing menial work because you're not as intelligent."

I didn't answer. He was a lot like Nelly. They were both embalmed in preconceived old-fashioned ideas, and I had no chance of making them change their minds.

Mr. Crocker asked me how old I thought he was. I said, "Sixty-three?" He walked away mumbling something.

An hour later, his wife called me to the office and said, in a mischievous voice, "I heard you told Sam that you thought he was sixty-three years old. Can't you see he's not that old?"

I tried to fix the situation. "I'm sorry, but to me he looks even older. I was being kind when I said he was sixty-three."

The women in the office were laughing, and one of them said, "If you keep that up, you might lose your job."

I doubted Mr. Crocker would fire me. I was the only guitar teacher he had. Besides, I truly had no idea how old he was. Al was thirty-eight years old and Mr. Crocker looked old enough to be Al's father. The next time someone asked me how old I thought they were, I was prepared to say that I have no idea.

I was making a lot of money teaching and felt very lucky being paid for something I would have done for free. I absolutely loved teaching guitar. In the mornings and until 3pm while my children were at school I taught mostly adults. When the boys got home from school, Nelly would not take care of them, so I took them to work with me. They waited in the waiting room doing their homework. My students were telling their friends and family and my classes as well as private lessons were growing steadily every month. Al got promoted to manager at Bonds and that meant a better salary too. We were doing well financially. I began to send money to Mama every week.

Ralph's teacher, Mrs. Roylond, called asking me to meet her at school. It was something about Ralph's behavior being less than desirable. Nelly and I waited patiently in the hallway for Mrs. Roylond to come out of the classroom. The teacher seemed frustrated and she was crying when she said, "Your son Ralph is very difficult to control. He does what he wants and doesn't care about consequences. It's like he doesn't know the difference between right and wrong. What's the matter with him?"

I felt sorry for the teacher. Ralph was used to getting what he wanted, and I couldn't tell her his grandmother was to blame. Nothing was accomplished from the brief hallway meeting.

On the way out, Nelly said, "I have never seen a teacher cry over a student. She's obviously too young and inexperienced."

~ *Chapter Six* ~

AT THE EDGE OF DARKNESS

1970

Spring of 1970

Al called me a hippie every time I expressed my opinion concerning equal rights for minority groups and freedom of choice. Long live America and its diversity!

When Al first started saying I was weird, I used to get upset, but soon I began to enjoy the thought that I was different. I didn't want to be like him or anybody else. The way God had made me was the way I wanted to stay.

Another silly letter from Mama arrived. "Don't ever think a man and a woman can be friends. There's no such thing as a platonic relationship. Men only have one thing on their minds, sex. Make sure your husband goes everywhere with you where there might be another man that will desire you." Mama had read too many old-time novels, like *Madame Bovary*. That was the only thing making sense to explain all the nonsense she came up with.

During my once-a-year checkup, Dr. Adler said, "You have little pieces of tissue growing around your uterus. That's the reason you're having problems using the diaphragm.

Don't worry, it's a very simple procedure and you only have to stay one night in the hospital. All women need a D&C after having children."

"What's a D&C?"

"That's the name of the procedure."

I trusted Dr. Adler and I didn't mind going to the hospital for one day. It would be like a mini vacation away from Nelly.

I was put to sleep through the D&C procedure, and when I woke up, Dr. Adler said I was doing great and could go home the next morning. A week later I went to see him at his office to have the stitches inside of me taken out.

Dr. Adler removed the stitches in his office and sent me home. But I felt so sore from the procedure that I stayed in bed until the next day and must have been very tired because I didn't wake up until nine the next morning. Nelly and the children had already had breakfast. I felt bad I wasn't doing anything to help downstairs, and decided to get up and do some house chores. I started by making my bed. When I bent forward to tuck in the bottom bed sheet, I felt something wet slip out into my underwear. I took a look and it was a big red blob made of blood. So I thought it would be a good idea to lie down and stay still, but another red blob came out. It wasn't painful; it was just a weird feeling. I decided to call Dr. Adler since I had never seen anything like it. He was not available. About an hour later he called back and I told him what was happening.

"You're hemorrhaging," he said. "Get to the hospital immediately."

I went down to the playroom where I found the kids and Nelly watching television. I told her what was happening. "Dr. Adler wants me to go to the hospital as soon as possible because I'm hemorrhaging." I was scared. I looked at Ralph and Steve, wondering if I was going to die at the hospital and never get to see them grow up. I wished they were older so they could comfort me and take my fears away. "Just go lie down and wait for Al, he should be home soon. After he has his dinner, he will drive you to the hospital." She said calmly.

When Al came home, I came downstairs, and sat quietly at the kitchen table watching him eat his favorite meal, spaghetti and meatballs. I kept my legs tightly crossed so the blobs would not plop out.

"You don't look too good. Are you okay?" he asked.

"Oh, I'm fine. I'm just waiting for you to finish eating so I can ask you to take me to the hospital, because I'm hemorrhaging."

He wanted to see what the heck I was talking about, and when he looked at my underwear he freaked out. "My God!" he yelled. "You're bleeding to death!"

He wrapped a blanket around me like a diaper so that I would not bleed all over the front seat in the car. The blood was gushing out into the blanket and down my legs. The kids and Nelly were in the backseat. When I looked at Al, I saw a look of panic in his eyes and I knew I was about to die. In the emergency room, I must have passed out because I don't remember anything except for a nurse slapping at my wrists.

I woke up hearing a familiar voice next to me. "Ronnie! Ronnie, are you awake?" It sounded like Nelly. She was lying on the bed next to mine! She was laughing as she told me, "I faked a heart attack and requested to stay in the hospital in the same room as you."

Dear God, why? Why was she there? I couldn't escape from her, not even in the hospital. It just wasn't fair! And I cried. But then I felt guilty when I realized how much work she had gone through to stay by my side. She had done it out of love. How many friends or even family members could say they had sacrificed themselves to be near the one they loved by faking a heart attack? I thanked her for caring and tried my best to feel at peace with my situation.

When visiting hours were approaching at the end of the

day Nelly said, "Put on some lipstick and fix yourself up so your husband doesn't worry about you when he comes to visit. You look absolutely terrible. There's nothing worse for a man than to see his woman dying."

She was right. Even *The Bride's Book* I had read in Portugal and had brought with me to America said, men don't like sickly women. So I put on some lipstick and combed my hair the best I could. Al came and told me not to worry. He had taken a few days off from work and would be taking care of the kids when they got home from school.

Nelly went home a week later. Every two to three days I was wheeled out of my room and into a surgery room down the hall where Dr. Adler packed my insides with sponges and strips of gauze material, trying to stop the bleeding. It was very, very painful when he pushed and pressed the gauze material inside of me. I cried a lot and sometimes I screamed.

Every time he finished packing my insides he said, "Looks good. Looks good and firm."

I was then taken back to my room. But it wasn't working because even if I lay very still, the blood kept gushing out through the gauze material.

Summer of 1970

The days had turned into weeks and then months. Nothing had changed, except I had been so long in the hospital that I began to believe I wasn't ever going home. They kept me on plasma instead of having blood transfusions. Dr. Adler told me blood transfusions were not as safe.

Some nurses were made in heaven and others came directly from hell. I had learned that much in the hospital.

A young, heavyset nurse came to check on me one evening. She lifted my bed sheet to see if I was bleeding and said, "You're so skinny and tanned. How do you do that?"

"I have been in this bed for three months. Maybe it's the contrast of my body with the white sheets?" I thought she was being friendly and dared to say, "Since you're here, would you mind peeling that orange for me? " I pointed to the orange laying on my side table. "I have tried, but I don't seem to have the strength to cut through the skin with a butter knife."

She said with a disdainful tone, "You look healthy enough to do it yourself." She walked away.

Another nurse came in my room one morning and was taking out my food tray when she noticed I had not eaten breakfast. "I don't blame you for not eating this junk. I'll be right back with something nourishing."

She brought me oatmeal. "I made it myself," she said. "You need to eat if you're going to live. You're very young, so you might have a chance."

I was paying close attention to Ms. Josie. She cared.

"Listen to me," she said in a maternal tone, "your blood has been changed several times with plasma, and when you leave this hospital you might develop diabetes or who knows what. After what you have been through, I would not be surprised. You must watch your diet. If someone gives you an apple and a piece of apple pie, which of the two are you going to choose?"

I took a chance when I said, "The apple."

She smiled. "That's right, the apple! Remember what I'm telling you. Refuse the sugary pie. Water—you must drink lots of water, but purify it. You must purify it. There are too many chemicals in the water system nowadays. You go to Sears and get their best purifier. I'm coming here to see you every morning and I will bring you fresh fruit and oatmeal for breakfast." And then she hugged me. Ms. Josie was my hospital angel.

Ms. Josie explained to me that D&C stood for Dilation and Curettage and Dr. Adler had scraped and stitched my insides. If I had known that ahead of time I would not have been so eager to have it done.

Autumn of 1970

Al and Nelly came to see me at the hospital. Al was wearing his favorite pink shirt, which had always struck me as odd for a man to wear. I looked at him and for no other apparent reason I began laughing. I laughed and laughed, and the more he asked me, "What's so funny?" the more I laughed.

Al and Nelly stared at me—from the serious looks on their faces they must have thought I was going crazy. The more they stared at me, the funnier the pink shirt looked. Tears were coming down my face as I laughed uncontrollably.

Nelly brought her hands up to her face and covered her eyes. "Al, your wife is not acting normal. You'd better call a nurse in immediately." He did, and the nurse put a hand on my arm trying to calm me down.

"Are you going nuts?" the nurse asked.

"No," I said, pointing at Al, "look at his pink shirt. I think it's amusing, that's all. I spend the days looking at the walls. What's wrong with laughing at something silly?"

The nurse left the room after saying to Al, "Your shirt is definitely different."

"As long as you're okay, that's all that matters." He kissed my forehead

"I'm fine, honestly, and besides, I feel warm and cozy."

"Are you still bleeding?"

I didn't answer. He lifted the bedsheet and screamed, "Oh, my God, you're lying in a pool of blood!"

"It's okay, Al. This happens every day, but it doesn't hurt. If you say something, the nurses are going to call Dr. Adler and he's going to come back to the hospital and pack me again. I just can't take the pain of packing. Please," I begged him, "don't say anything to the nurses."

"Screw the nurses and screw your doctor. I want something done right now. I want a second opinion right now. Can't you see that he's killing you?" He stormed out of the room, yelling down the hallway. "Where is that darn freaking doctor?"

Ms. Josie came in and I said, "Please get my husband to stop yelling. The doctor is going to come back angry and hurt me."

"It's about time something gets done about your situation here in the hospital. It's been months. Your doctor needs to get with it."

I heard Dr. Adler's angry voice in the hallway. He was talking to Al. "Yes, I can stop the bleeding but she'll need to have her uterus removed, which will mean no more children. Are you ready for that?"

"Screw the children. I want my wife to live."

"Okay, if that's what you want; it's your decision not mine. I'll do the surgery right now."

They wheeled my bed out of my room and down the badly-lit hallway. It was late in the evening. I was terrified that he was going to pull my uterus out with his bare hands and then pack my insides with gauze like he always did when trying to stop the hemorrhaging. I grabbed his sleeve, "Please, Dr. Adler, don't be angry with me or my husband; he is only protecting me."

He looked away and didn't answer. He and another man wheeled me into the operating room and then Dr. Adler said, "Don't worry, soon you'll stop bleeding."

Oh good, I thought to myself, I'm going to be fine, or I'll die. Either way, no more pain.

I woke up once during the surgery with a tube down my throat. I was choking. I heard Dr. Adler's annoyed voice telling someone to stop me. I was doing my best to pull the tube off when suddenly I was out like a light once again.

When I woke up, my hospital bed was in the hallway. I

begged for water but there was no one around. I tried to get up but couldn't move. Sometime later I woke up back in my room. I was not sure what had been done to me.

Dr. Adler came to see me after what I believed was a day later. He asked me to stick my tongue out, and after touching it with one of his fingers he said, "Well, you're not dehydrated; that's good."

I couldn't tell if he was angry with me or just cranky. "I'll be back in a few days to remove the stitches from your lower abdomen." He left and I pulled down the bed covers to see what he was talking about. I was surprised that Dr. Adler had cut my belly open. I didn't realize it was going to be a real operation, with stitches and everything. I couldn't lie down on my left side; it was too painful.

Two days after the surgery I experienced excruciating bladder pain. I knew it was the bladder because I had not urinated since the surgery; I wanted to urinate, but nothing came out. Nelly and Al came to visit me and found me crying, "I can't stand the pain anymore! Someone, please help me!"

Just then, Ms. Josie, my angel-nurse came in the room. "I'm going to call your doctor immediately. He makes me so angry." I believe I heard her mumble, "The old bastard," as she walked away.

A priest walking in the hallway heard me screaming and came into the room. "My daughter, you're in a lot of pain, aren't you?" he said in a very soft, gentle voice.

"Yes," I cried out. "It hurts so much that I would not mind if someone killed me. I really can't take it anymore."

He put his hand on my head and said, "Do you believe in Jesus Christ? Because if you do, he will take your pain away."

I looked at Al and Nelly and, since they were Jewish including myself, I begged them forgiveness with my eyes.

"Yes, I believe! I believe in Jesus!"

My God, what pain could make someone say or do! I

quickly asked God to forgive me for saying I believed in Jesus because what I meant to say was that I believed Jesus existed; but I believed there was only the one God. Then I waited for a miracle. The pain stopped.

The priest made the cross over me, and after a short prayer, he left the room. I was about to say I was experiencing a Catholic miracle when the pain returned agonizingly. I began screaming, "Help! Help! I can't stand the pain. It's horrible. I want to die! I want to die! Someone kill me, please!"

Ms. Josie came back smiling. "You're going to be fine. I got hold of your doctor and he gave me the okay to insert a little tube toward your bladder."

"Oh no," I cried. "No more surgery, please."

"No surgery, honey. This will get rid of the urine, which is what's causing the pain. Just relax and let me help you."

The urine came out like a torrent of relief. I cried again, but this time they were tears of relief and joy. I recalled when Aunt Heydee and I were taking a walk in the countryside and there was no place to go to the bathroom. Finally she found a bush big enough to hide behind. When she was done she came around with a bright smile, "Veronica, there's nothing more gratifying than peeing when you have been holding on for too long."

It wasn't until the next morning that it dawned on me the conversation in the hospital hallway between Al and Dr. Adler prior to my surgery. Al had fought for me. He had taken control of the situation by speaking up. He had saved my life, he was my hero. I had two wonderful sons and it didn't seem important to me at the time that I couldn't have any more children, I had Al's love and devotion. I felt complete.

Thank God Al was visiting when a nurse came into the room and said, "C'mon, let's have you turn over for your daily injection."

I turned on my side unquestioningly but Al said, "Why is my wife getting a needle?"

"Well, isn't she Mrs. Oswald?"

"No, she's not Mrs. Oswald! Her name is Ronnie Esagui! How about asking her roommate sleeping in the next bed?"

I had just learned a very important lesson. If a nurse gave me a pill or wanted to give me a shot, I would always ask why, what for, and most importantly, who was she looking for?

Mr. Crocker came to visit me and gave me a book called, *Future Shock,* and another book on how to make paper plane models. I was starting to think he was a nice person when he said, "You're lucky you had this operation. Now you can have sex and not worry about getting pregnant. My wife is like a baby machine and sex isn't even good between us."

Just the thought of sex with him spoiled the rest of my day.

Dr. Adler had cut me from three inches below my belly button straight down to my pubic bone. He was far from being a seamstress. The stiches were irregular and made the cut a pretty nasty sight. He was not open to conversation while removing the stiches. I waited until he was done to ask the most important question on my mind. "When can I go home?"

"You have not bled since the surgery. It's safe to say, you can go home in three days." He left without showing any signs of joy.

I missed Ralph and Steve. We spoke on the phone everyday but that didn't tell me what was going on at home. I had visions of Steve getting beaten up and crying, "Mommy, Mommy, please come home!" It had been a long time since we had seen each other. What if they didn't recognize me as their mother anymore? I might not recognize them either; it had been over six months since I had last seen them.

I thanked God for being home again. The kids were very happy to see me and I wanted to keep them next to me forever. I cried with joy. They had gotten taller. We sat on the couch downstairs hugging each other and Nelly brought me a cup of tea and sat next to us. It was going to take me a few days to get adjusted to my new environment as a wife and a mother.

Once I went upstairs and saw myself in the bathroom mirror, I understood why they kept staring at me with such solemn faces. My eyes had sunken in, and I looked like a grayish-yellow skeleton.

Dr. Adler's office called. I asked the nurse what was it about and she said, "It's a personal matter and he wants to see you and your husband no later than tomorrow". On the way to his office Al said, "Maybe Dr. Adler is going to offer you free care to make-up for almost killing you in the hospital."

"No way is he touching me again," I said panicking. "You stay with me and please, no matter what, don't let him take me into his examining room."

"Stop biting your nails," he said. "He's not touching you. I'll be there to make sure."

Dr. Adler remained seated behind his massive mahogany desk when we entered his private office. He didn't make eye contact with us and seemed uncomfortable as if annoyed by our presence. He asked how I was doing, but the lack of concern in his voice and cold glare made me feel like he could care less. He handed us a piece of paper, "My lawyer has asked that you both sign this form, it states you won't be suing me for what happened." I handed him the paper back. "Don't worry, Dr. Adler, I'm not going to sue you. You're a doctor, you did your best."

He didn't say thank you or show any emotion except to push with one finger, the paper back toward me. "I still need your signature and your husband's."

"After what you did to my wife you have a lot of nerve to ask us to sign this kind of document." I put a hand on his arm trying to calm him down. Al looked at me and then grabbed the paper. "Let's just sign the freaking paper and get the hell out of here."

We were sure Dr. Adler was just as happy to see us leave.

I made an appointment to see Dr. DeCicco, our family doctor. He was the only one I trusted. His gentle manner reminded me of my Uncle Augusto, who was a medical doctor in Lisbon, Portugal.

Every night I suffered from nightmares as if I was still in the hospital. They felt so real that when I woke up, I had to check between my legs to make sure I was not in a pool of blood.

If Al had not spoken up to Dr. Adler, I would still be bedridden in the hospital, if not already deceased. I had to climb the stairs at home very slowly so I could catch my breath while holding on to my sore guts. I felt very old and decrepit.

Dr. DeCicco, performed a brief gynecologic exam on me and then talked to us in his office. "Dr. Adler should have his medical license revoked. I have never seen anything so damaged. You are raw inside" He said to me. Then he looked at Al. "I don't recommend intercourse until your wife recovers completely. It will probably take a year or more to heal."

"I'm just happy my wife is alive," Al put his arm over my shoulders "I'm willing to wait as long as it takes for her to heal." I smiled and gesture with my eyes how much I appreciated his understanding. Dr. DeCicco gave us the name of a gynecologist in Freehold and advised me to wait at least until the spring because I was too tender to be examined.

Ruth called. "What's the matter with you two. You have to sue the bastard, he's not a doctor, he's a butcher." But all I wanted was to forget what had happened and when it came to Al, it wasn't in his nature to sue anyone.

Winter ending 1970

For Christmas, Nelly bought us a modern teak wood dining room table and a matching china cabinet. There were two strict rules to follow; it was to be used only when we had family over, and I was not allowed to touch it, not even to dust it. She would take care of it by using special oil made specifically for teak.

Winter of 1971

The honeymoon was over—Nelly was back to being the mean mother-in-law and grandmother. While the kids were in school, I used the time to lie down and take it easy. I had to get strong and healthy quickly if I was going to save my children from her. I needed to get back to teaching and start making money again.

Mama sent me a copy of her first published poetry book called *Ansia de Viver*, which meant "desire to live." The next one was already being prepared for publishing, and it was called *O Meu Mundo*, which meant "my world." I had to admit it; I didn't understand or appreciate poetry.

Al, Nelly and I were called to Ralph's school for a private meeting with Mr. Rogers the school principal and Mrs. Warner, Ralph's teacher. It all started after Ralph decided to show off in school his bilingual expertise and some of the kids in his class were picking up some of his lingo. Mr. Rogers stood from his chair and walked toward us with an accusing finger. "By speaking several languages at home, you're seriously hurting Ralph's education. You need to stop."

Al waved his hand in the air and said, "Hey, I don't speak Portuguese, Spanish and much less French. My mother and my wife are the ones with the bad habit. I have tried to stop them, but they don't listen to me. Half the time I don't have any idea what they are talking about. I agree with you, it's very confusing for the children, I'm sure. They already have enough with English."

"They have no problem understanding us." I said defensively. "It's good to speak other languages." The principal filled his chest with air like a rooster ready to sing his morning wake up call, and pointed to the mini American flag on his desk. "Do you see that flag?" He didn't wait for an answer. "We are in America, and English is the only language to be spoken. Do you understand?" Like a parrot, Mrs. Warner repeated, "When in America you speak American." I couldn't believe my ears. I had never heard anything so dumb in my life. Nelly and I were speechless. In Portugal, besides Portuguese we all had to learn French, Latin, and English in school. It was part of our education. Learning other languages didn't make us less Portuguese.

When we left the school Al continued to harass us. "You guys had it coming. It's about time you speak only one language at home."

For the sake of not having to put up with Al and, being called back to the principal's office to be scolded like criminals, Nelly and I agreed to abide to their moronic demands.

~ *Chapter Seven* ~

MAMA

1971

Spring of 1971

Al wanted to visit Niagara Falls again for our week-long summer vacation. Walking was still very painful and the idea of sitting in a car for hours scared me. I was weak and shook a lot. But I wanted to do everything I could to make Al happy. I owed him my life.

I snuggled up to Al in bed. "I don't think I'll ever be normal again down there. It still hurts inside when I stand or walk," I said apologetically.

"I don't mind waiting until you're strong enough to have intercourse." I knew why he had no problem waiting. He preferred oral sex. "You're very lucky that you had the surgery," he said. "Now you don't have to worry about getting pregnant or contend with the usual mess of menstruating every month. Do you know how many women wish they were in your shoes?

It wasn't until that very moment that it hit me; my dream to have a little girl wasn't ever going to happen. I didn't consider myself lucky. If anything I felt like a curse had been put on my head. Al went to sleep and I cried myself to sleep.

My best birthday present that year was life and being with my family. I thanked God a lot more heartily when I blew out the candles on my birthday cake.

I went to see Dr. Gynor, the gynecologist, recommended by Dr. Decicco. After the exam he said, "Dr. Adler must be an old doc. He should have used the laser technique to do the D&C procedure instead of stitching."
"You mean Dilation and Curettage." I said stressing out the double t's in Curettage.
"Are you French?" he smiled.
"After what I went through I refuse to call it D&C for short."

Summer of 1971

Nelly didn't want to go to Niagara Falls and stayed with Ruth and Joe for the week we would be gone.
When we went on vacation, I always reminded the kids, "If you fight with each other even once, it will be the last time you come with us." The bluff always worked.
The kids were very well behaved, but it didn't seem like much of a vacation because I couldn't run or play with them. One morning we were walking in a park and my insides were hurting so bad from standing that I laid down on the grass. I was scared of starting to hemorrhage again and being taken to a Canadian Hospital. I whispered to the kids, "Mommy's tummy is hurting and I have to lay down. You just play around me and daddy will take a picture of us as if we are having fun, okay?" Al took several pictures as I pretended to be enjoying the moment by acting silly, bringing my arms and legs up in the air as the kids rolled around in the grass. I remained on my back even after the kids got tired of playing. "Oh, this cool grass feels so good, so refreshing." I said. "Let me lie here just for a few more minutes."

"You can cool off at the hotel where there's air conditioner," Al said impatiently. I got up and didn't share my fears with him. I kept saying to myself, *Men don't like sickly women.* I also didn't want to be like my mother, always complaining with aches and pains. I was glad when we got back home and I could lie down as needed.

Mama came to visit us again but without José. She took us all by surprise; she had lost more than half her weight and she looked great. "When you told me the heart specialist had given me a couple of months to live on account of my weight, I decided to kick death in the butt. I also wanted to show you how strong-willed I can be." When it came to showing the power of inner strength and the will to live, Mama made a big impact on me. I felt proud of her.

I was in the kitchen making breakfast when Nelly turned to Mama and said disdainfully, "Do you know your daughter doesn't use soap to wash her face in the morning? Isn't that terrible?"

"Well, it seems to be working for her. She doesn't have a wrinkle on her face. Maybe you and I should do the same and see if it works."

Once again Nelly said good-bye to her sister and took off to Long Island even though she had been there a month before.

Wherever I went, I took Mama along. I was enjoying her company a lot more, probably because I was starting to accept her as she was, or I was becoming more mature, or maybe both. I still missed the mother/daughter closeness I wished for, but beggars couldn't be choosers. Growing up without a loving connection between us had created a permanent invisible barrier. All I could do was play my role as a daughter and hope things changed for the better.

We went to Atlantic City and the kids had fun on the boardwalk and we went to the pier to see the horse jump off the pier and into the water. Mama bought a whole bunch of fake jewelry, for herself and for gifts to take with her to Portugal.

Mama loved McDonald's burgers and pizza. We went to Asbury Park with the kids and had pizza. If Mama had the opportunity to live in America, she would adapt perfectly to the American way of life. But with José needing her at home, she would have to stay in Portugal.

One evening our neighbor Robert called. Barbara, his wife, had tried to commit suicide and was in the hospital. I took Mama with me. Barbara looked terrible. She had cut her wrists and was heavily medicated. Robert asked Mama if she spoke English and Mama said, "Yes, I do. Give me money, money, money." She emphasized the words by rubbing her right fingers together. "Money, money, money."

Robert said, "Can you say something else?"

"Money, yes, yes… give me money, money, money." Everybody was laughing—except me.

The next day I took Mama to the music school so she could see where I worked, and she played the piano so loudly that Mr. Crocker asked me to take her out of the store because she was annoying the customers. The way Mama still put on her heavy make-up, the way she dressed, and all the jewelry she wore made her look like a gypsy. When we went to Shop Rite to buy food for the week, I pretended I wasn't with her even though she looked a lot better than the last time she had visited us.

One evening we were on the way to play bingo when Mama saw her mother's ghost. Mama was all excited about it, "Seeing my mother is always a good omen; it means I'm going to win." For a few seconds she seemed to be in deep thought and then added, "Veronica, after I die, would you like me to visit you?"

"No, please. Don't do that. You'll scare me to death. I don't want to see ghosts. Please Mama, whatever you do, don't show up as a ghost to me."

Braving A New World

"Okay, if that's what you want. I won't return after I'm dead."

I took a deep breath of relief. We all die sooner or later, nobody lived forever, but whatever came ahead, I preferred to learn all about it when the time came. It would be more exciting that way. While I was alive I wanted to live in this world, where God put me. The way I looked at it, the next world belonged only to the ones already there and not to the ones still living here.

Mama did win one bingo game and she acted as if the thirty-five dollars she won were a million dollars.

After Mama left for Portugal, Al told me he didn't mind if both my parents came to live with us, as long as they didn't bring José along. "That's a nice offer," I said, "but my parents would never leave my brother in Portugal to contend on his own." As I expected, Al said, "No way, that's out of the question to have José living with us."

Truthfully, I didn't want my parents living with me. I had enough with Nelly.

After a few days of pondering and looking for an answer I could live with, I came up with what I thought was an excellent strategy, to convince Nelly to spend a few hours a day away from home.

I was a nervous wreck, and it took a lot of deep breathing and courage to ask her to sit down next to me so that we could have a heart-to-heart talk in the kitchen. It was going to be my first time trying to reason with her. I hugged her, then held her hands and looked into her eyes and smiled, so she understood I meant well. "Nelly, you work too hard all day doing housework. I have an idea that I think you're going to like a lot."

"What are you talking about?"

"How about taking up a hobby? Something to take you out of the house so you can have a little fun?"

She was looking at me very seriously. I thought, "She is

assessing the possibilities. This is going better than I imagined." I went on. "If you join a senior center you can learn to make pottery, paint, and make friends your own age. You're still very beautiful and you might even meet someone special." I winked at her.

She stood. "You are nothing but an ungrateful bastard. After all I have done for you. You're trying to get rid of me!"

"No I'm not. Nelly, you need to have other interests in your life, besides us. It's not healthy for you to stay home all day."

"How dare you tell me to go to a senior center and find a hobby? You know how I feel about old people. I'm not taking on any hobbies, I don't need hobbies. I have enough work to do here, taking care of you and your children."

I felt like a fool and went upstairs to my bedroom to cry.

Al no longer had to contend with swallowing my front tooth. I saw a dentist and he made me a permanent bridge. I couldn't get over how real it looked; it was a perfect match with the other teeth and the roof of my mouth loved feeling plastic free. Thanks to Barbara's suggestion, I had lost my most secret fear—taking a bite of an apple or a corn cob and in the process, become toothless. I would always be thankful for her suggestion, but I was sad to say that Barbara attempted suicide once again and she was successful. Her husband put their house for sale and he and little Lisa moved away. Nelly and I prayed for Barbara's soul.

Autumn of 1971

I changed my mind about the Beatles. I was still not a big fan of their music, but I was thankful for their easy songs because my students could start playing some of their tunes within a month or two of guitar lessons. Being able to play a popular song was very satisfying to a beginner student.

I had started teaching again but it wasn't easy climbing the steps all the way up to the third floor where my teaching rooms were located. I held on to the railing and pushed myself up one slow step at a time Thank God for blue jeans! They were good for everything that ailed me; in the past they had helped with back support when my lower back was hurting, and in my present situation wearing snug jeans was very comforting as it held my insides in place.

Learning to play rock and roll was still one of my dreams. But I had the worst luck finding a teacher. One guy I called said, "You know how to read music and you also teach. What can I possibly teach you?"

"Rock and roll."

"There's no such thing. You need to get in a rock band and start playing then."

Mr. Crocker had said the same but I didn't feel as confident as he was about my capabilities. There was always something new to learn. I knew that because I still couldn't play like my idol, Eric Clapton.

Out of desperation, I settled for a classical guitar teacher. Mr. Zarkevich was the only one I spoke to who was not worried if I knew more than him. He lived with Valeria, his second Russian wife of sixty years in a house he built from an old chicken coup. The house smelled like raw egg yolks and boiled chicken feathers. The ceiling was very low and the rooms were very small, but that seemed to be okay since he and his wife were shorter than me. Mr. Zarkevich was 92 years old and the sweetest man I had ever met.

"Oh no," he said, "I look sweet now, because I'm very old, but I was a very bad man in my younger days. I ran around with lots of women. In those bygone years I loved them and left them. Worst of all," he wiped a tear with the back of his hand. "I left my first wife and baby girl in

Russia to go work in Turkey, and I never returned." He wiped another tear. "I'm very sorry I did that to my family. For the last twenty years I have been writing to the consulate of Russia in New York City trying to see if I can locate my daughter. Her mother died ten years ago." He had no success with his inquiries and feared the worst. While in Turkey he worked very hard as a bricklayer, but in his spare time he showed a natural gift for playing classical and gypsy guitar and also the balalaika, a three-stringed Russian instrument that looked like a small triangular mandolin. By joining a gypsy style band of musicians, he finally made it to New York City where he became very well-known and even played classical guitar with the famous Andres Segovia, his beloved and close friend.

At the end of the guitar lesson, Mr. Zarkevich liked to play some of his old records. He had a lot of memories connected with those records. We sat quietly listening and I noticed his eyes getting glassy as he took a few deep sighs. I paid Mr. Zarkevich for a half hour private lesson once a week, but he didn't let me out for at least an hour. He still played his antique balalaika, and at the end of our guitar duet session, sometimes he asked me if I didn't mind accompanying him with my guitar while he played the balalaika. He taught me to strum gypsy style, and the lessons consisted mostly of playing duets. Playing duets helped me with timing. He said the reason his arthritic fingers were so limber was because of the copper bracelets he used, one on each wrist. Copper helped to fight the crippling arthritis that in the last few years had been trying to take over his fingers.

Strangely enough, I was starting to enjoy playing classical music. It was like when one hears a boring song on the radio, but it grows on you after hearing it over and over again.

Mama wrote, "Sex is good for anything that might ail you,

and if you don't have sex on a regular basis, you'll get sick! Are you having sex? You have not answered my last letter."

While growing up, my sex education had been a narrow straight path when it came to learning anything from her. She used to say with conviction, honeymooning was a serious health hazard and masturbating caused worms to grow inside our sexual organs while other children less lucky went blind.

I pretended her letter had gotten lost in the mail. Sometimes that happened.

Just like I didn't understand my mother, I also didn't understand Al's way of thinking. He was very good to me and I should not have been complaining since he supported anything I wanted to do, but I wished we were more alike. It bothered me that we didn't have much in common when it came to life's values. For example, when I bought two new coffee tables for the playroom, I told him, "I'm going to put the tables outside on the curb. Someone passing by will pick them up for sure since they're not damaged."

"If they want coffee tables, let them go out and buy their own." He broke the coffee tables into pieces and put them into the garbage.

We had no use for the tables, so why not share them with someone needy? Al and I did not see eye-to-eye on many things principally when it came to caring for others who were less fortunate.

Several times while growing up, my family had been destitute and furniture was a very precious commodity. I had not forgotten those difficult days but I was also grateful to have experienced them, they had taught me the value of everything we tend to take for granted.

I got a call from the school principal. He wanted to know why Ralph and Steve wore the same clothes. I explained to him and the teacher seated in his office that my children's clothes were clean and used only one day and then washed. Before the school year started, I purposely bought them the same clothes so they wouldn't fight over what the other one had. If each had five shirts and five pants that were exactly the same for each day of the week, they would feel equally loved. The principal and the teacher were still upset and didn't understand my purpose, and felt they should have different clothes, as if school was some kind of modeling agency. Nelly was with me, so I couldn't go into detail about the reason for my madness.

Nelly went out the next day and immediately bought a whole wardrobe for Ralph—exactly what I was trying to prevent from happening.

When I put Ralph in Cub Scouts, I deliberately waited for Steve to be of age to join too. But it didn't matter what I did. Nothing helped. I had no solution. Thank God for my guitar and teaching. When I was away from home I had no stress and I was the happiest woman alive.

Winter ending 1971

Mr. Zarkavich was poorer than I thought. One day I got to his home a little too early for my guitar lesson and caught him and his wife having lunch. The kitchen where they ate reminded me of the set for *Alice in Wonderland*. Everything was tiny. He asked me to join him and Valerie at their kitchen table which was just big enough for two small people. I felt like a giant seated on one of their tiny wooden chairs. I told them I'd already had lunch, but Valerie insisted I have fresh peppermint tea. She poured the hot water from a tiny porcelain teapot which matched the tiny porcelain blue tea cup with scalloped edges and gold banding. They ate cottage cheese with saltine crackers. Afterward they had cottage cheese with honey. That was their lunch.

"The meal is the cottage cheese and when you add the

honey, it becomes dessert," said Mr. Zarkavich, smiling.

I felt bad when Valerie handed me a container of grilled eggplant and tomatoes to take home for my family. I felt like I was taking their dinner, but when I refused it they got offended, so I took it.

Ralph and Steve were absolutely overjoyed when they opened their Christmas presents that year. Afterward, they confessed, the previous Christmas they had gotten hold of all the hidden presents under my bed. They opened and closed everything carefully, but the result was that they knew what they were getting and it took away all the thrill and excitement of opening their gifts for the first time.

Life was a constant lesson, which was also kind of frightening if we didn't learn the first time. Probably the reason someone came up with the quote, history repeats itself.

Winter of 1972

I was very lucky. My students came for music lessons because they wanted to learn to play the guitar and not because they were forced to do it, like the students who had to attend public school. One day one of the girls in class said, "Wouldn't it be great if it snowed really hard today and we have to stay here with Ronnie for days and days until the snow melts?" The others agreed.

It was a great feeling to be loved and appreciated by my students

As if Steve didn't have enough problems in his life, suddenly and for no good reason, the palms of his hands would crack and bleed. I took him to a dermatologist who prescribed some medicated cream to be applied every night before he went to sleep. He had to wear plastic gloves to bed to make sure the cortisone cream didn't get wiped off.

It smelled weird and made his skin look thinner. My instincts told me the medicine was a nasty drug in cream form I threw it away and began applying Vaseline instead.

The pharmacist in Freehold had been right; Vaseline did wonders for the skin. Steve's hands began to look normal again.

I told Mama about it and she wrote, "Steve has the hands of a saint and just like Christ's hands used to bleed, so does Steve's." I didn't know Christ's hands bled except for when they nailed him to the cross. I didn't share with Nelly or Al about Mama's belief. They would not agree of course, and most likely use that as another excuse to torment Steve.

Being the only guitar teacher at the music school had its advantages. I was very busy. I made a lot more money teaching classes, but I preferred to teach private lessons because it was not so demanding on my throat. I often lost my voice. Al liked to say, "Men would love you as a wife." He was just kidding of course because we didn't really talk to each other much. We didn't think the same way about anything and I preferred to remain quiet than have a disagreement with the man who had saved my life. That was the least I could do.

I no longer had bleeding nightmares concerning what I had gone through in the hospital, but if I talked about it, I was guaranteed to have a nightmare that night. When I woke up from such a nightmare, I could not help myself from imagining the atrocities done in the so-called hospitals in concentration camps when they would do medical experiments on healthy young men and women. I felt like my agony was nothing compared to what they went through, and felt ashamed that I still complained over my personal ordeal.

Lately I was also experiencing a creepy kind of dream that was not only turning into a nightmare but becoming an omen. It was always the same type of dream, I would be walking inside a museum with Egyptian artifacts, and little by little a sense of doom would take over me as if I was trapped inside a pyramid and I couldn't breathe. I always woke up out of breath and with heart palpitations. One or two days later after the Egyptian dream, I would get sick with a cold or a sore throat. I could understand what I went through in the hospital could give anyone nightmares, but the thing about the museum had me puzzled because it was like a warning about my future health.

Mama's letters made me feel like I was committing a crime by not sending Ralph and Steve to Hebrew school so they would be ready for their Bar Mitzvah when the time came. I couldn't tell her that neither Al nor Nelly supported such idea and I was just as guilty. Mama's relentless letters kept coming and finally I gave in to her. I registered them for Hebrew classes, after regular school hours, at the Jewish Temple in Freehold. After a month I took them out. They were skipping classes and spending the time in the pizzeria down the street. Of course I got very upset when I found out, but at the same time, memories of my mother having me learn Hebrew returned and I remember it as being one of the most tedious events in my life. I decided not to force my kids into anything their hearts were not into. I probably should have forced them to go for their own good, but force to me meant living in a dictatorship like when I was growing up in Portugal.

Thanks to Ralph and Steve, I had become non-ticklish. They could no longer make me laugh by tickling me. I concentrated and concentrated to maintain my wits as they liked to tickle me every chance they could. They tried a few times more, tickling me under my arms and on my feet, but they finally had to give up. Ha, ha! The mind was very powerful!

I got a bass book and started to teach myself electric bass guitar. A month went by and when Mr. Crocker heard me play, he said I sounded good enough to teach. They booked me with two new bass students.

It was Papa's turn to visit us. I was very concerned because I knew he was going to criticize and analyze everything I said and did, just like when I was growing up in Portugal. I didn't know how I would react to his behavior since I was no longer a child.

Papa had read a book by an American doctor who professed to have the cure for schizophrenia. In his book, Dr. Williams assured his readers that certain vitamin deficiencies caused mental illness and even death. Papa's mission was to meet with Dr. Williams in Pennsylvania and he was bringing José to be examined and treated. Mama and Papa had scraped every penny they had for such trip. Mama wrote, "If we can save our son, then no price is too high for us to pay."

There was one thing I did that I never thought I was capable of doing—sometimes I hit my kids. I couldn't stand it when they fought with each other. I didn't care what the reason was. To me they were both at fault and if they fought, they got punished. When I was a kid, I had sworn I would never, ever hit my children, but Ralph and Steve could easily try a saint's patience. I told them over and over again, "It's your choice: if you fight, I will get the belt and beat you both." Most of the time I would trick them into running away from me and they'd run upstairs and hide in their bedroom and lock the door behind them. Then I would warn them, "If you don't make peace with each other, I'll kill you both when you come out of the bedroom. Brothers are supposed to love each other and that's all there is to it."

Sometimes it worked and they acted all chummy when

they opened their bedroom door, but at other times I could hear them beating each other and that's when I banged my closed fists on the door, screaming at them, and getting ready with the belt when they come out. "Okay you got it coming,".

~ Chapter Eight ~

PAPA

1972

Spring of 1972

Nelly left for Long Island the morning Papa arrived. Papa and José were to stay with us for about three weeks, and Monday I would be driving them to Philadelphia to see the doctor who we hoped would cure José's schizophrenia with vitamins.

It broke my heart to see my brother José. He was totally gone, mentally and physically. But Papa had changed a lot for the better. He had developed a sense of humor that I was never aware of. He told me with a beaming smile, "In the airplane to the United States, the stewardess told me I reminded her of Maurice Chevalier, the debonair French actor." He winked at me and added, "I am old, but handsome."

Papa still spoke pretty good English, and wherever we went he made himself understood. He learned English in high school while he was growing up in Berlin, Germany, where he was born. For most of his life, he had been living in Portugal and speaking only Portuguese. At sixty-nine years old, he still had a fantastic memory. I could only hope to be as healthy as him when I was his age. When he was forty-five years old he had been diagnosed with a serious heart condition, but it did not seem to be affecting him in any way, shape, or form.

I told Papa, "In America men don't wear a jacket and tie unless they are going to a wedding, or some business meeting. Besides, it's too hot to wear those kinds of clothes. You and Jose need a light, comfortable summer outfit."

"Americans are very wise and practical," he said with a certain twinkle in his eyes. "I want to look American." The next day, I took him and my brother to the mall and he bought a pair of shorts and a t-shirt for both of them.

I freaked out when after lunch Papa said, "Your mother told me you are a guitar teacher, so let's hear you play something good."

I was trembling when I sat across from Papa with my acoustic guitar. He said, "Thank you, my daughter." He sat back in his chair, crossed his arms and closed the eyes as if expecting to hear some incredible tune. I picked a simple Bach piece I could show off with. When I finished playing, I looked at him. He was crying silently and wiping the tears with his handkerchief.

I had seen Papa cry once, when he lost his business many years ago, and I was still a child. I didn't feel like it had anything to do with my playing, but one never knows. He asked me to sit closer to him. He had something very important to tell me and he spoke quietly with his Portuguese-German accent. "Verónica my daughter, I want to ask you to forgive me for not being involved in your life and your brothers, while you were growing up. My main focus was to work and to make money to keep the family fed. Now I realize what I lost during all those years." He wiped his tears and motioned with his hand that he was okay. "I lost out on the most precious thing I could have possessed—time with you and your brothers. I never got to know my children. Can you ever forgive me?"

"Papa, you did your best." I hugged him. "You were a good father. But I understand how you feel and I forgive you." We hugged again and I felt like a newborn child. He had aged into a kind, gentle human being. The barrier between us had dissipated like magic and I looked forward to getting to know him better.

The doctor in Pennsylvania said José had a zinc deficiency among many others, and Papa spent a small fortune buying all the necessary vitamins to take home. Personally, and I felt this very personally, José was the way he was because of our parents. They had driven him to insanity. Vitamins were not going to help him. He was still living in the same environment, just like Ralph and Steve were also stuck in the same environment with a grandmother who messed up their lives.

I enjoyed seeing Papa happy and smiling as he got a kick out of doing the most ordinary things I took for granted living in America. He enjoyed cutting the grass while seated on our riding lawnmower, and even asked me to take his picture. He saw me watering the grass and couldn't wait to try. "I have never used a water hose before." He took on the job with gusto as Ralph and Steve teased him to get them wet. José stood by the front door watching and smiling but he didn't participate in any activities, most of his days were spent sleeping, drawing geometric drawings or watching television. One evening I showed Papa how to light the barbeque grill outside. He was ecstatic. He had never done that either. Wearing just shorts and, my bright red apron, he used the long barbeque fork to hold one of the pork chops in the air and posed playfully for a picture.

One morning I took Papa and José to the Museum of Natural History in New York City. Papa asked me a question when we were in line but I couldn't understand him, as it wasn't clear. Then, just like I always did when I did not want people to think I was stupid I nodded and said,

"Yes."

But Papa got angry. "Why are you nodding your head like a dummy? Can't you hear me? Are you deaf? I didn't ask for a yes or no, I asked you, how much are the tickets?"

The fact remained, he was still Papa, the harsh German father I had grown up fearing. But since he had cried and asked for forgiveness, and he was leaving in a couple of days, I had to accept his rudeness as a small part of his old self.

Overall, I was thankful to God for giving me the opportunity to make peace within myself about my father and letting me see the sensitive, more human side of him.

Once Papa and José left to Portugal, Nelly returned from Long Island.

Another letter from Mama arrived. She did not give up easily. "I have not heard from you about your sex life. Let me tell you this—sex is good for the circulation, for the heart, for general pain everywhere. Sex is good for emotional stability, sex is good for a healthy relationship, and a lot more. This is my last letter to you on this subject because it looks like you are not going to talk to me about it. But remember, I am your mother and I know more about life than you do!"

Al and I were called once again for a meeting with the school principal. They had done an IQ test on our children. Steve's was normal, but he was going to need tutoring with math. Hmmm, just like me. Now, Ralph was a different story; his IQ was exceptionally high. We were advised to send him to private school where he could get a lot of attention. We were also encouraged to start saving money because Ralph was prime material for college, and he would most likely become a doctor. I wondered how much of this encouragement to put Ralph in private school had to do with the teachers trying to get rid of him.

Just in case they were right, I began looking into private schools. They all had one thing in common—they were extremely expensive. It seemed to me a waste of money to put him in a private school and then have him return to our dysfunctional family at the end of the day. What I had to do was look for a place that would show him the world did not revolve around him. He needed to be away from Nelly—only then would he learn to take care of himself and not rely on her.

My guitar students were a compilation of adults as well as children and were from all walks of life. Sally, a thirty-five-year-old mother of five had me puzzled. It took a lot of courage for me to tell her what was on my mind but one day I said, "Okay, it's been a month, and every week you come to see me for a private guitar lesson, but you never even open your guitar case. I just sit here listening to you."

She smiled. "Talking to you is cheaper than seeing a psychiatrist."

"But I'm not a psychiatrist. I'm a guitar teacher and I feel like I'm taking your money for nothing."

"You may call it nothing but having someone listen to me is more valuable than you can ever imagine."

Then there was Mark, the nine-year-old boy with a learning disability. His mother gave him a bag of saltine crackers, and he ate the crackers while holding the guitar. When the crackers were finished, he put the guitar away into his case. He could not sit still for the whole half hour lesson. Most of the time it lasted five minutes, or even two minutes depending on how fast he finished eating the crackers. I told his mom, "I feel guilty getting paid for teaching him when he is unable to learn or even remember what was shown to him the week before." His mother said, "My son likes you and looks forward to seeing you. I only want him to be happy. I would pay ten times what the lesson costs just as long as I know he's happy." I hugged her and held my tears back thinking about my parents and José.

Summer of 1972

I loved drive-in movies in the summertime. It was so American! Ralph and Steve were always on their best behavior. Nelly loved Bruce Lee; she thought he was cute when he did his scream before doing one of his karate movements. Nelly could be a lot of fun, and at the drive-in movies, she was always nice. Al rarely came with us because he preferred watching television at home. We usually took sandwiches and potato chips and lots of candy with us. It was like having a picnic in the evening.

Paul, one of my new adult students only had one major request, I was not to play my guitar when teaching him; otherwise he duplicated what he heard. He played by ear and wanted to learn how to read music.

I was astounded when Paul told me he taught Jose Feliciano to play guitar. I was more than happy to abide by his wishes. I could never compare to him or Jose Feliciano. Paul was completely devoted to learning to play classical guitar the hard way, note by note. I could only wish I could play like him, by ear!

Because they didn't offer much sheet music for the latest popular songs, whenever a young student wanted to learn a popular lead or run, I had to spend hours at home listening to the cassette tape. For me, it was a stop and go thing with each note, until I found it on the guitar, and then wrote it on staff paper. I was getting more proficient as the years went by, but I knew I could never do what Paul, and others like him, did naturally. They heard a note and automatically knew where it was on the instrument. That was amazing to me. That was a real musician!

I loved it when the kids were out of school. In the summertime my student count went down and I had a lot more free time to enjoy our time together. We had a lot of fun going to the beach, having picnics at the park in Lakewood, and playing fun games like Scrabble, Battleship, and Monopoly. I always did well with Scrabble because I cheated. The kids were too young to know. As a mother and an adult and as the more knowledgeable one, I felt entitled to cheat, although they were getting smarter every day. Neither Nelly nor Al liked to play games.

Autumn of 1972

It took me a while to come up with another idea to get Nelly out of the house, even if it was just a couple of hours a day. I suggested she learn to drive, and then she could take off any time she wanted without having to depend on me. I offered to teach her to drive and she said she was going to think about it.

Winter ending 1972

Nelly finally made her mind up. She was going to learn to drive with me and then get her own car. I couldn't be happier. My intention was to make it as pleasant as possible so she wouldn't quit. I recalled what Al did to me when he taught me to drive, so I spent a long time patiently showing Nelly what each thing in the car was for. Wheel turned left, wheel turned right. Pressing the gas pedal on the right moved the car. Brake pedal to the left of the gas pedal stopped the car. Thankfully this was an automatic so she didn't have to worry about a clutch. When she said she was comfortable, I said she could turn the key.

 I had been in a roller coaster once in my life and that's what Nelly's driving reminded me of—especially when the roller coaster cart suddenly dropped. It was a mind-boggling experience! Nelly was even less coordinated on the road than Al.

She drove over the sidewalk and missed a tree by a few inches because she turned the wheel too slowly. I didn't want to give up on her, so I offered her a short break.

"Take a deep breath. Relax. You can do it."

"Okay I'm relaxed." She put her foot down on the gas pedal and began driving toward a parked car.

"Use your breaks! Use your right foot to stop the car. Stop the car!"

She drove into the parked car but barely touched the car's bumper. She had no idea of distances and her reflexes were very slow. In my opinion she could not learn to drive; it was too late at her age.

When Al got home from work I motioned for him to follow me upstairs. "Whatever you do, don't try to teach Nelly to drive." I warned him. "She's dangerous behind the wheel and should have a professional teacher controlling the car in case of emergency."

"You're picking on my mother. I taught you to drive and I can teach her too. She doesn't need to pay some jerk for that."

My feelings were hurt. I decided not to say anything more. We had dinner and they left right afterward.

I began cleaning the stove and putting the dishes in the dishwasher. My instincts told me something horrible was going to happen. They were going to die, both of them. I was a nervous wreck waiting for a cop to show up at our door to give me the news. I sat down to play dominos with the kids. Then I heard someone at the front door, knocking. It was Al and Nelly. They had walked back from the accident and left the car stuck on a tree.

Instead of taking Nelly around our neighborhood like I had done with her earlier in the day, Al took her onto the back roads. When she drove around a corner, she drove into a tree. Nelly had bruises all over her arms and chest. Al was furious because he found out that Nelly had taken some "relaxing" medication prior to going out with him. Smart woman, she knew he was going to yell at her. But she was too relaxed to respond to quick decisions like using the brakes or turning the wheel on time.

Nelly bought Al another car as the one that hit the tree was beyond repair. We all went to the Volkswagen dealership and they picked their smallest model. When the five of us got into the car, I started to cry.

Al said, "What's the matter now?"

"When we get into an accident in this car, there won't be anything left of us. This is not a car. This is a motorcycle with tin walls."

Al called me nuts, but Nelly said, "If Ronnie has a premonition about this car, let's go back. I'll pay the difference for a bigger one."

Al made a U-turn and we returned to the dealership where he exchanged it for their largest vehicle. When Al got into his usual winter accident he would be a lot safer.

Nelly never again mentioned wanting to learn to drive.

For Christmas it had become a family tradition to take Nelly and the kids to Radio City Music Hall in New York City. It did not matter how long we had to wait outside in the freezing cold on a line that sometimes went around the block. We could not break our customary winter outing. It had become a yearly tradition, not to be broken.

For Christmas, Nelly gave Ralph her husband's books on pharmaceutical drugs. Ralph sat on his bed reading them as if they were children's books. She gave Steve a gallon of milk.

Ralph accidentally stapled one of his fingers. He was trying to see how the stapler worked. He didn't expect the staple to fly out of the staple gun at the speed of a bullet. I guess that's why they call it a staple *gun*. Ralph was very smart but very curious. He was a lot like Einstein in many ways, and even though he was only ten years old, I looked up to him as if he were a grown-up with inner wisdom.

I read somewhere that Einstein's mother found him, when he was a young child of course, in the chicken coop sitting on a couple of eggs trying to hatch them. That was something Ralph would do. Also, Einstein was not a good student and was terrible at math, just like Ralph. For Ralph's birthday I bought him a book about Einstein's theories. I knew it was early to buy a birthday gift, but once I found something good, I would buy it and hide it away. I looked at the book briefly and had no idea what it was about, but I knew Ralph would enjoy reading it.

Winter of 1973

My nickname had its advantages. When people called the music school for guitar lessons, they assumed Ronnie was a male teacher. I realized that a few years back when I entered the room to meet Charlie, a new student, who was a teenager.

"Where's Ronnie?"

"I'm Ronnie, your guitar teacher."

"You're a woman. You can't possibly know how to play guitar."

I looked fearlessly straight at him. "What is it you want to learn that you don't think I can play or teach you?"

"Led Zeppelin; I want to learn how to play *Stairway to Heaven*."

Talk about the perfect timing, I had learned that song not even two weeks prior, from Dan, the drum teacher across from my room, who was also a very good guitarist. Charlie was impressed with my playing, and he looked at me very differently after my little performance. He accepted me as his guitar teacher wholeheartedly.

Paul, my student who could play by ear, and I became good friends. Mama's presumption that men and women could never have a platonic relationship was proven wrong. But the truth was that I did not feel particularly attracted by his looks, and when it came to his intellect, he was very boring. I felt sorry for his wife.

Hava, another one of my adult students, progressed so well with guitar lessons that I asked her to be my teaching assistant with beginning guitar classes. She was thirty-five years old and had been born in Turkey. Her mother had been forced to marry her father after he kidnapped her. He was on his horse and grabbed her future mother as she was innocently walking down a street in her village. Hava was adamant, "I will never allow myself to be dominated by any man."

At first Mr. Crocker didn't like the idea of hiring Hava, but it was easy to persuade him when I asked him what he would do if something were to suddenly happen to me. Between the classes and private students I was teaching around one hundred and ten students a week and I needed to have a backup. Hava was a bit nervous about teaching, so I put Steve in private guitar lessons with her; that way she could practice teaching a child and feel more relaxed about her capabilities. Until then, Steve had been learning to play guitar with me. I felt confident in Hava's ability to teach; she was very patient and had been a dedicated student. Also, Hava had been looking for a job and she loved playing guitar.

~ *Chapter Nine* ~

MY SONS ARE MY WORLD

1973-1975

Spring of 1973

Earlier in the year, Steve was in love with Ms. Lacey, one of his teachers in school and couldn't understand why he couldn't bring her home. But after meeting Hava, he had a change of heart. I thought it was cute since he was only nine years old. He became an avid guitar player.

Ralph was into drums. I bought him a blue five-piece drum set. Ralph played drums, Steve played the guitar and sang, and I played my electric guitar. We used the den downstairs as our music studio. Because Nelly did not like people visiting us unless they were family, when she went away for a couple of weeks during the summer, I invited some of my most talented students to play with us. Steve sang out of tune, but he was so passionate about it and put so much feeling into it that Ralph and I never said anything to discourage him.

For Ralph's birthday, Nelly bought him clothes and a pair of sneakers. For Steve's birthday, Nelly gave him her usual gift, a gallon of milk. Steve loved milk and did not eat much. I asked Dr. DeCicco if I should force Steve to eat, but I was told not to worry about it, since milk offered good nourishment. As long as he drank a lot of milk, he would be fine.

I sent Mama and Papa what I thought was an amusing picture of Al and me dressed as gangsters. We had our photo taken in Atlantic City in one of those specialty photo shops. Al dressed as a gangster, smoking a cigar, and holding a rifle and I put on the costume of a saloon dancer, sitting on top of the bar next to him. Mama wrote, "We got your picture today. Your father and I are really worried about your way of making a living. Robbing banks can only get you both killed. Please think of your children."
I could not believe they were so gullible. I wrote back, explaining that it was only a joke! My parents were such characters!

Al got a kick out of people assuming he was my father. When we went out he always asked me to wear my hair in pigtails. Then he made jokes about it. "Yes, my wife is very young. I stole her right out of the cradle." It was embarrassing. I wished he would stop treating me like a child. But I did not mind when I was with Ralph and Steve and people thought they were my younger brothers because that's how I felt when we were together.

I got a letter from Mama telling me not to let the kids go to school on a certain day that week. Something bad was going to happen to them if they went to school. I read her letter and then out of habit I threw away all ten pages of mostly handwritten poetry. On Sunday I told Nelly about it and she said maybe I shouldn't send the kids to school on that day. The problem was that I could not remember which day of the week I was supposed to keep the kids home. I did not have time to write back to Mama and wait for an answer. I believed she said it would be that Monday.

Monday morning came and the kids gladly stayed in bed sleeping. When I went downstairs to do the laundry, I couldn't believe what had happened during the night. The glass ceiling-lamp in the hallway by the den's door had dropped off the ceiling and splintered into pieces the size of small diamonds all over the tiled floor. Their school clothes were in the den's closet downstairs. If Ralph and Steve had gotten up that morning to go to school, they would have cut their feet since they always ran downstairs like bats out of hell without their shoes on.

I wrote to Mama, thanking her for her forewarning and she wrote back, "I think my premonition was for Tuesday, not Monday. I'm glad my grandchildren are okay." Since her letter came a week later, we already knew Tuesday had been fine. Somehow her thoughts and mine got mixed up, but between the two of us we came up with the right day. I started believing Mama did see into the future.

Summer of 1973

I made the mistake of going to New York City with Al, Nelly, and the kids. What possessed me, I don't know. We were walking on one of the city's streets and Ralph and Steve were walking ahead of us. Nelly was complaining about it and Al yelled, "You boys better walk along with us, by our side."

Neither one of them would listen, so Al grabbed Steve by the arm and slapped him across the face, chipping one of his front teeth. Steve was crying but Al didn't even say he was sorry. He said, "That will teach you to listen to me."

I cleaned the blood from Steve's lip and yelled at Al, "What about Ralph? Why is Steve always getting punished for everything? This is not fair! They were both walking ahead of us."

"Stop being so dramatic, I didn't slap him that hard."

"Hard enough to break his front tooth. He's just a child

for Christ's sake." I cried. But what I wanted to do was hit him back, hit him across the mouth, just like he had done to Steve. Slaps like these were why I now hated Al. I hated how he was so mean to Steve, his own child. I was so heartbroken with what happened that my only way to deal with the anger I felt was to emotionally distant myself from him. When he slapped Steve, he had slapped me. I had just lost whatever respect I had for him and with it any affection I had left for him.

I received another letter from my parents, but this time Papa did more than just sign his name at the end of Mama's letter. "Veronica, I'm glad to inform you that I finally tracked down the man who used to be my business partner. He is living with his wife in Buffalo, New York." He added his address and phone number and asked me to give Walter, his ex-partner, a personal message. "Time has gone by, but your wrongdoing has not been forgotten. You stole from me, and then ran away, like a coward to America, leaving me and my family destitute. Now it is time to give back the money you stole." I promised Papa the next time we went on vacation to Niagara Falls we would stop in Buffalo, and I would seek out Walter and give him my father's message in person. I was very young when it happened but I remember my parents having to sell everything they had and my mother picking dandelions from the backyard to make soup.

It was absolutely delightful when Nelly went to Long Island. There was so much freedom. To celebrate her first day away, I went to Shop Rite and bought every kind of cheese that looked interesting. Ralph, Steve, and I had a cheese party. The three of us always had a blast when we were by ourselves. I used every hour we had together to do interesting things.

I would have loved the opportunity to travel to faraway

places with my two sons and have wonderful and exciting adventures like I used to read about when I was their age. Sandy Hook, on the New Jersey shore, was one of our favorite places. We would look for treasures washed ashore from sunken ships and search for buried treasure chests left hidden by the pirates who used to roam those shores a long, long time ago.

One day the boys and I were walking around the outskirts of Spring Lake, admiring the huge homes when we spotted what appeared to be an abandoned mansion. The front door was not locked, so we went in and roamed through the rooms looking for secret passages in what looked like a library, and then we went downstairs into the dark, mysterious cellar. When we were starting to go up the steps to leave, a tall dark silhouette showed up silently at the top of the cellar stairway. We screamed and so did the shadow. It then said, "I'm the janitor. What the hell are you doing down there?" We stared pathetically, waiting for repercussions from the man with a broom. He yelled, "You and your two little brothers better leave right now or I'll call the police."

Autumn of 1973

Paul and I went to a classical guitar gathering and from then on we got invited to meet each month with other classical guitar lovers. It was only for an hour or two on a Saturday afternoon and Al encouraged me to go without him. He was not into classical music or interacting with people he did not know. He said, "Most likely I'll fall asleep in front of everybody." He also had the bad habit of saying whatever came into his mind and then laughing about his own joke. At the classical guitar meeting we listened to each other's playing and stayed open to creative criticism afterward. One evening Paul brought a friend named Peter to one of our guitar meetings. Peter was also a guitar instructor. I didn't connect with him. He seemed to be untouchable and when some of us asked him to play the guitar, he said, "I'll be playing at Brookdale College next month if you want to hear me play. Here are some brochures about my guitar concert." He sat like a stiff doll in the corner of the room looking at his nails and avoided making eye contact with anyone as if he was superior to us.

Winter ending 1973

Al had told me several times, "I can't wait for our sons to be old enough to be on their own and out of the house, so it will be just you, me, and Nelly." I was not looking forward to those days. I loved my children and I did not feel complete when they were not with me, except when they fought like cats and dogs with each other. Then I felt I had no problem killing them myself.

To my complete surprise Al offered to take Ralph out on a father and son type of outing over the weekend. He had never done anything like that with either child. Nelly must have told Al to take Ralph out and spend time with him.

"What about Steve?" I asked.

"No, it's only Ralph and me."

"That's not fair. How is Steve going to feel when you take Ralph out and he's not included?"

We argued back and forth, and finally Al walked away saying, "Then it's neither one of them."

I knew neither Al nor Nelly loved Steve like they loved Ralph. It was a fact and I could do nothing about it, but I was going to fight tooth and nail for equal rights for both of them for as long as I had a breath of air in my lungs. Since Steve had been born he had been mistreated and despised as if he were born with leprosy. I was devastated over Al's irrational behavior, even if it was created by his desire to keep peace with his mother who could nag anyone into madness.

I felt alone and detached from being a real mother. When people asked me if Ralph and Steve were my brothers, they were getting closer to the truth than I could admit. Yes, Al gave me the freedom to do what I pleased, but as we had started to grow apart, I saw him as my father and Nelly as my mother. I had to stay busy all the time so I could go on living without going crazy. One of the thoughts keeping me from going crazy was remembering what happened to Aunt Ligia, my mother's younger sister in Portugal. One week before her wedding, her fiancé called it off. Aunt Ligia went into a depression. She had to be put into a mental hospital and they administered electric shock treatments to her brain. I did not want to end up like Aunt Ligia as once I accidentally put a finger into an electric socket when I was a kid and I did not like the feeling of electricity.

Winter of 1974

Steve showed an interest in taking tap dancing so I signed him up for a class at the music school where I taught guitar. Steve was ten years old, and I thought he was going to quit once he found himself as the only boy in a class of eight girls. I was wrong. Steve loved being surrounded by girls and was having a great time. It did my heart good to see him smiling when he came out of the class and he could not wait for the next lesson.

Nelly was upstairs when I heard her crying out for help. We all ran to see what was going on and found her lying on the floor. She had hit her head on the corner of the wall when she tripped and fell. Al screamed at her for being clumsy which I thought it made no sense. Nobody falls on purpose. That's why it's called an accident.
    I was the one taking her to see Dr. DeCicco, our family doctor. I was the one rushing her to the hospital every time

she said her heart bothered her. Considering Al's detached attitude toward his mother, I really worried that if I were not home, Al would ignore her complaints and she could die from lack of medical attention.

When Nelly got her flu shot, she got seriously ill. I could not comprehend why people got the flu shot and expected not to get the flu after they had put the sickness into their body.

Dr. DeCicco even came to our house to see her. "I don't know what to do for her," he said, while twisting his hands. "She's such a nice lady. I just don't know what to do to help her." He had tears streaming down his face.

Except for my Uncle Augusto in Portugal, Dr. DeCicco was the most sensitive and caring doctor I had ever met. I liked him a lot, even after I had called him on the phone to make an appointment, as I had a really bad cold and I needed some medicine, and he asked me not to come to his office because he didn't want to catch it.

Spring of 1974

Al and I went out once a year for our wedding anniversary. Nelly watched the kids for us that night. After I fed them, I played with them. We went up and down the steps and we ran around the house until they were exhausted. Then I gave them candy and goodies to make them happy, got them into bed, and waited until they fell asleep. It was not easy; they knew I was up to something.

Al and I always dined at Van's, in Freehold, the most sophisticated restaurant around. Actually, it was the only one around employing waitresses who wore white aprons. I didn't really like their food, but I loved the dessert of chocolate mousse and the complimentary appetizer basket with olives, sliced carrots, celery sticks, French bread, and a great cheese dipping sauce. The dinner was very expensive, but we only splurged like that once a year. Then we went to the movies. Sometimes we even went dancing. Al did not like to dance; one or two slow dances and he was ready to go home. I would have loved to stay out and dance all night.

Summer of 1974

On our visit to Niagara Falls we stopped in Buffalo, New York, and the first thing I did was to call the number my father had given me. Walter's wife, Helga, answered the phone. I told her who I was, and that I needed to speak to her husband. She was very emotional and wanted to know how my father was doing and said she needed to see me too. She was on her way to work, and asked me to stop by during her lunch hour. She worked at Sears, in the women's clothing department. Helga cried when she hugged me, and I didn't have a chance to say much. "My husband died four years ago," she said. "But before he died, he told me he was sorry for what he did to your father. Please tell your father he's very dear to my heart. Please tell him that for me. Tell him I'm sorry for what my husband did to your father and family."

Everything that needed to be said no longer seemed important to me. It was time for closure. I promised her I'd write to Papa when I got home. I knew my father would forgive his dead ex-partner.

During the summertime, I got to collect unemployment because most of my students from Marlboro and Freehold went away for vacation. Music lessons basically came to a stop.

Having so much free time on my hands kept me busy with architectural projects around the house. Yet each idea was not always well received as it meant more work for Al. But I found that if I kept explaining how well it would work out, he would begin to see it my way.

"Imagine a wider kitchen by taking down half the wall dividing the kitchen from the dining room. It will make it more spacious, more modern." I said.

He was worried the wall might be a load-bearing wall. I told him I would take full responsibility for the project, and crossed my fingers behind my back.

The kitchen looked a lot bigger afterward and even Nelly was impressed.

We always watched television downstairs in the playroom while we had dinner. It was a lot of work putting everything on TV trays and carrying them downstairs and then back up again. There was nothing like eating while seated at a regular table. I said to Al, "How would you like to sit comfortably at the kitchen table, eat, and watch television at the same time? Imagine, no more crumbs in the couch downstairs!"

The idea of a television in the kitchen went well. I figured out how to put a small television into the kitchen cabinet after we changed our old stove for a more modern one. The kitchen took on a more contemporary look after that. We were all happy.

My supreme summer project was to create a laundry chute. It was not easy to figure out where to put it. But one morning as I lay in bed thinking, it hit me like a lightning bolt—the broom closet upstairs was the most direct route to downstairs. I got Al to make a hole in the bottom of the broom closet and to attach a wide, flexible plastic tube leading straight down. A large mailbox was inserted at the bottom of the laundry chute as the receiving container which stood about a foot between the washer and the dryer. Nelly was delighted. No more carrying or throwing the laundry down the steps.

I loved playing architect. Maybe I was one in my past life because I loved construction and creating ideas from existing spaces.

The next project was a fun one. I did it with the boys'

guidance. I cut a rectangular hole into the wall between the playroom and the laundry area. Al was impressed with how well the space I cut worked out and how easy it was to slip in a fish tank.

We had a few gold fish for a while but they didn't do well, so we bought two gerbils, and the kids and I spent hours watching them play.

Autumn of 1974

Paul mentioned he would like to start a classical guitar society with me. I told him Mr. Zarkavich and Hava, would be great people to have in our group. He agreed to meet them but made it clear that he also wanted his friend Peter involved in it, as Peter had a lot of connections with other important musicians.

Winter ending 1974

Al had no hobbies. If he had some kind of outside activity, we would have something to share and talk about, but he only had one interest in life—watching television when he got home from work. He was willing to go out for dinner once in a while, but it was always the same two restaurants, Chinese or German. He never did anything out of the ordinary. It amazed me how he could eat a whole gallon of ice cream in one evening of TV watching, but never deviated from vanilla flavor. On the plus side of all that, he gave me complete freedom of doing anything I wanted on my own.

The Classical Guitar Society was formed, but it was not the same fun-filled relaxed atmosphere I had enjoyed when we used to practice with other musicians at their homes. There were monthly dues and obligatory monthly meetings, and Paul and Peter made the decision of who was going to be what in the Society. Paul made himself the president with Peter as his silent partner. They voted Hava as the vice president, Mr. Zarkavich as the consultant, and me as the secretary. Being a secretary meant taking notes and numbers down, which I hated doing. I wrote Paul a letter, graciously resigning from the group. Mr. Zarkavich was not happy either and he did the same. Hava called and said if I was quitting, so was she.

I thought I was going to die of embarrassment at Mr. Crocker's Christmas party. Al and I were walking around talking to the other teachers, when the husband of one of the piano teachers said to Al, "I see that you have a horse's head as your tie pin. Are you into horses?"

Instead of Al telling him it was a scout pin from one of our boys, he said, "Yes, I am. I'm into horse shit." The man looked at him, than looked at me not knowing what to say after that remark.

I just walked away like I always did when Al said something embarrassing.

Winter of 1975

The kids and I were hanging out listening to some records in the living room when Ralph said, "We have a lot of land on the side of our house, why don't we get a built-in swimming pool?"

"Yeah, Mom," said Steve, "during those hot summer days, it would be great to have a place to cool off."

"When I was a kid, my brother Max-Leão and I used to dream about having a pool in our backyard," I said. "Even when we offered to do the digging, our parents didn't go for it." We all laughed. "In those days it was just a kid's pipedream. But in America, dreams are meant to come true, right? Let's do it."

They were very excited to get involved in the planning.

Braving A New World

We did some research, and even got Al and Nelly interested in the project. An in-ground pool would increase the value of our home, and I could afford to pay for the construction with all the money I made teaching guitar. It was a unanimous vote. The following summer we would have a built-in pool on the side of our house.

Mama sent me a picture of Papa and her standing on their back porch, holding hands. She wanted Steve to put his hands on the picture and heal her heart and the inflammation in both her ankles, and to also heal Papa's kidneys that were not functioning well. I didn't tell Steve the reason why or he would think I was nuts, instead I handed him the picture and let him hold it in his hands as he examined it. I understood why Mama thought Steve had some kind of magic healing power. When she came to visit us she asked Steve to put his hands over her heart and the pain went away immediately. On another occasion she had a headache, and she asked him to put his hands on her head and the headache disappeared. Another time I think Steve was only seven, I woke up with a sore neck, and Steve gave me a quick neck massage and the muscle pain was gone immediately, but to me it only meant one thing, he possessed a natural instinct for doing massage.

Al volunteered to work two nights a week at the Freehold First Aid Squad. He loved the thrill of sirens and urgency. He always wanted to be a cop, but because of his hearing loss on the right side, they would not take him. Al blamed the sound of bombs exploding close to him for destroying his hearing when he was in the Air Force during the Korean War. Both his knees had also been injured from constantly jumping into foxholes during attacks. "The war in Korea was not too bad except for the enemy night raids. My captain could not take the stress and one day shot himself in the head."

"Poor man, that's horrible."

"He was a coward, that's how we all felt about it. War is war. But we also had some good times when we went to town. I had "wonderful" experiences with the geisha girls—most likely dozens and dozens of children are now walking around Korea with dark curly hair and eyeglasses like me." He laughed.

"Really? That's horrible. You don't mean that."

"I was single. What do you expect?"

"Have you thought of going to Korea and trying to find your kids? I wouldn't mind adopting them."

"We have enough with our two sons already."

I felt he was heartless for not taking responsibility for his own children.

Al was accepted as a member of the Squad, but they never tested his hearing. For a while everything was going well, until they realized he couldn't hear well enough to check someone's vitals, so he was asked to drive the ambulance. I knew it was not going to last once they saw him driving. The idea was to get the injured to the hospital in one piece, not to have another accident on the way there.

Al drove the ambulance twice before they politely informed him they had someone else with more experience, but he was welcome to come along.

When he would receive an emergency call in the middle of the night, he was dressed and gone in the blink of an eye. When he returned, I couldn't wait to hear what had happened.

One night when he was called in, the lady was already dead when they got to her house. She had died from the surprise birthday party given to her by her family and friends. When she entered the house, she was so flabbergasted that she dropped dead. Nobody knew she had a weak heart.

When Al was driving his car the accidents he was in were mostly when the ice made the roads slippery. I almost expected it to happen every winter but this year it was not his fault. It wasn't even raining when a woman went through a red light on Main Street in Freehold and T-boned him. His car was totaled, but Al only got a few scratches on his forehead and a bumped knee. He always seemed to end up okay in car collisions of any kind. Thank God he never got hurt. Besides, like he always said, he was due for another car. Even though Al had a negative attitude toward people, politics and religion, I admired his positive attitude toward the ups and downs of his own life.

I got a call from Mr. Johnson, the school principal. According to Ms. Languard, Ralph's teacher, Ralph had blamed his grandmother for the way he acted. They wanted to know what was going on at home. Thank God Al, and not Nelly, came with me so I could tell them about our predicament. "My mother-in-law favors Ralph because he has her husband's name. I cannot reprimand him. She is always defending his actions even when he is a brat."

"We have no control over our children," Al added. "I hate to say this, but my mother runs the household."

"It's your duty as parents to put a stop to such nonsense," said Mr. Johnson.

"Yeah," said Ms. Languard. "You must have a talk with your mother and reason with her."

"You must be kidding." Al chuckled. "I've tried.. She won't listen. It's a waste of time to even bring this up to her."

"Very well, Mr. Esagui," said Mr. Johnson. "You need to make a decision. If you love your son, you need to take your mother to see a family counselor. He might be able to help her and your situation."

When we got home, Al had barely said anything about the need for Nelly to see a counselor when she broke into a crying frenzy. We followed her as she ran upstairs into her bedroom. She got into her bed and covered herself with the blankets. She yelled, "A counselor is nothing but a psychiatrist, and I'm not crazy."

Then she put both hands over her chest rolled her eyes toward the ceiling and taking deep breaths as if grasping for air, she said, "I'm dying. My heart... my heart...you're both killing me!"

She reminded me of Fred, the character played in *Sanford and Son*, every time he wanted his son to do something, he would put on an act just like Nelly. The same thought must have come across to Al, because he threw his hands up in the air and said, "There she goes with her acting." He left the bedroom.

I stayed with her, trying to comfort her just in case she was not faking. Then I felt sorry for her and told her she didn't have to see a counselor if she didn't want to.

As always when I got to work I immediately went upstairs to play my guitar before starting the morning classes. Mr. Crocker was in one of the upstairs rooms playing a guitar with the door open. Nobody else was up there but him, which was strange because he no longer played guitar. As I went past his doorway, I stopped and standing on the doorway I said, "Good morning Mr. Crocker." His guitar caught my eye and I said, "Wow, a twelve-string guitar. It must be more difficult to play than a six-string."

"It's all the same. You should be able to play it without any problem." He went back to playing and I went into my teaching room. I was practicing a new tune on my guitar when he came over, pulled a chair right in front of me for himself and handed me his twelve-string guitar. "See if you like the way it feels."

I strummed a few simple chords and said, "I really like the sound, but I don't care for the way it makes my fingers hurt from pressing two metal strings at the same time." I was still holding the guitar when he grabbed my face between his hands and kissed me on the lips. Nasty, disgusting, gross—that's all that was going through my mind. His lips were bigger than Al's, and very soft. I felt like he had just raped me and my face went red. My next thought was, *Do I slap my boss and lose my job, or act like his kiss is a fart in the wind and just keep playing as if nothing happened?* I realized instantly that I didn't have the nerve to say or do anything except to look at him as if he didn't exist. I gave him his guitar back without a word. I guess he didn't have the courage to kiss me again, and to my relief he left to go downstairs. I went to the bathroom and washed my lips with soap and water. I hardly ever talked to him! What could I have done to make him act that way? It was my fault. I had talked to him and he thought I liked him. If anything, I found him disgusting—a married man kissing me like that. I did not tell Al about it. I felt terribly ashamed.

Nelly was complaining of chest pain, so I called Dr. DeCicco and he asked me to take her to the hospital to have X-rays done. While doing the X-rays, something went wrong and they had to revive her by using electric pads on her chest. They broke her ribs. The poor thing had to remain in the hospital for a week.

A month prior, at a barbeque party given by the Freehold First Aid Squad, Al had slipped and fallen and broke two ribs. He couldn't breathe from the pain. I knew enough about anatomy to know the ribcage housed the lungs. If one broke it had to hurt like hell to breath. Lucky for him to be surrounded by the First Aid Squad volunteers, they put him in an ambulance and took him to the hospital at full speed.

I was taking Ralph to school to pick up an assignment he had forgotten to bring home when I became inspired to use nature as an analogy to the value of education. "Ralph, look at the trees. Do you notice how some look healthy, tall, and proud? That's because they had the right nourishment and proper food as they grew up. The others you see are kind of sickly and never developed enough, possibly because of a lack of nutrients in the soil. It's the same with education. You can learn to be somebody of value, or you can grow up to be like those small sick trees on the side of the road. The choice is in your hands about your future."

"I know what you mean," he said. I believe he did. Even I was impressed, I didn't know I had it in me.

Steve and I were at McDonald's, having a burger and fries, and I was telling him to hurry up so I could get to work a little earlier.

"Mom, why are you always rushing? What's so important that you can't even take your time to eat with me?"

"Because, I am losing time from practicing my guitar and..."

"Mom, if you keep rushing through life like this, you'll get to the end a lot faster than you want and you'll miss everything in between." Wow! That was the heaviest thing I had ever heard, especially coming from an eleven-year-old.

Both Ralph and Steve were my greatest inspiration when it came to appreciating life. They were both very young but they were also very wise in their own ways.

On my way to pick up the kids at school, I left Nelly at Britts department store and went through a McDonald's drive-through for some French fries. Munching away on salty fries and singing along with the radio, I put on the signal to make a left turn, and just as I was about to turn into the school parking lot, a car crashed into the back of my car at full force. Even though I was wearing my lap belt, I still went flying into the steering wheel with my chest and hit the windshield with my forehead. Then I fell backward as the seat broke from the impact. It all happened like the speed of lightning, yet at the same time it seemed as if it happened in slow motion. When the seat broke loose and moved backward, I was still tied into it by the lap belt but couldn't reach the brakes or the steering wheel. I saw the huge tree looming in front of me and I clenched my teeth, and closed my eyes tight, anticipating the impact. The car stopped once it hit the tree. I opened my eyes and realized I was in my first car accident. The whole world was going to learn that I listened to loud rock music and ate McDonald's fries. I immediately turned the radio off and began picking as many fries as I could to put back in the paper bag. Blood was dripping down my face from my forehead to my shirt and my hands had fries covered in blood. My chest was hurting from hitting the steering wheel and it was difficult to take a full breath. I suddenly realized that I should get out of the car as soon as possible; smoke from the engine, which was wrapped around the tree, could only meant one thing the car was going to explode. I kicked the door open with my feet and crawled out onto the grass as far from the car as possible. Then I sat on the side of the curb with one hand on my bloody forehead and the other on my achy chest.

    The girl that had rear-ended me came running toward me screaming, "Oh my God! I killed her! I killed her!"

    "It's okay, I'm not dead," I said, waving at her. "I'm just bleeding from my head."

    An ambulance seemed to appear out of nowhere. Someone must have called them. I gave them the music school's number. "Please call them and tell them I'll be late to teach guitar lessons today."

    My car, my poor beautiful red car was smashed at both ends like an accordion.

    "Please call my husband at work, my mother-in-law at Britts, and my children at school. They are expecting me.

The kids will have to take the school bus home." I was assured that everything would be taken care of. They put me on a stretcher and took me to the Freehold hospital.

"We need to stitch your forehead," said the ER doctor with a syringe in his hand. "I'm going to give you a little shot to numb the area."

"Oh no," I said, "I'm very allergic to pain killers. All painkillers! Just stitch my head and do whatever it is you have to do, but no shot."

What was pain anyway? Nothing could be as bad as when Dr. Adler used to pack my insides with sponges.

"Get someone to hold her hand," said the doctor to one of the nurses.

"Would you like someone to hold your hand?" said someone by my feet.

"Okay, I guess so." I wondered how holding onto someone's hand was going to help. Then a nurse appeared. He was blond, blue-eyed, and very good-looking. I smiled back at him and squeezed his hand. I didn't feel a thing except for a prickly feeling on my forehead.

They wanted to keep me in the hospital overnight. The first words out of my mouth as soon as Al came to get me were, "Thank God you're here. Please get me out of this hospital." After my last hospital experience, I did not stay in hospitals if I could help it.

I was hurting all over when I got home. Nelly told me not to worry. She had called the music school and canceled all my classes, and had also called my private students for the week. "No one has shown any concern for you when I told them you would not be in because of being in a car accident." She laughed. "Even when I called one of your male students, his response was, 'Oh, okay.' And he hung up on me."

She enjoyed giving bad news. Even if it was true that no one gave a hoot about my well-being, I thought it was very unkind of her to convey such lack of concern toward me.

Nobody wants to know if they die nobody cares.

I called Hava and she said not to worry, she would cover for me until I was ready to go back to teaching.

The next day I looked like I had been beaten with a baseball bat over my face and body. I was black and blue everywhere. The car insurance requested I send them some pictures and Al took several of me with a mini skirt and a short-sleeved shirt. I looked my very worst ever. My eyes were almost swollen shut and it hurt to open them. I put Vaseline over my eyelids so the skin did not hurt so much when it stretched to open my eyes. We were worried I might go blind. Al took me to an eye doctor. When the doctor looked at me he said, "Oh dear, I have never seen anything like this. Your eyes are oozing."

I didn't want to hurt his feelings by telling him it was Vaseline. He said my eyes had hematomas, whatever that meant, and he was going to send a report immediately to the insurance company regarding the injuries I had received.

Al came out of the doctor's office laughing his head off. "Yeah, it's called Vaseline hematomas! What a jerk of a doctor. It tells you how much he knows."

Spring of 1975

A month went by and I got a call from the car insurance company. They offered to pay for all the medical bills and they were going to send me $1,000 for all my suffering. I didn't know how to thank them; that was something I didn't expect.

I bought another used car for $650 and with the rest of the money I put a down payment on a new refrigerator at Sears. Now that was what I called a lucky accident.

Al and Nelly went to the dog pound and surprised us with a dog. Al named the dog Sheba. She was a blonde mutt, very big but very friendly. Steve was upset that he did not have a part in picking the dog he liked, but it was hard to surprise someone if you let them know ahead of time what you are going to do. Ralph was fine with the dog. Sheba was a good, loving dog, and I was sure they were all going to be friends once they started playing together. It was a good idea to get a family pet. It was a first for me too. My brothers and I were not allowed to have pets, not even a bird.

Nelly decided to have fun and asked Steve to choose a couple of numbers. Too bad we didn't buy the ticket. The lottery came out a week later with the numbers Steve had picked. I said, "I do not want Steve or anyone to know about this. Swear to me, that you'll never ask him for any numbers again."

"We could be rich."

"No, I'm his mother and I forbid you to do such thing. If you do I'll curse you so badly that you won't be able to enjoy the money you make. He's a child and I want him to have a normal childhood."

She agreed to keep it a secret.

The excavation for the swimming pool in our yard started with a slight problem. A sump pump needed to be installed first. It was discovered that the river up the street from us flowed right under our property. No wonder all our neighbors' homes with cellars got flooded when it rained a lot. But if everything went well, that summer we would be swimming in our own backyard pool. We were all very excited about it.

Summer of 1975

It did not matter that I took Sheba out for a walk twice a day. She still ran away every chance she got. If the front door was not locked, she knew how to push on the screen door and off she went like the Flying Nun. She came back two or three days later covered in dried poop.

The kids and I were the first ones to jump into the pool. They quickly learned to swim and I practiced my one and only swim stroke I knew, the belly-frog, while keeping my head above water. I did not like to get water in my eyes. Al went into the pool only to clean it. Nelly did not know how to swim but she liked to waddle in the low end and I kept an eye on her. The past summer while visiting Joe, she had almost drowned in his above-ground pool when she lost her balance. The whole family was in the pool and I was the only one who noticed her going under and pulled her up.

I went to see the doctor who took out Steve's and Ralph's tonsils and adenoids. I wanted to know what was wrong with my jaw. It hurt ever since the car accident and it was not going away. He looked at me, asked me which side was hurting; came back with a needle, and gave me a shot on the right side of my face before I could even stop him. The shot was so painful that I cried. He hugged me, and said, "You'll be fine in a few minutes, I'll be back." He left. He came back about ten minutes later and tried to hug me again saying that I had beautiful green eyes. My heart was speeding up and I felt weak and jittery. I knew I was having a reaction to the shot because I could not be touched. I pushed him away. He left. A nurse brought me a glass of water and told me to stay seated and relax. I recognized the same symptoms I had experienced when having a shot at the dentist and grabbed a Benadryl capsule from my purse. I waited patiently for it to take effect. I felt angry that the doctor didn't ask me if he could give me a shot and didn't even tell me what it was for He also had no right to hug me and patronize me as if I were a child. He was disrespectful.

It was right there, while I was waiting to feel normal

again, that I arrived to a logical conclusion, he had pulled out Steve's tonsils and adenoids for no good reason except to make more money. I would never forgive myself for such blunder. I would never go back to his office again. What he had done to my son and then to me proved once again why I should never trust a medical doctor. Just because they went to medical school, it did not make them gods or give them the right to do as they pleased. I left his office without a clue as to why he gave me a shot in the jaw. *Filho da puta*! Bastard!

Autumn of 1975

A group of teenage boys from the opposite side of our community began disrupting our peaceful neighborhood during the night. The Redhead, as everyone called him, was the leader of the group. Everybody was too scared of retribution, so no one did anything except to call the police anonymously. When there was a robbery in our neighborhood, the Redhead and his gang got taken away. But it only lasted a few days because they were still in their teens. Everyone was waiting for the Redhead to reach adulthood so the police could keep him in jail.

The group particularly liked to hang out by our fence on the side of our house where we had no windows to observe what they were up to. The side of our yard was the ideal place for a private party. The next morning we found their empty beer bottles and cigarette butts all over our lawn.

Theresa and Mark her husband lived kitty-corner from us. Her husband was afraid for Theresa's safety and asked us to keep an eye on his house when he was at work. He placed barbed wire, broken glass, and a few animal traps on the inside of his tall fence.

The Redhead must have found out about it and took his revenge on Theresa. She had a miscarriage after someone called her on the telephone and blankly told her that Mark, had died in a car accident, and she should come down to the morgue. Of course it was a lie, and even though we did not have proof, we all knew it was the Redhead. It was frustrating to know he got away with it.

One day Al complained, "Ralph is very selfish. He puts as much as he can onto his plate, not caring if there's enough food left for everybody else. He always grabs the bigger piece of meat, always thinking about himself first."

The opposite was true with Steve. When he served himself, he took a small amount of food onto his plate. But if he went for seconds he got yelled at for being greedy. In my opinion, Ralph was smart to pick the big piece. At least he was guaranteed not to go hungry. If Steve went for seconds or grabbed the biggest piece out of the serving dish, he would get smacked.

Maureen, one of the piano teachers at the music school where I taught, knew I was looking for a private school for Ralph, and she recommended Valley Forge Military Academy in Pennsylvania. According to the information they sent us, they offered a great academic program, and when Ralph saw the brochures, he was excited about it. The school was quite a ways from home, yet it was close enough for us to visit him on weekends. The tuition was $5000 per year, but if I kept teaching, I could take care of that and also make enough money to send Steve the following year.

Steve was beside himself when I told him he would be able to ride horses at the Academy. He could not wait to leave. I was not happy at the thought of losing both my sons, but I had to protect them the best I could.

Al was called in the middle of the night by the First Aid Squad to help pick up someone who was injured while riding a motorcycle. When Al returned, I asked what had happened and he said, "Oh, a young punk got what he deserved. He was riding away from the cops who were trying to get him for speeding, so they had to put up a cement barrier on the road. They stopped him all right! He went flying when he hit the barrier and broke his neck when he fell off the motorcycle." He got into bed, turned over, and went back to sleep as if nothing had happened.

I stayed awake thinking about the dead motorcyclist. Someone had to mourn for his young rebel soul; and besides, I probably got the news of his death before his mother did.

The store where Al worked, Bonds, at the mall, went out of business, and closed down all its other stores. Al went looking for work at the R&S Sporting Goods store near Shop Rite, and lucky for him, they hired him because he had a management background from working at the Bonds clothing store.

Al loved his new job. He could walk to work if needed, and most importantly, he would be working in the gun department.

Mr. Crocker called me into his office. "Your boys are no longer welcome in my music store. They're out of control. They threw stones into the toilets and locked all the bathroom stalls from the inside."

"That's impossible. How could they have locked the doors from inside?"

"They obviously slipped back out underneath the doors. I had to pay someone to open the doors and fix the toilets."

I asked Ralph and Steve about it, and they said Mr. Crocker was lying. I believed them. But I needed my job.

I arranged for Steve to go directly from the school bus to his friend Matthew's house. I paid Matthew's grandmother, Mrs. Irving, a real pleasant older lady who lived two streets from our house, to babysit him while I taught guitar classes in the afternoon. Ralph went home, but I encouraged him to stay with his friends Stephen or Tom until I got home from teaching.

I took turns taking the kids with me to work. Mr. Crocker did not seem to mind if I only took one. Steve was still enjoying his guitar lessons with Hava and as a special treat; I lent him my Yamaha electric guitar to play at home. But that was not enough; I had to get my children out of the house. Ralph came first because he was harder to handle. He did not listen to his father or me. He was even talking back to Nelly. He was stubborn and had a bad temper. One day he punched a hole in the wall going up the steps in our house. According to Nelly, he did that when he got infuriated with her. But Ralph was very bright and was aware of the way he acted. I heard her scolding him over some stuff in the garage, and when I went in to see what was happening, he had teary eyes and said, "I hate her. She treats me like a baby. I'm ready to leave for the military academy and get away from her."

"I hope you know that your Mrs. Irving is teaching Steve to play cards," announced Nelly one day when I got home from teaching.
"So what's wrong with that?"
"She's making him a gambler, that's what."
"I rather he becomes a gambler than to be subjected to your constant badgering."
"Call it whatever you want. I already told you, for me, it's a challenge to debate with Steve."
Crazy, freaky woman. Debate my foot—more like mental agony before she smacked him.
Besides having to cope with what to do about my kids, a new problem had developed. Al was falling for Sarah, an employee at R&S. All he did was talk about her. One evening while we were having dinner he said, "Poor Sarah,

she is such a sweet, girl I can't understand how she puts up with a lousy husband who doesn't appreciate her. This afternoon she came to me crying that she couldn't find her purse and she couldn't go home. She was worried someone had taken it, so I hugged her and gave her a little kiss on the cheek to make her feel better."

"Did she find the purse?" I kept my eyes on my plate so Al couldn't see how much I hated that woman.

"Yes, it was in the back room." I bet it was. What a crock! I had seen Sarah. She looked at Al like a cat in heat. I could just see her looking at him with sad eyes and puckering up her lips saying, "Pity me, pity me, take me home and put me to bed. You're the only man that is kind to me and I need you to protect me against my nasty, cruel husband."

Of course I didn't let my thoughts be heard. I just kept eating. She was trying to steal my husband. She should be working on her marriage, not someone else's.

Winter ending 1975

Some kids (the neighbors said it was the Redhead and his gang) decided to have fun throwing raw eggs at the windows in our neighborhood. It happened over the weekend when we went to visit Joe and Ginny in Long Island. When we got back, we found one of the glass panes in our bay-window broken, and raw dried eggs all over the curtains and the carpet. I put a plastic bag over the broken window to keep the cold wind from coming in and tried to wash the carpet. The living room smelled like a chicken coop and the egg stains in the carpet were not coming up. The curtains were no better. It was the weekend. I would have to wait until Monday to call the home insurance company.

We had paid house insurance for over twelve years, but

when we put a claim for the carpet and curtains to be cleaned and the glass pane in the bay window to be replaced, they gave me a hard time. I was done with insurance companies.

The way I figure it, if every twelve years we got hit with raw eggs, the cost to have the place cleaned and a window replaced was a drop in the bucket compared with what we paid every month to the Mafia House Insurance Company.

December 23rd, R&S had a little Christmas party later in the evening, at one of the employee's houses. It turned out to be at Sarah's apartment, Al's victimized coworker. I took a good look at Sarah as she sat cozily next to Al on the couch, after bringing him a glass of Coke with ice, his favorite pop soda. She was a thirty-five-year-old emaciated woman with pimples all over her face. She obviously didn't bathe because her hair was greasy and she had bad body odor. I was no beauty pageant judge, but I felt like Aunt Heydee was right when she used to say, "A man can be turned on by any woman, no matter how ugly, as long as it inflates his ego; a damsel in distress is enough to do it."

In Sarah's case it had to be her body stench he was attracted to. It matched his when he went days without showering. He used a washcloth nightly to wash under his arms, but in the morning he bathed on cheap acid-like cologne, which gave me a nasty sinus headache. Al had the notion that if he washed his hair more than once a month he would go bald. That would explain why he had so much dandruff. I hated scratching his head, which he wanted me to do while he watched television.

Winter of 1976

I was just a teenager when Mama caught me reading a romantic novel. While growing up I was not allowed to socialize or have friends my own age; there was no television, only books. In the winter I was busy with school but in the summer, the days seemed extra-long while vacationing with the family at some seaside town not too far from Lisbon. I could only sit on the sand and stare at the ocean eating potato chips for so long, and when it came to walking I was to remain within Mama's eyesight. One day I found a small bookstore around the corner from our summer house that rented only romance books. I had never read a romance novel. I rented one and found a quiet spot in the park. I couldn't put it down. It was all about love and passion things I was forbidden to even think about. I had found the perfect mental entertainment. For about a dollar I could get five books, enough to last about two weeks of reading. One morning I was sitting on the sand just a few feet from Mama and my brothers, when she suddenly stood by me and bending over she briskly pulled the book from my hands. "What are you reading? I called you and you didn't answer me. What are you reading that keeps you so engrossed?" She opened the book randomly and to her shock, and mine too, it was the page where the author described Maria and Roberto kissing passionately on the lips. "I forbid you from reading this type of garbage do you hear me? It will put nothing but nonsense into your head. I'm throwing it away."

"You can't," I wanted to cry but I didn't. "I rented it from the bookstore; I have to return it along with four other books."

"You give me the other books and I'll return them. You are not allowed to read any books unless I check them out first."

But by then I was already hooked on romance, and to take it away from me meant no more dreaming of love and prince charming. So I started writing my own novels in my mind, and to tell the truth, I found a world of undying love that was even better than in the novels. It was tailored and created by my own imagination while I sat on the same spot on the beach staring at the sea.

Mental writing was one of the things keeping me feeling alive through my marriage. But one night, the unexpected happened. Al went to work and, as always, he kissed me goodbye before leaving. I was still in bed and I thought I was awake when I heard footsteps coming up the stairs and then into our bedroom. I figured it was Al, but when I felt him getting into my bed I realized that Al had already left. I tried to open my eyes to see who it was, but no matter how hard I tried to open my eyes, I couldn't, as if they were glued shut. My heart started to beat faster as I felt his lean body against mine. It was pleasurable in a definitely spooky manner. I knew it wasn't a normal event, but I wasn't fighting it, either. Afterward, I fell asleep.

When Al came home, I asked him if by any chance he had come back upstairs to bed after he said goodbye that morning

"Nope."

I told him what had happened, and he laughed. "Probably a ghost came to visit you. It sure wasn't me."

I was not scared. My ghost lover made me feel good. So, once in a while after Al went to work, I started thinking about him and, sure enough, he showed up. I did not try to see his face. Of that I was just a little scared.

Mama freaked out when I wrote to her describing my dreams. She said my ghost lover was to be told to go away.

"Veronica, I'm begging you to stop the morning affair with the ghost. He is a ghost and the more you invite him over, the more he will want to be with you. You need to stop the affair immediately or he will take your soul with him and you'll die."

I stopped wishing for him and he did not return.

Al was screaming at me in one of his moments of switching between being Dr. Jekyll and Mr. Hyde, and poor Steve got hit for being in his way. I cried so much through the night that I had to wear sunglasses the next morning to keep the light off my blood-shot eyes and to hide the fact I had been crying. Mama had warned me several times, "Tears, because of their salt content, will burn the eyes and cause blindness." I wished I were dead, but I could not make such wish wholeheartedly because if I died, my kids would not have a mother. I called myself selfish for having such negative thoughts and a weakling for not speaking up to Al or Nelly.

The next day Nelly and I went to drop off Al's lunch at work and, as he came out of the store to the car, Sarah came out running after him. She wanted to meet Nelly.

When we left, Nelly said, "You'd better watch out, that girl is a cutie."

I didn't say anything, but I became aware at that very moment I had nothing to worry about. I was not only cute myself, but I was also smart and unique. I was one of a kind.

God only created awesome things, even when we did not agree sometimes. I would start enjoying my cuteness. From then on, I would have more important things to think about, like getting my children out of the house including myself. If Al liked Sarah more than me, it was his loss, not mine. I really did not care anymore. I would no longer feel jealous; it only wasted my time and sucked up my energy. From then on he could talk all he wanted about Sarah and how sweet she was. As a matter of fact, I would be delighted if he divorced me, married her and took Nelly to live with them, and then we would all be happy.

I decided to go back to school.

The guitar lessons I got from Mr. Crocker were for reading music and playing guitar. I was a teacher, but I did not feel like a genuine teacher. I had no music degree.

The next morning I went to Brookdale Community College to sign up for classes. They asked me if I had a

Braving A New World

high school diploma. I lied and said yes. They wanted to see it.

I asked Mama to go to my old high school in Lisbon and get a copy of my third year high school diploma. I figured no one at the admittance office would know the difference since they did not read Portuguese.

Mama got a copy of my certificate and then proceeded to "fix" my passing grade from a 9 to a 16 using one of her bad, drippy ink pens. The lady at the admittance office said, "This high school diploma has been falsified!"

I thought I was going to die from embarrassment, but at the same time I felt like patting myself on the back. I had been right—they couldn't tell if it was a high school diploma or not because it was written in Portuguese. I explained to the office lady, "My mother changed my passing grade trying to make me look smarter than I am."

Lucky for me, she said to forget about the Portuguese diploma. It was just as easy for them to test me to find out where I could be placed. I was amazed at this opportunity. I did not share my school plans with anyone, not even Al.

Wonder of wonders! I passed the tests, except for Math and English. I was very proud of myself, considering I had only finished the third year of high school and that had been eighteen years ago. I was getting older but my brain was still young. The people at the college told me they would help me to follow a curriculum toward earning my high school diploma. I loved Brookdale Community College!

Ralph left for Valley Forge. Dropping him off at the school was no different from abandoning a newborn on the steps of some church. I reasoned it was for his benefit. The more I stayed away from home, the better I felt emotionally. The more money I made teaching, the quicker I could send Steve away. With Ralph gone, they were picking on Steve a lot more. I had to come up with another five thousand dollars; it meant ten thousand dollars a year for both kids to go to private school. Too bad I had spent so much money building the swimming pool—oh well; it was no use crying over spilled milk.

As soon as Steve took his bus to school, I left for my early morning class at the college. Nelly and Al believed I had morning classes to teach. I planned on taking only one class each semester. My plan was to do really well with each subject and still be able to increase my teaching hours in the morning.

Being in school opened a world that I did not even know existed. I no longer had to stand at the kitchen window looking at life going by. I had opened the front door, and I was walking among the living. I enjoyed learning and making friends. I walked across the campus to my classroom with an exhilarating feeling of accomplishment. I had made it to college.

~ *Chapter Ten* ~

VALLEY FORGE, NO MORE

1976

Spring of 1976

Valley Forge didn't turn out to be what we had imagined. It was more like a prison for my son. Ralph told me horrible stories, like marching in the cold, freezing snow and doing guard duty outside like a soldier. It was like being in the service except he was still a child. Steve was not going to like it either. But at least they would be away from their grandmother. I did not know what else to do. I had tried to encourage Nelly to get involved in outside activities but she had refused. I tried getting Joe and Ruth to take Nelly for half of the year. She was their mother too, but they always found an excuse to back out.

I didn't put up much of a fight when Al said he was taking Sheba back to the Humane Society. I guessed he dropped her off in the woods to fend for herself. That was what everybody did when they wanted to get rid of their dog. "If I had taken Sheba to the dog pound, they would have gassed her for sure," Al told me.

In the back of my mind, I know Sheba was not going to make it without food all alone in the woods.

I was getting high honors at school. The exams were set up with multiple choices! I had never heard of anything like that in my life. In Portugal, if you could not write the answer on a blank piece of paper, you failed the test. I was looking forward to getting my high school diploma and then taking classes in music, oceanography, world history, tap dancing, theatre, and much more. College was like a smorgasbord of knowledge and I was ready to take in every single morsel.

Summer of 1976

Ralph came home for a month of summer vacation. Having both my sons at home made me feel alive again. Except for having to teach a few classes at the music center, I stopped attending Brookdale College. I wanted to spend as much time as possible with the kids. One morning Ralph wanted to have a private talk without Nelly around, and we walked to the little park behind our development. When we bought our house, the home association told us about the park they were going to build. Twelve years later a bench and a swing showed up by the green tainted lake.

We sat on the bench and then Ralph begged me not to send him back to Valley Forge. "Mom, I hate my life there. Besides marching in the freezing cold early in the morning with rain, snow, or burning heat, there's one bully kid there who likes to get behind me and squeeze my neck until I almost pass out."

"You need to let one of the teachers at school know what's going on. Don't worry; I'll talk to them when you go back to school."

"Mom, it's not just the bully and the hard physical work I have to do. I want to enjoy my childhood. I miss being home with my family and my friends. I want to come home."

"Impossible. That's totally impossible. If you come

Braving A New World

home, I'll have to contend with your grandmother spoiling you rotten. I can't stand the thought. I'm sorry but that's not going to happen." I stopped crying and then added, "All I can do is to take you to karate school so you can learn to defend yourself from the bully at school." I tried hugging him but he pulled away from me.

I took Ralph to karate, and he said he was enjoying the classes, but three weeks later the teacher went around the room showing how he could make a kid pass out by pressing on their neck with two of his fingers. I got a knot in my stomach from watching the kids passing out. What an idiot!

I took Ralph out of the class. I could only hope that with what he had learned so far he could defend himself.

Ralph was going back to Valley Forge the following week, but I was very worried, he had told Nelly about a man who liked to hang around the school talking to him and another boy. "As an adult and a stranger he has no place in the lives of young boys," she said. "Who knows, he might even be a mass-murderer of young boys."

I confronted Ralph about it but he only knew him as Mr. McCarthy. He was a pilot and had offered to take Ralph and his friend for a ride on his airplane.

When we took Ralph back to school, I alerted the "general" in charge of the school to be aware of our fears.

I figured out why a few days before something bad happened to me I always had the same nightmare about a museum with Egyptian artifacts. The only possible explanation was that it had to do with the old Monastery of Jerónimos in Portugal, where as a child, my family had tried to force me to look into a tomb containing a dead soldier. The nightmare triggered my survival instinct. That nightmare represented death or sickness. But I did not welcome the warning because it did not stop it from happening. All it did was make me worry for nothing. Aunt

Heydee always said, "Facing your problem is the only way to get rid of it."

Since Al and I were making plans to go to Portugal the following year, I planned to visit the Monastery of Jerónimos. I would bravely look at the tomb of the Unknown Soldier and face my fears, hopefully stopping the nightmares once and for all.

Autumn of 1976

I prayed every night, "Please dear God, protect Ralph from any harm." I did not sleep well.

Steve ran to his bedroom and cried on his bed as usual every time Nelly or Al abused him verbally or physically. I sneaked upstairs and tried to comfort him by telling him that as soon as I had enough money he could go to Valley Forge too, and he would be happy going to school with Ralph. Together they could help each other against any bullies. Even though I knew what Ralph was going through, I believed Valley Forge was their only salvation.

Winter ending 1976

At the end of the year, I always offered my students the opportunity of having a recital. But because I had so many students who wanted to participate, and because the other teachers also asked me if they could incorporate their students into it, I suggested a recital every three months.

For the Christmas recital, Steve played a classical piece from Aaron Shearer, his favorite classical composer. Steve was a real musician, always very relaxed about performing in front of people. The recital turned out to be very entertaining when a very young pianist, properly dressed in his black mini-tuxedo and bow tie, performed a Mozart piece. The room was silent as the adorable nine-year-old sat appropriately at the bench and extended his fingers, rolling them smoothly across the piano keys. Everything was going well until he missed a key.

"Fuck!" was the loud and clear word out of the little boy's mouth.

Parents and other children looked at each other and then at his piano teacher who stood frozen staring into the crowd with an apologetic look on her face.

My voice teacher at Brookdale College asked me if I would play with the school's orchestra for their Christmas show, as they need a guitarist. I was very happy to do it. But I had to tell Al about it. That night when we were in bed, I gave him the news and asked him not to tell Nelly since she might not agree with me attending college.

"You're right," he said. "She won't be happy about it. Why didn't you tell me you were going to college?"

"I was afraid you would be against it."

"I don't care if you go to school. If it makes you happy, I'm happy too." He kissed me on the forehead and then we snugged together. I was happy, very happy and before I fell asleep I thanked God for providing me with such an understanding husband.

Al came to see the show on opening night and took a picture of me holding my red Yamaha electric guitar. I felt very accomplished as a musician, playing along with the orchestra in the concealed shadow of the pit. I wasn't concerned about anyone recognizing the guitar "stolen" so many years ago from Mr. Crocker's music center.

Winter of 1977

Ralph showed up at our doorstep. He had run away from school. It was snowing but Ralph didn't care, he just wanted to come home. A woman saw him on the road hitchhiking and offered to drive him to New Jersey. She was gone before I could thank her.

I drove Ralph back to the military school the next morning even though I couldn't stand the thought of taking him back. We hardly spoke to each other on the way.

A week went by since I had left Ralph at the Valley Forge Academy. I couldn't sleep at night, visualizing Ralph in the military school, marching like a criminal in the freezing cold snow of Pennsylvania and I, his mother, had done that to him!

Papa had gotten upset when I wrote to him describing my life as having my hands tied behind my back and drowning, but it was true. I was losing both my children, but what else could I do, I asked myself. By Spring I'll have enough money to pay for Steve's tuition. But what about now, how do I contend with the emotional and physical abuse he is suffering at the hands of his father and grandmother. I felt like I was going crazy. Teaching and going to college keeps me busy, but without my children, I have no reason to come home. What am I doing here, I asked myself again. That was the night I concluded, I'm done with Al and Nelly. I no longer need to live with my husband and his mother. I make enough money to be on my own. All night long I could hear Aunt Heydee's words of wisdom, "Grab the bull by the horns and do what you have to do."

Before leaving for college the next morning, I went to my neighbor's house, Mrs. Shapiro, and gave her a condensed version of my life. I told Mrs. Shapiro I would be staying at the motel on Route 9 until I found an apartment.

I sat at her kitchen table and, after writing a letter to Al, asked her to personally give the letter to him when he got home from work in the afternoon. My letter to Al was short:

Braving A New World

Dear Al,

I am sorry that I have to leave you, but I am not coming back. Living with Nelly has not been easy. She is the one that is married to you, not me. I have lost my children because of her. Don't worry, I will continue to work, and every month I will send you money to cover our sons' tuition so they can have a good education. Please forgive me for doing this, but I am not happy.

Love, Ronnie

After grabbing a raisin muffin and some milk at the college's cafeteria, I attended my math class. Afterward, I went to work and taught a few private guitar students as well as the afternoon guitar classes. I didn't do a very good job teaching as my heart was not in it, and I could feel myself shaking all day long. For dinner I picked up some French fries at Burger King and then went to McDonald's for a hamburger. Then I went to Shop Rite and got myself a large bottle of water, chocolate cookies, and candy, and settled down for the night in the motel where I had told Mrs. Shapiro I would be.

I didn't care for my motel room. The smell of stale tobacco and mildew made me sneeze and cough for a while.

I understood why they called those types of motels a "one-night stand." No one could live in one of their rooms for another night without developing some kind of respiratory illness. Not much care had been invested in keeping the rooms clean. I sat on one of the chairs trying to empty my mind of all thoughts. I didn't want to go to bed. Soon I got tired of staring at the wall in front of me and opted for lying down. I felt it was more sanitary to lie on top of the bedcover and I opened the window for some fresh air. When it got too cold I closed the window. Before long, a flaming dragon twirled itself into the darkness of the room, oozing itself from the ceiling above and carrying me into a nightmare of smells, shapes, and ghosts so frightening that I woke up shivering with a pounding headache.

I got up to drink from the bottled water and then sat in bed holding my head with both hands, trying not to lie down. Someone was knocking hard on the door. It was the motel manager. My neighbor Mrs. Shapiro was on the phone.

"Come home," she said. "Your husband got his brother Joe to come over and take your mother-in-law and all her stuff in a U-Haul back to Long Island with him. She's gone! Your husband loves you and he wants you back."

My goodness, it was a miracle! A real miracle. If that was true, I no longer had to send my children away. I should have written a letter and left years ago. I wondered if I was dreaming.

Al was waiting for me outside our house. It was three in the morning. He ran to me as I got out of my car. He hugged me, apologizing for the mess we were in.

"I should have called Joe and asked him to pick up Mom a long time ago," he said. "We had her living with us for fourteen years. Now it's their turn to do the same for the next fourteen." Then he hugged me again and said, "From now on, it's only the two of us."

"Yes you and me, and our two sons." I said firmly. How he could forget the kids was beyond me.

We sat on the sidewalk in front of our house and I told him I would be going to Valley Forge the next day to bring Ralph home. I was very happy when he said he would like to come with me.

I was going to do everything possible to save our marriage and be the best wife I could possibly be.

Ralph was emotional with joy when we told him he was

free to come home. The principal/general in charge of the school asked us to allow Ralph to finish the semester; that way he could attend his graduation. Ralph agreed to it.

I thanked God for everything. I was never so happy in my life.

Steve stayed with Mrs. Irving for the ten days when Al and I were in Portugal, visiting my parents. The idea of flying again had me in knots. Aunt Heydee had written, "Don't be a fool; you know how flying affects your ears. Don't do it. Let them come and visit you instead."

I needed to prove to myself that I could handle a plane ride if I wanted to travel and go to faraway places. Something had to exist to help people like me. Maybe it wouldn't be so bad, maybe my ears were stronger and it wouldn't hurt too much.

There was hope after all. Our pharmacist advised me to take Benadryl to dry up my sinuses and chew gum to get rid of the pressure. Besides taking a bunch of presents with us for the whole family, at Mama's request, I also carried two hamburgers from McDonald's in my luggage just for her. I slept on the way going and coming, and my ears did pretty well except for when we landed in Lisbon and upon returning to New York. The Benadryl helped tremendously because my ears didn't hurt as bad as the first time I flew, when I first came to America.

About fifteen years had passed since I had left Lisbon, the city where I was born. The brick wall outside the airport conveyed a very clear graffiti message, GO HOME YANKEE. I was no longer welcome in my country. It was also with sadness that I saw the dirty, broken-down sidewalks. The city was overcrowded with cars and parking was basically non-existent; motorists used the sidewalks for parking. I now understood the meaning of "You cannot turn back the hands of time."

Nothing was the same—even the apartment where I had lived as a child had shrunk, and so had my parents.

Everything as I remembered was gone.

Al was bored stiff listening to us speaking Portuguese all day long and I did not blame him. I was glad to get out of the house for daily trips but we were expected to be back for meals. We did not have much time to ourselves. My parents were adamant about us being home with them for breakfast, lunch, and dinner, and back before dusk since the streets of Lisbon were not safe after dark.

Mama had become a recluse. Her heart was weak and her legs gave in too easily. Papa went out every afternoon to do errands, and every morning he was at the farmer's market promptly at seven. Al and I went with Papa one morning. Breathing the smell of fresh fish, vegetables, and fruit brought me back to the days when I was a child and would visit the same open market. Al complained about everything, including the lack of refrigeration and sanitation in the market.

Papa got a real kick out of talking to the vendors, as they all knew him by his first name. We visited family, family visited us, and time just went by. Little cousin Haim, who had held the tail end of my long wedding gown, had grown up into a handsome man.

He kept saying, "I can't believe it's you, Verónica. You have not changed one bit since you got married; if anything, you actually look younger." I always liked my cousin Haim.

Now, Cousin Salomão was another story. He wanted to see me, but Al and I had to go to his office way across the city because he was too busy to leave his practice. Salomão had a crush on me when he was forty-five years old and I was fifteen. He asked Mama for my hand in marriage and thank God she had asked me if that was something I wanted to do. Of course I immediately said no, and I remember crying just to make sure Mama understood that when I said I would rather kill myself than marry Cousin Salomão, I meant it.

Braving A New World

He basically ignored Al and flirted with me. I didn't like Cousin Salomão fifteen years ago, and my feelings toward him had remained the same. The only reason I visited him was because Mama said I had to go see him. Cousin Salomão was her cardiologist.

That night Al wanted to have sex with me after saying, "Salomão was drooling from his mouth staring at you. He wanted to get into your panties."

I told Al I had a headache and turned over to sleep.

The next morning we went to visit the Monastery of Jerónimos with the intention of visiting the tomb of the Unknown Soldier. I was going to come out alive and well. To my surprise, everything I remembered was gone. I could not believe my eyes. A heresy had been committed. The room I was looking for had been divided with self-standing wire panels from which some mad artist's paintings were hanging. The monastery had turned into a despicable modern art gallery!

Since my dead soldier was gone and not a trace of scary old Egyptian and Portuguese relics were present, I was sure my nightmares would also be gone from that day forward.

The strangest part of the trip was when Al and I went to one of the banks in Lisbon to change traveler's checks. My parents came with us. I was waiting in line, when a slightly bald, chubby man tapped on my shoulder and said in a perfect British accent, "Verónica? It's you, my sister Verónica, right?"

"My name is Verónica, but you're not my brother." I walked away from him, and pushed through the crowd to meet with my parents, both waiting on the lobby's bench.

"A man came up to me and asked me if I was his sister."

Mama said to Papa, "I wonder if Max-Leão is in Portugal."

Just then, the same chubby guy approached my parents and said in Portuguese, "This is my sister Verónica, correct?"

"Yes, Max-Leão. It's your sister," Papa said casually. Mama added with a certain pride in her voice, "Your sister is visiting us from North America."

My mind was racing—that man couldn't possibly be my brother. I tried to show some emotion, but I didn't have any as I hugged him. It had to be a cruel joke. The last time I had seen my brother he was fifteen years old. He had dark thick beautiful hair. He was handsome, tall, and built like a model. The man I was hugging was a stranger.

Like the gas stations in New Jersey, one on every street corner, so were the banks in Lisbon; and out of all the banks in Lisbon, my brother and I had chosen the same one on the same morning. His wife, Patricia, was outside in their car waiting for him. They followed us to our parents' apartment, but things did not go well. Not much had changed since my parents had disowned him for marrying Patricia. Time had passed by, but the wounds were still open and bleeding. My parents had not told him that I was coming to Portugal and since my brother and I did not correspond with each other and I did not have his address, I was not able to let him know of my visit. My brother was angry at my parents. I could sympathize with him. Our parents insisted they did not know Max-Leão was in Portugal. Obviously they were still not communicating well with each other.

Aunt Heydee came into the living room, grabbed my arm and took me into the dining room to complain how Max-Leão had mistreated her over the last few years. "He's an ungrateful bastard. After all I did for him when he was a child, he shows me no respect."

Max-Leão had followed us down the hallway and hearing her speak in those terms, started defending himself and accused her of being a "user" among other things. It was ugly. I curled back into my old shell of being Verónica-the-Speechless. There was nothing left between Max-Leão and me except the ignorance of a misunderstanding.

Al hardly spoke to my brother because he felt Max-Leão was boasting about his antique cars and all his farms, and as such Max-Leão was nothing but a jerk. In the back of my mind I felt guilty, confused, and afraid to offend anyone. Staying non-committal was my only defense.

I was dying to talk to Max-Leão and Patricia in private and explain to them that the letter I had sent to them years ago had not been my own words. I wanted to ask them to forgive me for being an idiot, but once again, I lacked the backbone to speak up.

Maybe someday Max-Leão and I would meet again under better circumstances. That was all I could hope for.

~ *Chapter Eleven* ~

THE PURSUIT OF HAPPINESS

1977-1981

Spring of 1977

Ralph's yearly graduation was conducted in a military version called "pass in review" and it was a grand performance that included marching and a military band. He looked very handsome in his uniform, and Al and I were very proud of him for finishing the full term at Valley Forge Academy. I knew it wasn't easy.

There wasn't much to pack. While at the military school Ralph wore a uniform which he was glad to leave behind. I held his hand as we walked away and drove home that afternoon.

We moved the television from the playroom into the living room, and the kids and I began making plans to turn the playroom into a real playroom. When the deliverymen came to our door with the pool table, they asked me if my mommy was home. I told them that I was the mommy. Couldn't they see that Ralph and Steve were my sons? They were putting the table together and one of them asked my age. I told him thirty-three and he said, "You look like a teenager. I bet you drink milk with all your meals and don't drink alcohol or smoke. That's probably the reason you look so young."

I kept nodding my head up and down and saying yep, yep, yep. I didn't know what else to say.

Before they left he said, "I'm twenty-five years old and I feel and look like an old man. I am going to change my life around and start taking care of myself. You don't realize how much you have influenced me. Can I shake your hand before I leave?"

I shook his hand and wished him good luck with his health and future. I also wondered how I could have influenced him, when I hardly said anything. I assumed he was just being charming.

I asked Ralph and Steve where they would like to go in the summer for our two-week vacation, and they said, "Disney World in Florida."

"How about taking the train to Disney and staying in Florida for five days, and then we fly to the island of Jamaica for a week?" They freaked out!

They both had seen the advertisement on television for Air Jamaica showing the flight attendants as beautiful island girls serving steaks along with exotic drinks with little umbrellas. Al was just as excited as they were.

Summer of 1977

Our vacation to Florida and the island of Jamaica was a magnificent family experience. But I did not care for the overnight train to Florida. I could not sleep in a sitting position. In the morning, I found Ralph and Steve still sleeping perfectly comfortably; half-hanging out of their seats as if an invisible mattress was under them. Al snored through the night, bobbing his head around while seated in a slouched position.

I was dazed and confused when we got to Florida. The

lack of sleep developed into a headache with back pain to match. "I hope you guys don't think I'm a weakling," I said. "But from now on if we have to travel overnight in a train, I'll need a private cabin with a real bed where I can stretch out." I knew they did not understand my suffering since they woke up completely refreshed.

Money was no object on this trip. We stayed at the best hotel, and each kid got twenty dollars for personal spending. I wanted them to feel independent. Steve bought himself a Davy Crockett fur hat at Disney World. Ralph liked playing in the game room.

One night we went to see the hotel's show, "Cabaret." The girls were dancing and singing, "Money makes the world go round..." One of them sat on Steve's lap. We all thought it was very manly of him, but also frivolous when he gave the girl his last five bucks.

The flight from Florida to Jamaica turned out to be a real letdown. Al, Ralph, and Steve kept saying, "Where are the girls, the drinks, and the steaks?"

Commercials lie!

We stayed at the Hilton Hotel in Ocho Rios, where the kids gorged on the daily buffet by eating mounds and "Anybody not snoring?" mounds of watermelon. Al was having a fit over it because he felt that watermelon was not food and, with what we paid at the Hilton, they should get their money's worth.

When Steve joined us for breakfast one morning, I noticed he wasn't wearing his Davy Crockett fur hat. "Did you lose your hat, Steve?"

"Our waiter is very poor and he told me he wished he could buy a hat like mine to give to his nine-year-old boy."

"But you loved that hat," I said.

"I felt sorry for him. Imagine Mom, he loves his son but can't afford to buy him gifts."

Steve has a heart of gold.

Except for mealtimes, we hardly saw the kids. They

were busy swimming and playing pool, but we did get together one morning to go horseback riding. Well, almost. Once I got on top of my horse and realized how high I was seated, the idea of falling was too much to endure. Al said if I didn't go he wasn't going either. So the kids went alone with the group. About an hour later, the guide came galloping back ahead of everybody, waving Steve's t-shirt stained with blood. Al and I panicked, waiting for the kids to arrive on their horses. It turned out that they were both fine. Steve had developed a bloody nose and used his t-shirt as tissue. The guide for some wacky reason had decided to use Steve's bloody shirt as a flag.

That same night Al and I were at the hotel's dining room, waiting for the boys to join us, when we got an emergency call from Ralph. They were both still in their room, but for a good reason. Steve had found a tick on his butt and was crying. The tick had probably been riding on the horse's back until Steve got on. We got a needle from the front desk and Al heated it with a couple of matches. There we were with Steve lying in bed with his pants down, crying. The tick let go after a while and came out when we burned it. The whole thing was funny later, but it was awkward and frightening at the time.

The next morning we all took a trip down a muddy but very scenic river on a primitive riverboat made of logs tied together with ropes. The mosquitoes had a feast on Steve's naked back. Our river man told us the island was going through a drought and most of the green vegetation was gone. We had nothing to compare it with, so to us it looked like plenty of luscious, green vegetation all around. The river man also commented, "I cannot understand why rich Americans come to Jamaica, a poor ugly island with nothing to offer. If I was rich like you I would go to America for vacation."

One of the most memorable moments of our vacation for me, was when we were walking to town to buy some carved wooden masks for the playroom, and I heard an incredible tune coming from someone's house. I was entranced by the style and beat. I had never heard anything so unique and moving in my life. Al said, "You are definitely weird, it's nothing but jungle music." To me it was like music from heaven; fun and happy. It was called reggae.

Two days before we left the island, I thought it was a good opportunity to have my hair done into an Afro. It only lasted a few hours. Al hated my new look. He took my picture just for the fun of it, and then asked me to go back to the beauty shop and get rid of my kinky curls. I had to agree with Al, my hair looked better in its normal state, straight.

Except for Al and me catching a temporary skin infection after we went swimming in the ocean on our last day in Jamaica, we all had a great time. Besides the wooden masks, I came home with three coconuts carved into monkey heads, to decorate the side of the house facing our pool.

Three weeks after hanging the monkey heads, they disappeared. Of course we blamed the Redhead, but we couldn't prove anything.

At least twice a year we get an unsolicited visit from a photographer who would not take no for an answer. When the doorbell rang, Ralph and Steve ran to see who it was. The man said, "Is your mommy home? I'm here to take your family pictures."

I was standing by the kitchen's entrance listening and thinking, *Darn it, how am I going to get rid of him?* Suddenly, and I don't know what got into the kids, but they ran up the steps to me—Ralph grabbed me by my feet and Steve by my wrists—and they started swinging me from one side to the other. I was laughing and the kids were laughing as the guy yelled from the front door, "Are there any adults in this house?"

That made me laugh even more; but when the kids started to carry me downstairs, I started screaming, because I was scared they would drop me on my back. "Put me down if you know what's good for you!" I yelled. They laughed.

"Put me down right now, or I'll kill you both with my bare hands!" They laughed even more.

"My heart, my heart feels funny and I can't breathe, I mean it. Put me down!" They put me down gently and ran laughing to hide in their bedroom. I was very angry with them for treating me like a child in front of a stranger, but upon second thought, I took it as an opportunity to get rid of the salesman. "There are no adults in this house. We're all orphans!" And I rapidly closed the front door.

Ralph was getting good at playing his five-piece drum set, and Steve still sang out of key but it didn't sound too bad. He was very passionate about his singing and put a lot of feeling into it. I played my electric guitar along with them. We sounded pretty good for a summer backyard rock band but I felt they should be playing with kids their own age. I asked two of my students to join our rock group. Richard on lead guitar and Mark on electric bass. Our neighbors' kids were the audience, and I served them Kool-Aid and Jell-O. It felt great to play the part of mom and hostess.

I loved being surrounded by kids, music, and sunshine, and swimming in the pool with them. I was enjoying the moment; life could not be any better. Steve and Tom were Ralph's friends, and Bill and Eric were Steve's friends. As for their parents, I never met them. All the other kids who came by to listen to the band knew they were welcome.

They all complimented me for being a cool mom, and Bill told me that I reminded him of Morticia Adams from the television show, *The Adams Family*.

After Nelly left for Long Island to live with her son Joe and daughter Ruth, I had hoped Al and I would get closer and have more in common, but nothing had changed between us. I was growing up with my two sons, and with each day I felt a wider gap between Al and me. Al had gotten over Sarah and to him everything was perfectly normal between us, but I did not feel the same way. He was not growing with me. Our philosophies about life were at extreme opposites and we were moving steadily away from each other. My children were the only ones who brought me emotional stability. They gave me a reason to look forward to life.

It was a great summer full of activities for the kids and me. Besides exploring the New Jersey shore and enjoying our favorite outing of looking for buried treasures in Sandy Hook, we also went into Philadelphia, checked out New York's museums, and took long rides into the Pennsylvania countryside. We would leave the house early in the morning and return just in time for me to prepare dinner.

Autumn of 1977

Steve had been born a kind and thoughtful person. Every week he called Nelly just to see how she was doing; he held no grudges. Steve initiated the phone call and then Ralph said hello to her and I did the same. We still went to Long Island to visit the family, and the subject of why I had run away and Nelly was living with them was never brought up. It was like nothing had happened, which made for a pleasant family gathering.

The kids and I were back to school in September. I continued to get high honors in my classes. Having an interest in the subjects I chose helped me to stay focused. That was the difference between high school and college—

Braving A New World

Ralph and Steve did not have choices in their curriculum, but I did.

Winter ending 1977

Al was only excited about one thing in life—retirement. "Al, if you retire, what are you going to do?"

"Nothing, that's what's good about retirement, I can watch television and relax." It had to be a joke since all his free time was spent watching television.

I loved chocolate and strawberry and pistachio ice cream. He only liked one flavor, vanilla. He hated New York. I loved New York. He hated driving. I loved driving. Anything more than half an hour on the road and he started with his usual, "Are we there yet? When are we getting there?"

Ralph and Steve were my best friends and buddies. They were only thirteen and fourteen years old, but we were in the same frame of mind. We thought alike. Ralph once said, "Dad will say something that makes sense, but then he continues on and on repeating the same opinion over and over again to the point of becoming frustrating and I don't care to hear it any longer because it's annoying."

Al meant well, but he reminded me of that irritating Felix Unger character from the television show, *The Odd Couple*.

Ralph came up with a real crazy idea. He wanted to drop out of high school. Steve heard him, and wanted to do the same. I told Al, "It's my fault, this is happening. When they come home there's no one to oversee that they do their homework. I'll stop working and get involved in their school projects this way they know that I'm serious about their studies."

"If you think that's going to help, go ahead, but I doubt it." he said.

The next day I gave the news to Mr. Crocker. His response was as encouraging as Al's. "It doesn't matter if you stay home or not, they're still going to do what they want. You're not going to be able to stop them." Then the real reason came out, "If you leave you're going to ruin me."

"Hava will be happy to work for you. I'm not quitting, I'm retiring and I won't be back after Christmas."

"That's ridiculous. Nobody retires at your age."

I promised him to return to teaching once my kids were adults.

Al and I were invited to Mr. Crocker's Christmas party. Mr. Crocker asked me to dance with him as a farewell dance and afterward he asked me to stand next to him. He then picked up the microphone and announced, "How would you all like to retire looking this young and beautiful? Don't you all wish you could retire at thirty four?"

Everybody laughed and applauded. I didn't feel guilty about my early retirement, my children came first. Ralph and Steve needed me more than ever.

Winter of 1978

Two months had gone by quickly but being a stay-at-home mom did not work out. I was stunned with a mixture of shock and disbelief when I found under Ralph's mattress, a large plastic bag with shredded dried leaves and a beautiful ceramic pipe. I was sure it was marijuana and I did what felt most natural; I emptied the contents into the toilet and flushed it. But the pipe was so beautiful I did not have the heart to throw it in the garbage. I hid it under my mattress.

I showed the ceramic pipe to Al when we were in our bedroom that night.

"This is it!" he got up from bed and started to put on his bedroom slippers. "I'm throwing him out of the house and into the streets like a bum."

"You're jumping to conclusions." I grabbed him from the back in time to stop him. "Ralph hasn't approached me yet about his "stuff" being missing. Maybe, just maybe, it belongs to one of his friends and he's holding it for them."

"If the police find the pipe in our house, you and I are going to jail, you know that right?" He paced back and forth with his arms behind his back like a politician about to face a crowd of supporters. "I want you to throw the pipe out immediately."

"Okay, okay, consider it done. But please don't throw Ralph in the streets. Let's wait and see what happens." I ran down to the kitchen and against my will, because I loved ceramics of any kind, I put the pipe into a paper lunch bag and put it in the garbage container to be picked up the next morning.

Nothing happened for two days, and then all hell broke loose. Ralph wanted his "belongings" back, and he was really angry, saying I had no business touching his things.

"I never touch your things, and you know it. I was changing the bed sheets and, as I tucked in the bottom sheet, there it was."

Ralph flipped out when I told him I had flushed the "grass" down the toilet. I had heard what happened to young people who smoked marijuana and I was scared for his life. Sometimes they went brain-dead, and a few had jumped out of a window thinking they could fly. I had seen it happen on TV shows and a lot of movies.

I called the Marlboro Hospital and asked to speak to a doctor in charge of treating drug addicts. I told Dr. Stupper about Ralph smoking pot and that Steve might also be involved, even though he had told me he would rather have beer. Dr. Stupper invited me to bring the kids and their closest friends to the hospital for a chat. He said most likely they were all doing it.

The next day I took Ralph, Steve and their closest

friends Bill and Stephen to the Marlboro Hospital. Dr. Stupper was very explicit about his patients' history. They were the final result of drug abuse.

Ralph and Steve and their friends came out laughing about it, saying that marijuana was far from being LSD, cocaine, or mushrooms.

Spring of 1978

I did some further research and found a psychiatrist at Riverview Hospital who was willing to meet with us. Dr. Burronet stared at me, then Ralph and Steve, and then at Bill and Stephen and then said, "Well, you all look healthy. None of you are obese." I stared at him in disbelief, he had no clue of what to say or do with us. He must have read my mind because he advised us to go across the street to what he called a halfway home specializing in addiction. Maybe there they could give us some guidance.

A young girl in her mid-twenties was the counselor in charge. She briefly listened to me and then asked me in a condescending tone to follow her to another room. She put her arm over my shoulders and said, "Look, your sons are fifteen and fourteen years old; it's about time you let them be. They're not drinking alcohol or smoking cigarettes, so what do you want?"

"I just want you to give them some counseling and let them know about the dangers of doing marijuana. They will not listen to me."

She kept her arm over my shoulders and would not let go. "You need to leave them alone. They need their own space. Mom, stop meddling in their lives."

How she dare call me Mom! What did she call her own mother? I moved away from her annoying embrace and went to get the boys waiting patiently in the lobby. I had to accept it; she was most likely a pot smoker and a drug addict. I felt sorry for her mother. "Camon," I told the kids.

"Let's get out of here." I didn't know what to say to them and I was glad they were also quiet on the way home.

For my birthday, we planned a barbeque in our backyard. It would be half an hour before Al got home and we thought it would be nice if we had the grill going. Steve offered to light up the grill, but something went wrong and his long curly hair got caught on fire. He didn't get hurt but his vanity did. I convinced him to let me pour some extra-virgin olive oil on his singed hair.

Ralph said, "Let's put a raw egg into it too, to give it some luster." Ralph and I were laughing our heads off as I poured the oil and Ralph broke an egg on Steve's head. The warm oil and the raw egg didn't do much for Steve's hair. He had to go to the barber the next day for a crew cut.

My mind was still very active regarding how I could save my children from doing drugs. Everybody I spoke to said marijuana was not as bad as LSD and other drugs, but I was worried that afterward, when the thrill of the marijuana was gone, they would continue to experiment.

I took Ralph and Steve to a theatre production at Brookdale College. The play's subject was about the results of addiction and its negative impact on health and the family. Ralph seemed interested and wanted to stay and talk to Dr. Harrison, the playwright. I assumed Ralph was finally starting to see the light. "Nice to meet you," he said, shaking Dr. Harrison's hand. "I really enjoyed the play. So tell me, doctor, when is marijuana going to be legalized?" I stepped back in shock.

"Most likely never since it's a drug."

"Yes, but in your honest opinion, isn't cigarette smoking a lot worse for your health?"

"It's too early to know the long-term effects of marijuana at this point. Maybe in ten years or so we will know for sure and can make an educated comparison."

"Yes, I understand that, but isn't cigarette smoking a lot worse for your health?" Ralph was not going to allow himself to be led off course. He firmly asked the same question again and again until finally the guy said, "Yes, I guess smoking cigarettes and drinking is a lot worse than smoking marijuana."

After the discussion with Dr. Harrison, I realized that Ralph would make a darn good lawyer.

Summer of 1978

Al was willing to do anything for me except stop using cologne. I cried one evening while holding my head between my clasped hands. "Al, the smell of your cologne goes up my nose and directly into my brain."

"It's all in your mind."

"That's right, now you said it, the headaches come from my mind, my brain, and it hurts like hell."

"You're weird. That's why you get headaches." He laughed and walked away.

I did not feel like we were married. It was a sinful thought but after being married for sixteen years, I sensed myself drifting away from our legal status.

Al loved me, and he supported anything I wanted to do, but I no longer belonged to him. I knew something was missing in our relationship but I did not know what it was.

Liar, liar, pants on fire. Yes, I knew what I was missing. The cologne was an excuse. I wanted romance, passion, adventure, having friends, excitement, and if possible, traveling across the universe to other worlds, other planets!

I loved taking the kids to Great Adventure amusement park. We had a family pass and attended all their evening rock concerts. Al never went with us because he only liked opera. He also did not like amusement parks.

While driving through the Safari at Great Adventure, we

Braving A New World

saw a cute little monkey sitting on the side-mirror of the bus in front of us. I snapped a picture and sent it to their main office. I felt like a professional photographer when a week later I received a letter asking my permission to use the photo in their advertisement.

We got a good scare at Great Adventure's Safari when we fed the camels but ran out of crackers. They surrounded our car and started chewing the cloth roof. Blowing the horn made them upset. They used their massive bodies to pound at the car. We were screaming that they might turn our car over. A ranger on a horse came to our rescue and took the camels away.

From that day forward we stopped feeding the animals and kept the windows up when we drove through the Safari.

I received a coupon in the mail for a free checkup at the new dental clinic next to the bakery where I used to work a few years ago. The dentist looked into my mouth and said, "You have two cavities that need to be filled as soon as possible. But before I do that, I'm going to refer you to one of my colleagues here to check out your gums. They don't look healthy." I was asked to pay $350 as a deposit and to return the next day to see Dr. Morris, their gum specialist.

Dr. Morris used a blunt instrument to point and pierce around my gums as he gave a bunch of numbers to a nurse standing next to him with a writing pad. "I hate to say this, but your gums are badly diseased. I'll need to cut back into your gums to remove the yeast growing deep within."

"Yeast?" I laughed. "Like yeast for making bread?"

"No, like the yeast infection women usually get down below."

"Below where?"

"Don't tell me you never had it or heard about it."

"I'm sorry but I have no idea what you're talking about.

Are you sure my gums have yeast? I have no pain."

"I really have no patience for this. All I can tell you is that you need three to four surgical procedures to reconstruct your gums. You're on your way to losing all your teeth within a year if you don't address this problem right now."

He sent me back to the office and a nurse at the front desk asked me to give her $950 as a first installment and to come back the next day for the first treatment. I gave them a check for the amount and, holding my tears back, I ran to my car where I sat in the parking lot crying uncontrollably.

A lady getting out of her car saw me crying and came up to my window to asked if I was alright. I told her the dentist had just told me I needed surgery all over my gums, and I was scared. "If I were you, I would get a second opinion," she said.

I sat in the car still crying and depressed when, across from me, I saw a car with a woman smoking pot and sharing it with a child seated in the back seat. The child couldn't have been more than two years old. I couldn't believe what I was seeing. Poor baby, born to a heartless mother! I cried even more.

When I got home, I told Al what the dentist had told me, and he agreed with the woman in the parking lot; I needed a second opinion.

I went to see Dr. Wise, the dental surgeon in Freehold who had pulled my wisdom teeth a few years back. After examining my mouth he said, "There's absolutely nothing wrong with your gums. Excuse my language, but those bastards are trying to take you for everything they can. These are the kind of dentists that give other dentists a bad name. You go and get your money back and if they give you a hard time, give them my name and tell them I said they are lying to you, there's nothing wrong with your mouth. Meanwhile, I'll take care of them."

I went back to the "highway robbery dental clinic" and

told the front desk person that I needed to speak with the owner. "What seems to be the problem?" she asked with a snooty tone.

"I saw Dr. Wise, a dental surgeon, and he said my gums are perfectly healthy and I don't need gum surgery. I want all my money back."

"Well, that's his opinion." She went back to scribbling on her large note book sitting on her desk.

"If you don't give me back all the money, I'm going to the *Asbury Park Press* so the public can learn of your dishonesty."

She took me into the back office. "Sit down and wait." She said a little less snobbishly. Ten minutes later she returned. "This check for $2,000 should be more than enough to cover any inconvenience you may have experienced. But first you must sign this document stating that we don't owe you anything else and you're happy with our services."

I signed the paper and left with the hefty check and a sigh of relief.

Ralph, Steve, and their friends enjoyed the rough rides at Great Adventure. They tried several times to convince me to go with them, but I could not stand roller coasters. I had gone on a roller coaster once when I first came to America and did not find any pleasure in feeling my heart stop or experiencing that empty-stomach-and-chest feeling when my seat dropped from a high point. It was not a happy moment in my life. I preferred to see the musical shows and go on the tamer rides like the merry-go-round.

One day, they went as far as carrying me by my feet and hands to a roller coaster. I had to put on the Nelly act. "My heart! Oh, my heart, I can't breathe. Oh, the pain, you're killing me!" They put me down and called me a fraidy-cat.

One evening it was getting close to leaving Great Adventure, and I started walking toward the entrance.

Steve's friend Bill and I bumped into each other. I told him I didn't like riding the big monster rides. He offered to stay with me and asked if I would go on the Ferris wheel with him, since we still had half an hour before we were all to meet. Bill was tall, blond, and his eyes were the bluest color I had ever seen. He reminded me of a very young Paul Newman. Before we parted, Bill said, "You're the coolest lady I've ever known."

I didn't tell him that I found him to be the coolest young boy I had ever met.

Autumn of 1978

Summertime with the kids had been a fun, busy time, playing music and games, having parties in the backyard, swimming, going on daily trips to New York City, Atlantic City, Sandy Hook, Great Adventure, and once we even went to Washington, DC. But once the kids started school, I went stir-crazy at home. I started taking morning classes at the community college but it wasn't enough to keep me fulfilled.

Mr. Crocker was thrilled when I told him I was done with retirement. Hava no longer wanted to teach. I had called him at the perfect time.

Christopher, my private guitar student, was a seventeen-year-old with a precocious attitude. During a lesson he said with a mischievously look in his eyes, "My parents will be away next weekend and I'm throwing a house party."

I responded as if I had not understood the subtle innuendo. "Aren't you going to be in trouble when your parents come back and find out?"

"They'll never know." He became very serious, his face taking on a sudden mature look that took me by surprise. "Will you come to my party? I would love to have you with me."

"I'm married and I'm your guitar teacher. That makes it doubly taboo for me to go to your party."

I bet his beautiful brown eyes and sweet smile got him any girl he wanted. He looked at me as if I were the love of his life as he played his favorite song and sang, "...'cause I'm hot–blooded, check it and see. I've got a fever of a hundred and three..."

Very much like Steve, I had always wanted to learn tap dancing, so I signed up for a class at the college. I felt awkward trying to follow the basic steps on the first day, but the teacher took a liking to me and helped me out. She even complimented my choice of shorts and wanted to know where I had bought them. "I got my shorts at Sears, my favorite store."

She liked the shiny black material. Tap dancing seemed fun—tap, tap, skip, tap.

"Suddenly the instructor yelled at the girl next to me, "Are you left footed? Or are you slow or don't you just have any talent?" The girl ran out of the classroom crying. I saw that and realized I would be next, probably at the next lesson if I didn't wear the same glossy shorts.

I got my full tuition back since I only attended the first class.

Whenever Steve's friend Bill had a cold, he would skip school and spent the day with me. Not once did I ever see Bill use a tissue to blow his nose. He followed me around the house as I did housework and I took him along to do my daily errands. His brother Kerry went to a school for kids with special needs. Both parents worked all day.

One of my adult guitar students asked me if I would play the guitar and sing at her church for the services on Sunday. After two Sundays of playing, I became aware of wasting the time I could have spent with my sons. Also, I felt like a hypocrite trying to put passion into songs about Jesus when I was of a different faith.

Once every two weeks I took advantage of the morning trips the college offered. For five dollars, the school bus took the students to New York City and to well-known places like Broadway, the SoHo galleries, Greenwich Village, and so on. Al was working and that was perfect since I did not want him coming with me and spoiling my day with negativity about the art or the city people. I enjoyed the freedom of being by myself.

I went to a bluegrass concert for the first time in my life. One of my older students had recommended it. I expected some silly, boring country music where I would yawn myself to sleep. Instead, I found the banjo to be the king of the stage. I felt my blood running like a wild cold river through the Sahara desert, quenching my thirst. The next day I went and bought myself a five-string banjo.

It was not easy to find a banjo teacher. Everyone I called played by ear. I was ecstatic when I finally found a real banjo teacher even if it was a forty-five-minute drive to his house.

It did not last long. Mr. Ballard went into a serious depression after my two lessons. His wife asked for a divorce and a large settlement. When I showed up for my third lesson he said, "I'm leaving town and won't be teaching anymore. I'd rather die than pay alimony to that bitch. Here, take the Earl Scruggs book with you and practice the tablature instead of music. You'll be playing banjo before you know it. Good luck."

A month later, Mr. Crocker heard me practicing the banjo and said I sounded good enough to teach.

I wrote to Mama about Ralph's girlfriend. "Rose is a skinny, unattractive, grubby-looking girl, what I would call a mother's nightmare. I told Ralph that I didn't like her and he was forbidden to date her. But he won't listen to me. He is in love with her. Mama, I'm worried that if she gets pregnant, they will get married, and the kids will look like her."

Instead of writing back, Mama called.

"Look what happened to your brother Max-Leão when your father and I tried to stop him from marrying the wrong girl. I'm telling you this from personal experience. If I had been smart and not made such a federal case about his choice, maybe, just maybe, he would not have married Patricia. The forbidden fruit is always the sweetest. Open your arms to her and do your best to show you like her. Ralph is very young, and most likely he'll have more than one girlfriend in his life. Trust me, if you do what I'm telling you, it will be over before you know it."

I guess I expected Ralph's first girlfriend to be not only a beauty queen, but also a female Einstein to match his intellect. I decided to follow Mama's advice. We all had lunch at a pizzeria and I was as nice as anyone could be. I invited Rose to our house and even started enjoying her company. What caused them to stop their relationship or if it was just a coincidence I would never know, but within a few weeks they were no longer seeing each other.

Mama had been right. I promised myself to stay away from my kids' love connections. Also, if some day they were to decide to marry someone who I did not care for, it was none of my business.

Dan, the drum teacher at the music school where I taught, heard me playing the banjo and asked me to join his bluegrass band, The Pine Brook Pickers. It was composed of three members; a husband and wife team who played the upright bass and the fiddle, and Dan on acoustic guitar.

We began practicing once a week. I had never cared for that style of music but the more I played with them, the more I began to appreciate it.

The kids had just left for school when Bill knocked at my door. "I have a cold and can't go to school. But I have an idea. You always take care of me. I would like to do something special for you as a friend. Come to my house and I'll make breakfast. I'm a very good cook."
 He made toast with butter and two eggs sunny-side up, with two slices of bacon on the side for each of us. We sat at his kitchen table eating and he did most of the talking. "I hate my father. He is very abusive to my mom and sometimes he hits her." He showed me her picture, a slim lady with white hair and a kind smile. "Isn't she beautiful? He said with pride. "My mother is the one who supports us. My father uses all the money he makes to buy liquor. My dream is to get older and bigger so that I can kick his ass. I want to beat him senseless and make him suffer for what he puts my mother and the whole family through, with his nasty temper. Would you like some orange juice?" I nodded. He got a container of Tropicana from the refrigerator and filled two glasses.
 "Ronnie, you're my best friend. You listen. Ralph and Steve are lucky to have you as their mother. My mom gets home from work too tired and there are things that I can't talk to her about."
 "You can trust me."
 "Last summer while spending a weekend at the youth camp, a girl slipped into my sleeping bag during the night and we kissed and hugged all night. I like her a lot but I don't know if it is true love."
 "Being a teenager is not an easy task. It's a lot like being a caterpillar before turning into a butterfly. The day will come when you will know it is love. I promise." He was happy. I helped him to clean the kitchen before I left.

Winter ending 1978

As a member of The Pine Brook Pickers band, it was necessary to become a member of the Musicians' Union if I was going to be performing and getting paid. Not only did the Musicians' Union get us bookings, but they also paid us union wages.

Al did not care if I was gone in the evening with the band, as long as we had dinner together.

Winter of 1979

I began taking voice lessons at the college because my school counselor told me it was the only way to get rid of my foreign accent. He was right—when I sang, I did not have an accent. But when I talked, it was just as bad as before. My voice teacher finally said, "You came to America as an adult, you will always have a slight accent." He saw the frustration in my face and added, "Don't be so disappointed, your accent is very charming."

I did not want to be charming. I wanted to be an American. I did not want to remain for the rest of my life, speaking defectively like my father, who had lived for over fifty years in Portugal, and still spoke Portuguese with a German accent. I guess accents were like tattoos, once you had one, it was forever.

College was a real blast. I befriended two other students who asked me to join them at Brookdale's radio station. Jim played the piano, Norman the bass guitar, and I played the acoustic guitar. That evening I learned an important lesson, a musician should always carry extra strings, and most of all, never leave their instrument on the floor without it being inside its case, protected. A microphone fell from the ceiling and hit the fifth string of my guitar. Luckily Al was home when I called and he brought me another A string.

Jim could not stop playing the piano at the end of our ten-minute performance. From being nervous or from wanting to play longer, he kept getting inspired and fifteen minutes later, we were still jamming until someone cut us off from the airwaves.

Joann, one of my younger private guitar students, and only eleven years old, asked me after her lesson, "Why don't we do real shows instead of boring recitals every six months?"

"Do you mean a musical?"

"Yeah, on stage, with singing and dancing. What do you think?"

"I don't see why not. Sounds like a brilliant idea!"

She was very excited and so was I.

I started asking my other students if they would like to be in a musical production. Everyone wanted to know when we would be starting rehearsals.

I had Mr. Crocker's blessing to go on with the project and I put out the word, anyone interested in performing was to show up at the music center the last Sunday of that month.

It was a great turnout and it got serious when one of my students suggested Kooky Clan and Ronnie for the name of our newly formed musical theatre group.

There were twenty devoted young people from the fifth to tenth grades willing to practice every weekend until the spring just to be the best they could be for our first vaudeville show.

I got the vaudeville idea from a couple of striptease shows that Al took me to see in Atlantic City. Of course I was not having anyone strip, but my goal was to intertwine between each musical scene the comedy relief needed to classify it as vaudeville. Ralph offered to play the drums, and Steve could not wait to do some singing, acting and dancing.

Nobody in Kooky Clan and Ronnie, including myself, had ever been on stage. None of us had any experience in theatre. I was stoked about the prospect of starting something so new and exciting.

Spring of 1979

After a month of running around looking for a place with a stage big enough to have a huge production on a zero budget, I was losing all hope. Then, one morning while still lying in bed, the answer came to me as clear as a bell ringing over my head. I would give all proceeds from the tickets to the Freehold Area Hospital. Being that it was a benefit; the Manalapan High School agreed to let us use their auditorium for a smaller fee.

Including Ralph on the drums, I had fifteen young musicians who could not wait to show off their musical talent. Seven parents offered to help with the selling of tickets up front, and would be providing homemade cookies and refreshments for sale during intermission. A lot of detail went into organizing everything. It reminded me of putting together a difficult puzzle.

For my birthday, I bought my dream car, a brand new white Ford Mustang, and I paid cash for it. No monthly payments. I liked the idea that all I had to do was put gas in the tank and drive.

Barbara Samanick, a young girl who lived two houses away from us, showed an interest in getting involved in the theatre project. Barbara, Ralph, and Steve used to play doctors when they were little, but now that they were all grown up and in high school, they were good acquaintances. Lucky me, Barbara was only sixteen but she had a natural talent for singing and dancing and her mom, offered to help us with make-up and wardrobe ideas.

David, one of my guitar students and a senior in high school told me he had a lot of experience choreographing musicals and offered his assistance. I called the theatre department at his school and the drama teacher confirmed his talent. I felt very blessed!

Mr. Crocker's wife taught me how to write to the newspapers and get free advertisements by addressing the mail to Community News Release. The date for our production was set—June 9, 1979.

I bought a new ribbon for my typewriter and I carefully began putting the playbill together, making sure not to forget anyone. No part was too small and all names had to be checked and re-checked to make sure I did not misspell them.

For the scene "Greased Lightning," I went to the Battleground Country Club and got them to lend me a golf cart in exchange for free advertisement in the program. I did not think the high school stage was strong enough to hold a real car.

I hired a driver with a school bus and took all the kids participating in our show to New York City to see the Broadway production of *Grease*. Everybody was keyed up about the trip. I didn't want to burst their bubbles of joy at seeing a real Broadway production, but personally, I was very disappointed with the simplicity of the set. I realized right then and there that anything I came up with would be a lot fancier.

Seeing *Grease* on Broadway gave me the confidence to pursue every empty cardboard grand piano box I could get my hands on. Mr. Crocker allowed me to store the flat boxes in one of the empty back rooms until I had the chance to start cutting them into shapes and painting them for the stage background. He had not bothered me for quite a while. The only stupid thing he did, which really hurt my feelings, was when we were crossing paths on the sidewalk outside his store, he handed me a small screw he picked up from the sidewalk. I looked at him, puzzled, and he said, "This is what you really need." He walked away laughing.

I made every effort to stay away from him as if he were the plague.

Summer of 1979

Two days before we put on our production, the music director for Manalapan High School called. "Your cast drove the golf cart into the pit and I almost broke my back with some of my students lifting the cart back onto the stage. I'm going to do everything possible to stop you and your theatre group from ever performing at our high school."

"I'm very sorry about what you went through with the cart. But I swear to you that when the cart was delivered to the school I personally gave the keys to the school janitor and I saw him locking the cart in one of the storage rooms. His name was Shawn and all you have to do is talk to him if you don't believe me."

He called a week later to apologize. Shawn confirmed what I had told him. Obviously some students had gotten their hands on the cart and used it to ride up and down the auditorium and when they got tired of it they just left it in the pit.

A Taste of Broadville was a great success to an almost full house. Considering the size of the high school auditorium, we had pretty good attendance. It didn't matter that two of the piano boxes I had painted as part of the set for *Mame* fell apart like dominoes during the scene. The audience was prepared for a musical comedy and thought it was hilarious.

I asked the stage crew to take a bow at the end of the performance. They deserved the applause as much as everybody else. I was called on stage as the producer. The applause was invigorating to the senses and I knew I was hooked for life on producing shows. The standing ovation was an incentive for everyone to ask right after the curtain closed when they could start working on the next production.

We only had one problem. David, our young choreographer, had an eye on Kathy since the start of rehearsals. She played the sexy blonde country girl in shorts and a low cut shirt, trying to run away from Bob, the dirty old man, between the musical scenes. They were only sixteen years old but make-up did wonders for both. During the second act, one of Kathy's contact lenses moved to the back of her right eye and seemed to be stuck, possibly melted due to the heat coming from the stage lights. Right after the show David offered to drive Kathy to the hospital. Everybody felt really bad about such unfortunate incident. We were worried about Kathy's eye, but we were a lot more concerned that once David got Kathy alone and showed her his sensitive side, she would fall into his arms, a victim of circumstance. None of us cared for David's macho attitude. The opposite was felt toward Bob, whom we all loved. Everyone felt he deserved to get the girl of his dreams, namely Kathy.

After the show, Mrs. Samanick, Barbara's mom invited the cast and crew to her home for a cast party. The highlights of the evening were discussed in full detail when we gathered to celebrate our first theatrical experience. One amusing incident happened when Mike, my bass guitar student, stood alone on stage and tried to play "Fire" on his electric bass. Maria and Barbara were to sing and dance while trying to entice Mike to stop playing and follow them instead. It was to be a humorous but seductive scene. The curtain opened and there was Mike standing on the huge empty stage. I looked up from the pit where I sat with my student musical ensemble and for the first time saw what Mike was wearing. He had on tight black pants that were too short. His thick white socks were an eyesore, and didn't quite fit his dressy black shoes. His battered black leather jacket was at least one size smaller than him. His hair was greased back and he was wearing sunglasses. He was trying to look like a cool rock star while holding his bass guitar, but he didn't have the proper clothing outfit. He looked like a nerd. He plucked his bass guitar but there was no sound coming from his amplifier. The audience was laughing hysterically as Mike stared at them with the most innocent look on his face as if asking, now what do I do?

The curtain closed and then opened again. Still, no sound from his amp, only his dumbfounded look that read, Help! It was just too much for anyone to look at him while holding a straight face. I was laughing with tears, along with the audience. The curtains closed again and once again opened. The spectators cheered on as Roy the stagehand came on stage, turned the small amp on, and took a bow. It was that simple. The tune "Fire" came on. There was a sigh of relief from Mike. Everyone agreed that was one of the funniest scenes on stage.

Steve got to act and dance in two acts and he did very well. Ralph also did a great job playing drums. I was proud of my two sons.

Steve was only fifteen years old, but he was a natural at dancing.

We started to practice every day with one goal in mind—to enter a disco dancing competition as a mother and son team.

Tom, one of my bass students, was taken to juvenile jail and then released after one month. He and a couple of his friends had broken into the neighbor's house and destroyed everything they got their hands on, just for the thrill of it. Tom told me he got a hammer and smashed the bathtub, and that was really the only thing he had damaged. He said he was sorry, so I decided to help his creative side instead of his mean side. He was thrilled when I invited him to join our backyard rock band.

I had a few complaints from my neighbors, but that was because they did not like music to begin with. All the neighbors' kids loved to hang out in our yard listening to the band. The parents did not know what they were missing.

Ralph went camping for the weekend with Stephen, his friend from up the street. I took Steve with me as my roadie to a mental institution in Philadelphia where the Musicians' Union had paid The Pine Brook Pickers to play for an hour. It meant less than fifty dollars each since our bluegrass group had grown with two more new members; Dan's new girlfriend on acoustic guitar, and her girlfriend with a four-string banjo.

On the grounds of the hospital, an old lady sat underneath a tree trying to pull her tongue from her mouth with both hands.

"What a waste of our time playing here," said Dan. "No one is even paying attention." He pointed to the old lady under the tree and then to another woman running in the grassy field, squeezing toothpaste into her mouth as one of the attendants ran after her, trying to stop her.

"Funny you should say that," I said to Dan and the other band members. "Watch the lady under the tree when we are playing and you'll notice that even though she's busy with her tongue, her left foot taps on the ground along with the beat of our music."

When Steve saw an inmate pulling her clothes off right in front of us he said, "Mom, please don't take this wrong, but the next time you play in a disturbing place like this, don't ask me to come along." It wasn't a pretty picture to see so many adults wearing helmets out on the lawn, screaming, and rolling on the grass uncontrollably. It was also very hot, which probably would help explain why the people who we thought were nuts were taking their hospital gowns off and rolling on the cool grass.

Al was very proud of me when I brought home my high school diploma. He wanted to frame it. "Everybody has a high school diploma," I said. "On a wall should be a degree; and in my case, a music degree is a lot more appropriate." That was my next goal.

Even though Steve and I were still practicing disco dancing and didn't have any place in mind where to show our talent he wanted to pick my disco outfit. We went to the Ocean County Mall and he chose a short strapless black and silver dress. I was very moved when he used his allowance money to buy me a small, over-the-shoulder mini-purse to compliment my outfit. All I had to do was get high-heeled black shoes when the time came.

I thought it was a great idea to have a motorhome with all the comforts of home. Everybody agreed, it was the best way to travel all over the United States. I was very excited about the idea of exploring the country as a family and the opportunity for Al and me to talk, and connect with each other.

We began visiting dealerships specializing in motorhomes and the brand Winnebago seemed to have all the pre-requisites we needed.

Playing with The Pine Brook Pickers was no longer enjoyable. I felt like I was being pushed away by the new girls in our group. They threw away most of our repertoire and began selecting what songs they wanted to play. Then they cut off my favorite one where I had a banjo solo. One meeting was called and Laurie, Dan's girlfriend, said, "Marlene and I wear long country skirts, and we want you to do the same."

"I'd rather wear jeans like I always do."

"Well, we have voted to wear skirts and you have to abide by the majority vote."

I decided not to play with them anymore. I liked jeans; they helped support my lower back and besides, as long as I wore my size six jeans, I was guaranteed to keep my butt from extending into size fourteen like them. I was having such a good time before the "girls" came along with their rules and regulations. Nothing lasts forever.

Our theatre group met to discuss a new name. Kooky Clan and Ronnie was outdated, and not a professional name. Everyone agreed with me, The Broadville Entertainers was a much better name, since what we did had a lot to do with Broadway and vaudeville styles of entertainment.

Autumn of 1979

I signed up for Oceanography as my next class in college. I thought it was very appropriate since I loved the ocean but didn't know much about it. I wanted to go to school for a long, long time, and learn everything I never had a chance to learn before getting married. Once Mama's plan for my pre-arranged marriage, became a reality she took me out of high school during my third year. In her opinion my rich American husband would take care of me and I didn't need any further education.

Most of the students at the college were a lot younger than me, but that didn't stop us from becoming friends, and going to New York City to the museums, art shows, concerts, and Broadway shows. I scheduled my outside activities in the morning, and on days I was not teaching. I always made sure to be home before the kids got home from school. They had talked about quitting, but they were still hanging on.

Braving A New World

Al lost his job; no reason other than they did not need so many employees. After a few weeks of throwing ideas around, I woke up one morning with a solution. Being a music teacher for so many years, I was very familiar with the companies selling musical instruments, books, and so on.

"Why not open a little music store?" I said to Al.

"You're out of your mind. I don't know anything about music."

"I know you don't, but I do."

I told him about the Collingswood Auction & Flea Market, open on weekends only. He agreed to take a look with me.

We found the perfect space for rent at the flea market, right between the egg-man and the banana-man stands, and inside the main building where it was nice and warm in the winter. Yes, it was a small; only four feet deep by twelve feet long, just enough space to put a narrow counter facing the foot traffic and still have room to sit behind it. Not bad for just $200 per month in rent. I painted the walls a mellow yellow, and with a black magic marker, I wrote the names of all the instruments we would carry. Al hung a strip of pegboard on the back wall and put up some hooks to hang strings, electric cords, guitars, electric bass, violins, banjos, and even a couple of ukuleles.

Being that it was a flea market-type of place, I was sure the less expensive the instruments were, the better they would sell. Being a guitar teacher for so many years I had all the contacts for purchasing the inventory we needed at rock-bottom prices. With a few small amps stacked up on the side, and a showcase full of small musical items like picks, kazoos, and other small items, it looked very appealing and professional. Al insisted it should be called Ronnie's Music Den and would not take no for an answer when I told him that "Ronnie" was not a good name. I felt it should be a big name, like Universal Music Den or

Collingswood Music Center. But his mind was made up. I painted "Ronnie's Music Den" on a plank of wood and hung it up for everyone to see.

Winter ending 1979

Ronnie's Music Den opened with a huge welcome by all the young people who lived in the area. On the first weekend, we not only made enough money to pay the rent for the month, but also enough to call it a good income to live on if it kept on going that way.

Al couldn't stop talking about how happy he was being his own boss, and had no intentions of looking for another job. "With what I'm making here on weekends, I would have to be a fool to kill himself working for some jerk someplace else."

Losing his job had been a blessing in disguise, confirming that everything happened for a reason.

Winter of 1980

After I did my Portuguese bargaining, I was able to get the price to buy our new motorhome down to $8,000. Thank God for my Portuguese upbringing where bargaining was looked upon as a needed skill in business of any kind. The Portuguese merchants expected it, and only a fool would pay without blinking an eye. It was a game of wits that both parties enjoyed. You always cut the price to half and then you worked it up to a happy medium between buyer and seller.

The motorhome had lots of closets and a kitchen with a stove and a refrigerator. The bathroom converted into a shower, the dining area had a table and chairs, and best of all, it had beds for five sleepy people. We could go on minivacations throughout the year. All we needed was gas.

"With what we are saving in hotels, we can eat like

kings making our own meals onboard," Al said.

We began making plans to travel to Virginia, Pennsylvania, and even Maine. I believed Al would soon love both kids equally and start enjoying travel since he would have all the comforts of home including a television, and lobster and steaks with French fries every day. I could not wait for the summer.

Rehearsals for "A Taste of Broadville II" had started and our cast had grown from twenty performers to thirty-six very talented young people. Even our music ensemble had bloomed into sixteen members, including a professional adult piano player. After we butchered his Polish name a few times, he asked us to call him Steve. The word got out in the community and Frank Condardo, a professional choreographer, from New York City, volunteered to direct and choreograph our musical production.

I found thirteen businesses who agreed to advertise in the playbill. That helped tremendously to help pay for the stage props. It also meant more money we could donate to Freehold Hospital and the First Aid Squad. We would be performing two nights, June 13 and 14, at Manalapan High School.

One day I came out of my teaching room completely discouraged with one of my guitar students. Vicki, the office manager sitting at the front desk kept blinking at me as I said, "I'm so frustrated with Johnny. I bet he doesn't even open his guitar case all week. He holds the guitar like a lazy person. He slouches off the chair and puts the guitar flat on his lap. I feel like kicking him in the butt. His parents are wasting their money on lessons."

"Are you referring to Johnny, my lazy son?" said a man dressed in a dark blue business suit right behind me. Vicki left the room.

I thought I was going to die as I muttered, "I...I

apologize about what I said. I didn't see you." No kidding! Then to show my personal concern I added, "I was going to call you about Johnny to tell you that you're wasting your money. His heart is not into music."

"I'm with you, but my son is going to learn to play the guitar if he likes it or not. You taught my neighbor's two boys and they are doing great; they even have their own band going. I don't care how long it takes. Johnny is going to play the guitar, and I don't consider it a waste of money."

Johnny's father should be the one to take the guitar lessons, but I kept my mouth shut.

Spring of 1980

Spring was in the air and with it came the bright thought of going blonde. I bought a bottle of hair color and waited until I was alone at home. My hair turned green. I ran to Shop Rite and bought two more bottles. By the time Al got home I opened the front door as a platinum blonde. "What the heck is that?!Oh my God, what did you do to your hair?"

I put my coat on. "I have to get to work. Do I look that bad?"

"You better use a scarf, that's all I have to say."

Mr. Crocker liked my new look but everyone else didn't. I did look better with my "own" dark hair, so when I got home I colored it back to black. Still, it was fun to be blonde for a couple of hours.

No matter how much Al and I tried to talk him out of it, Ralph dropped out of high school. "Mom," he said, "my most exciting experience was a few years ago when the teacher said to the class, 'Let's all go to the laboratories,' and I thought finally we were going to do a science project of some kind. It turned out it was the lavatories, not the laboratories."

He planned to get a GED and then come September, join the Air Force. His mind was made up.

We used our motorhome twice. Once we went up north to the Tri-State area, and another time to Virginia. Al drove all over the road, cutting off other drivers without even realizing it. It was not so bad when he drove his car, but behind the wheel of a large vehicle like our motorhome, he was a lethal weapon. Our lives were in jeopardy. I had to do all the driving if we were to return home in one piece.

I did notice a funny smell in the motorhome but I was the only one who detected it. I sneezed a lot; my eyes got red and watery, and I woke up with a rash on my chest and arms every morning. I did not have the courage to complain because Al and the kids were fine. I was the only one with problems.

Nobody used the pool anymore, and the yard was too much to take care of. I was afraid of bees. I had never been stung by one and did not intend to change my luck. Al cut the grass but that was it.

When I was a kid, my cousin Esther and I were seated on a park bench, just talking, and a bee stung her on the arm. They say if you don't bother them they won't bother you. Sure; go tell that to my cousin, who screamed like hell from the pain, and to all the people who died every year from being allergic to bee stings.

Nelly was not going to return and with Ralph in the Air Force in September, our home was getting too big for us. I said to Al, "If we sell our house we could use the money to buy ourselves a nice little ranch house. We can pay cash for it, and we won't have a mortgage anymore, just utilities. Just think of it—we will be debt free."

"I like your idea. It makes a lot of sense as long as it is a one-bedroom house. Let the kids go find their own place, they're big enough to take care of themselves."

What a horrible thought! I loved having my sons with me. They were the ones who gave me some form of sanity. Yes, I had the occasional problems when it came to Ralph smoking and Steve drinking, but it was a matter of time when they would outgrow the teen phase and find themselves on the right track. The Air Force would help Ralph to grow up, and when Steve was old enough, he could also join and get the heck away from his father.

I blamed myself for my kids' behavior. I had waited too long to do something about it. They had grown up feeling insecure; that was the only thing I could rationalize to explain what was happening. Smoking and drinking gave them a sense of euphoria and belonging.

We put the house up for sale with a Realtor on Thursday. Friday night I baked an apple pie to make the house smell good after the Realtor called to say she had someone interested in looking at the house Saturday morning.

Saturday afternoon, we got a call from our Realtor that the couple who had come in the morning commented on how comfortable the house was, from smelling great to looking great. It sold that easily. We ate the apple pie with glee.

Summer of 1980

We found the perfect ranch house in Kona Park, an adult mobile home community for people fifty years old and over. Al was thrilled. "We no longer have to deal with the Redhead or any other crazy teenagers around. I'm looking forward to the quiet nights," he said.

By moving to Kona Park, we would still be living in Freehold, which kept things easy for me, like my commute to work. I was thirty-six years old, but Al had just turned forty-eight, and that made us eligible enough to live in the adult community. The seller of the ranch house was a nice old man who was willing to wait for his money until we got all the papers signed with the real estate lawyers. It would take at least two months before all that was taken care of.

A Taste of Broadville II was another smashing success. My inspiration for writing the script for the comedy between scenes came from what I had seen in Portugal for the New Year's celebration. Every year a few college students would walk the streets of Lisbon with the "New Year Newborn" sucking on his milk bottle while being pushed around in a stroller. The baby was a full-grown man with hairy legs and he was naked except for the diaper and a bonnet. Two male students were dressed as the parents. I used "the family" to walk across the front of the stage while the curtains were closed, to keep the audience busy while the set was being changed.

We made a lot of money with *A Taste of Broadville II*, and the donations to the hospital and the First Aid Squad gave us a sense of accomplishment. The show had many flaws but they turned into brilliant moments of theatrical history for us. When the curtains closed and pulled one of the ropes off the side and tore a girl's skirt off, the applause was intense as she ran off the stage in her underwear. I dressed two young boys as cops to maintain an air of respectability. They took their roles to heart and the audience was convinced they were policemen. That was, until they had to break their cover to be in one of the more fervent scenes, "Disco Inferno."

Steve acted in the "Farm," "New York, New York," and danced in the disco scene of "Marathon." Ralph played the drums and I played the electric guitar with the orchestra. After the show was over, we all met at our house in the old neighborhood, to celebrate the two nights of entertainment. It was a large cast and crew and some of their family members had also joined in the festivities. The house was alive with music and people. "Why did you invite all these people in our house?" Al was not happy. "You know I don't like strangers coming in here."

"I know you don't, but it's just for tonight. We have no other place to have a cast party." Just then Wendy came in screaming, her brother Mike had been knocked out in front of our lawn and was suffering from amnesia. I rushed out and found Mike on the ground looking up at everybody without any idea of where he was or who he was. Steve started crying. "It's my fault if he dies. I should have defended him from those bullies. They ran into the woods but I'm gonna go after them and beat them up."

I tried to hold Steve down with two others. But he was drunk and took off. I ran into the house and called for an ambulance. With a house full of kids, Al and some of the parents offered to stay and watch them until I got back from the hospital. Wendy and I followed the ambulance to the emergency room. She gave me a complete account of the incident saying, "Three boys from another neighborhood came over and asked for beer. Mike made a fist and told them to get off of his property or he would let them have it. One of them made a fist and hit Mike on the head. When he fell to the ground out cold, they ran away."

Mike's father came to the hospital. "Ronnie, I don't know how you put up with kids like him. Mike has been nothing but trouble since my wife and I adopted him."

"Who is he?" Mike pointed to his father.

"I'm your father, you stupid moron."

"I don't know him," Mike told the doctor and me.

"Mr. Robinson, you need to be a little patient," said the doctor. "Your son has temporary amnesia from getting hit in the head. Just give him a few days at home and he'll be back to normal."

"That's what I'm afraid of, doc." He laughed. "Let's go home, Mike."

"Home? Where is home?"

Before Mike left the hospital with his family, he gave me a hug and whispered in my ear, "See ya later, Ronnie."

I stared at him, dumfounded. What kind of amnesia was that, I asked myself. I had to credit him as a darn good actor, he even fooled the doctor. I drove home praying to God that Steve was okay. Ralph and two other boys had found him in the backyard of one of our neighbors, curled up between some bushes, crying because he'd had no luck finding Mike's assaulter. I put him to bed and went back to joining the party, by sitting next to one of the parents, sulking. One of the mothers gave me a hug and said, "Don't blame yourself, it's not your fault." But I felt I should have been more aware of what was going on outside the house. I thought Ralph and Steve had everything under control. Apparently they thought that too when they hid the beer in the bottom of our pool.

Al and I took a trip during the week to Virginia in our motorhome. On the way back I swore it would be our last trip together. I planned to sell the motorhome as soon as possible. Traveling with Al had to be the most stupid mistake anyone could make. He reminded me of Mr. Magoo, oblivious to anything around him. As a safety measure, I drove home, but for me to drive every single hour hearing him complain about every possible subject coming into his head was beyond my endurance. It crossed my mind that if I listened to him hour after hour I might get brainwashed and begin thinking like him about life. I had seen movies where a lot of people had been caught up in some fanatical religious group. They listened to the sermons over and over again until their brain was fried and they were unable to think for themselves. That scared the hell out of me.

On the way home, Al started talking about Republicans versus Democrats. He was a Republican. I hummed a tune in my head. Al did not like to listen to music on the radio, only the news.

We finally moved. Our ranch house was a dream house. It had lots of tall, wide windows and a large futuristic round modern kitchen, a spacious living room and dining room, and a master bedroom to die for. It even had an extra bedroom which was not too big but okay for Steve to use for another year until he went into the service like Ralph. When Ralph came to visit us he could sleep on the pullout couch in the living room.

Our new home was so new it even smelled like plastic, similar to inside the motorhome.

I got a call from Freehold Regional High School asking me if I was available to teach adult guitar classes in the evening. I always thought in order to teach at a high school one should have some kind of degree, but they didn't even ask. Of course I accepted the job.

Autumn of 1980

The place where we had bought the motorhome had sold their business to another company. I called them to see if they were interested in buying our motorhome. I described it as being like new.

The new owner said, "Even if it is in such good condition as you say, I can't give you more than $10,000 for it." I almost passed out and so did Al who had told me if I got half of what we paid for it would be a miracle.

I drove the motorhome to their lot right after I got off the telephone. We only used it a couple of times, including once to move some of the houseplants and a few delicate housewares from the old house to the home in Kona Park. They agreed it was impeccably clean and in great condition.

They handed me a check for $10,000. They never asked us how much we wanted or even how much we paid for it. They were definitely not Portuguese.

Except for constantly sneezing and coughing, I loved everything about our new house, but I still did not look forward to coming home. My relationship with Al was far from ideal. After dinner I was expected to sit with him and watch television; one police series after another. I did not mind watching one show or one movie, but truthfully, I could think of better things to do than watch television. When we got into bed he would give me a condensed version of the news he'd read in the newspaper, and then he wanted me to suddenly become amorous.

"I don't care to hear about the news before having sex. Let's talk about something else."

"You never read the newspaper. I bet you don't even know who the president of the United States is." He laughed and then tried to fondle me.

Something had to be wrong with one of us and I could only hope it was not me.

Ralph left for the Air Force. I helped him carry one of his electrical transformers as he carried the other one, plus his luggage, onto the airplane. I had no idea why he was taking both transformers with him, but it crossed my mind that since he always had wished he was born a hundred years into the future perhaps he was going to continue to experiment with the idea. When it came to science and research, Ralph and Einstein would have gotten along well. Even though I cried as we waved goodbye, I was relieved when he left. He had found a career and his future was going to be bright.

I felt sorry for Steve who was still stuck at home.

Winter ending 1980

For the next production of *The Broadville Entertainers* we kept our old cast but we needed a bigger one. Barbara and I held auditions for *The Time Machine*, a musical I wrote about a punk rocker named Jones Van Prince who is told by his doctor that he has terminal cancer. Upon leaving the doctor's office, Jones runs into a homeless old man, and out of desperation, Jones gives him all his money. In turn, the old man gives Jones a small box which has special powers. The box turns out to be a time machine and transports Jones to the year 3001. There he meets Laseria, a female doctor who cures him. Of course they fall in love, and together they begin traveling back in time. With each decade marked by the different musical style, Jones Van Prince learns a lesson about music and how it has changed to be what it is today. It took me two weeks to write the plot, but when it came down to having it polished, I needed someone who was better at English than me. Barbara was excited when she read my script, and we spent a few afternoons polishing it.

What I loved most about producing and writing a play was the freedom of writing my thoughts and giving life to the words. Growing up in Portugal at a time when there was no television and the radio was a luxury, everyone was dependent on the art of communication, such as storytelling. Everyone enjoyed talking and listening. Writing a play was the closest I could be to being home listening to some amazing story.

A lot like Ralph, I loved the idea of time and space travel. The play was right up my alley.

Besides becoming my writing partner, Barbara helped me to organize the music to fit the plot from 1980 to 3001.

I sent the *Asbury Park Press* a little blurb about our next theatre endeavor, and they sent a news reporter to interview Barbara and me. The interview and our picture took a full page of the newspaper. We were sure that type of media coverage would provide us a larger attendance.

Winter of 1981

"I have a feeling that I'm allergic to our house," I said to Al one morning when I couldn't stop sneezing.
"How can you be allergic to it? You really are weird." He shook his head and laughed.
"Okay, look at my eyes. Take a good look at my eyes."
"They're red. But that doesn't mean anything."
"I'm fine all day." I sneezed. "And when I get home..." I sneezed again. "My throat feels like..." I sneezed twice. "Feels... like... it's closing on me." I blew my nose several times and sneezed again. "I feel dizzy and nauseous..."
"There's nothing wrong with this house. It's all in your head. Good thing I married you or you would be living in Greenwich Village with all the other oddballs."
He did not realize how appealing that sounded to me.
On the other hand, Mr. Crocker told me I should be living with him in the French Riviera, his favorite place on earth. Then he said, "I can see you driving a yellow Porsche." I told Al about it and of course he laughed and told me not to pay attention to Mr. Crocker because he was a dirty old man. I had to agree with that.

With each show I produced I was getting better at prioritizing what needed to be done way ahead of time. The thought process of organizing each detail to make a production successful put me into an exuberant state of creativity. It was hard to turn off once the ideas came flooding into my mind in the middle of the night or woke me up earlier than usual.

Spring of 1981

Ralph and Steve had never been great buddies growing up. If anything, they were more like adversaries. I was surprised when Steve said, "I miss Ralph."

Steve was lonely. Worse than that, he no longer took verbal abuse from his father, and responded back just as aggressively.

One day I heard a muffled crying coming from Steve's bedroom. I found him sitting behind his bedroom door, as if hiding away. Soon he would be turning seventeen and seeing an almost grown man falling apart emotionally was too much to bear.

"Mom, I can't stand the way Dad talks down to me. Why does he do that?"

Al was in the living room watching television. I kept my voice to a whisper. "I don't know. All I know is that you have got to get out of here. This environment is not healthy for you."

"I can't stand it anymore. I'm going crazy."

"I understand how you feel. Dad is not going to change the way he is. Let's put our heads together and think of what to do."

"I want to go into the military service like Ralph, and I'm not going back to school, either."

"Oh, my goodness you're going to quit too?"

"I want to go in the navy."

"Okay, okay. But you still need to finish high school. Without a high school diploma you can't do much of anything. How about getting a GED like Ralph and when you turn seventeen you can go into the Navy."

I encouraged him to come to work with me and use the time to study for the GED and also to start looking for a job so he would be away from home as much as possible.

Al was home during the week, but on weekends he worked at the flea market.

Braving A New World

When I was a kid, Uncle Augusto, Mama's brother, had diagnosed me with Juvenile Arthritis and prescribed me medicine which tasted horribly sour, and did not help a bit with the pain in my legs. Mama had me sit for hours in the sun hoping the heat would help. But the only thing working for me was to massage my legs as hard as possible until the harshness of kneading masked the bone pain. The problem never went away; and it continued to be an enigma to me. Sometimes weeks went by where I was perfectly normal and then the pain hit me out of nowhere. Al said I should take aspirin for it but I refused. I needed to know the cause and then take care of it.

Having a high tolerance for pain helped. I stopped complaining since it did go away after a few agonizing days.

It was about three in the morning when the phone rang.
"Hello," said the male voice.
"Hello. Who is this?"
"This is an obscene phone call. I want to fool around with you."
I shook Al to wake him up. "Al, I'm having an obscene phone call! Do you want to hear it?" I put the phone between our ears and tried my best not to laugh. "Excuse me, can you say that again?"
He did.
"Thank you. Now, can you say something else a little more exciting?" I couldn't help giggling.
"I want to come over and fool around with you."
"You already said that. No offense but what you're saying doesn't sound obscene to me. Can you say something else?"
He hung up.

I decided to try out for the dancing audition at Great Adventure in Jackson. I wore a short, tight multicolored dress and white boots. I took my portable cassette player, and when it was my turn to show how I could dance I put on the tape from *Fame*.

I believe the reason I was not nervous was because I was only trying out for the fun of it. I smiled at the panel of four judges and just imagined I had been a dancer all my life. Since there was no way I could memorize a bunch of specific steps, I made them up as I went along.

At the end of my routine, I knew I had done okay when a woman asked me to follow her to a dressing room where two women took my measurements. I did not have the courage to tell them I was auditioning just for kicks. One of them gave me a contract to enter my personal information. I wrote the wrong address and phone number and for my birth date I did write May 7, but lied about the year.

Mama and Aunt Heydee would have been proud of me for taking twenty years off.

My desire to someday dance on stage had been fulfilled.

Besides the *Asbury Park Press*, other newspapers gave us plenty of coverage for our original musical play, *The Time Machine*.

We all agreed, our show was very professional because everything went very smoothly. The party was held at Barbara's house. No pool, no beer, and no tribulations.

There was nothing to stop me from visiting my parents in Portugal; I took a well-deserved week off. I found my parents to be more demanding as they had gotten older. Their maid was constantly running down the long hallway attending to their needs. The distance to the bathroom from their bedroom was too much for Mama's weak legs, even with a cane to support her. She had fallen several times. There was only one way to take care of the problem—get rid of the thick brick wall and the glass window situated between their bedroom and the dining room. Then Mama would only need to walk half the distance to reach the bathroom. I was able to dismantle the window and then borrowed a hammer from the next-door neighbor and began striking the wall as hard as I could. Except for a few superficial dents the wall was like the rock of Gibraltar. I had forgotten that the houses in Portugal were not built like those in the United States. I couldn't even make a hole into the brick wall.

I hired a construction worker to handle the job and an entrance was created. My parents were delighted.

The days were spent sitting with my parents and talking to family visiting. Aunt Morena, Mama's sister, was disappointed I only had one lipstick to give her. I promised the next time I went to Portugal I would bring her two lipsticks.

Aunt Heydee said it wasn't healthy for me to stay home day after day cooped up with my parents; I needed at least one day off. She invited me to go to Estoril, her favorite beach. We took the train, just like in the old times when we would go to the beach together. It was as if time had stood still except the roles were now reversed. She wanted my advice concerning a personal dilemma of the heart.

"My dentist likes me a lot and asked me on a date. But he is seventy-one years old. He is too old for me. If he asks me to marry him, I just don't have the patience to take care of an old goat."

"Seventy-one is not that old." I knew she was eighty-one, but I didn't say anything out of respect for her.

"Are you kidding me, Veronica? On the way out of his office I patted him nonchalantly on his shoulder and he almost fell over. He'll never be able to keep up with me. You know that, don't you?"

"Going on a date doesn't mean you have to marry him. Can't you just enjoy his company and leave it at that?"

"I'll give it a go, but what I really need is someone in his early fifties."

The poor thing; chronologically she was old, but physically and emotionally Aunt Heydee was not a day over twenty-one.

Two days after I got back from Portugal I woke up with severe dizzy spells, even with my eyes closed. Any slight movement and it felt like I was twirling into a vacuum. Al called an ambulance and I was taken to the hospital.

Dr. DeCicco said I probably had a middle ear infection. He prescribed some medicine and told me to stay in bed for at least a week.

Wrapped in a blanket, I used the lawn chair in the backyard and spent the next ten days lying outside, where the sneezing and coughing subsided.

Steve finished taking his GED and got a job at a restaurant but he also went out drinking and came home late into the night. One evening I stayed up writing him a letter about how I felt and that he was hurting both of us. I put the letter on his bed. It was four in the morning when I heard him coming in.

The letter didn't do any good. With the money he was earning at Van's restaurant in Freehold, he bought a used motorcycle. I was now scared for his life.

Summer of 1981

Steve advised me to never, ever, under any circumstances send my food back to the kitchen when eating at a restaurant. "Most cooks are extra sensitive about their cooking and can't take any form of criticism," he said. "You're lucky if they just spit on your food."

Steve got his GED, sold his bike, and signed up to be part of the medical team in the Navy. His dream was to be a nurse. I could not be happier. He was finally in a safe place away from home. I could only hope and pray that when

Ralph and Steve came out of the service they would have grown into mature men and gained some wisdom. They both needed structure and a goal in life, and I believed being in the military was a good start.

Steve sent us his picture in uniform, and on the back he wrote, "Dear Mom and Dad, I love the Navy. This is the best place to be. Thank you Mom for being my friend, and for helping me to make up my mind to go into the service." I put the card in my photo album and thanked God for everything. I was proud of my two sons.

Autumn of 1981

Steve made the news. He sent us a newspaper clipping with a picture showing him with other Navy medical personnel during a training drill concerning a nuclear disaster. I could not be more proud of him! I put the newspaper clipping with his post card.

Winter ending 1981

Steve called in the middle of the night. His voice was palpably bright and cheery, "Mom, I'm in love."
"That's wonderful Steve." Gosh, he was safe away from home, and in love. "Wow, tell me all about it. So you met someone special in the Navy?"
"Yes, she's the admiral's wife. She's a beautiful black girl who got married about a month ago but she's very unhappy."
Good thing I wasn't standing or I would have dropped on the floor. I did my best to maintain calm and asked what any mother would say in such a situation. "What's her name?"
"Belinda."
"Belinda, hum what a lovely name. But, aren't you

afraid once the admiral finds out, your goose is cooked?"

"Don't worry mom. She told me she loves me too and is going to ask her husband for a divorce. If her husband refuses, we're planning to run away."

Al was now awake and asked, "Who you talking to?"

"To Steve," I covered the phone with my hand and said, "Shhhh, I'll tell you in a minute." My goodness if Al was to hear Steve's situation directly from him he would blow his top. At the speed of light I recalled Mama's words of wisdom, "Always welcome your son's choice of girlfriend otherwise it's guaranteed he will marry her just to spite you."

I said to Steve, "How about waiting until Belinda gets a divorce and then if you need a place to stay with her, you can come and live with us."

"Thank you Mom, I knew I could count on you."

After I hung up, I began to cry for my stupid son.

A month went by and we did not hear from Steve. On a Saturday afternoon he showed up at our door. His ship was stationed at the Brooklyn dock, and he had hitchhiked home. He had been very sick for a month with a high fever; the reason we had not heard from him. Steve was skin and bones. He had no idea what he had, but they had him quarantined. I was glad Al was at work.

Steve went out with his friend Jeff. When they returned a few hours later he was inebriated when he hugged me and started crying on my shoulder. "Mommy, Mommy, I don't want to die, I'm too young. Once the admiral found out about his wife and me, he had me transferred from my ship onto an old oil tanker. I've seen the hulls; they aren't going to make it across the ocean. Mommy, Mommy, I'm going to drown." He cried and cried and then he walked outside, and went straight over the railing on the deck and fell flat on his face. Jeff helped me to carry Steve into my car and we took him to the hospital. I was worried he might have a concussion from the fall. Jeff used to be one of my guitar students and he was Steve's age. They'd become good friends when they performed in my very first musical production. While we waited for the doctor to come and tell us what to do next, Jeff held my hands and rubbed my fingers tenderly. I didn't have the courage to pull my hands away, since I knew Jeff to be a kind and sincere friend.

The doctor told us that Steve was fine but needed to stop drinking and needed help. No kidding. I had thought the military way of life would put some sense into his head but I was wrong. When he got home he went to sleep in his room.

Steve woke me up at three in the morning by shaking my shoulder and whispered. "Mom, I need to get back to my ship, like right now or I'll be in a lot of trouble."

"I thought you were on vacation." Al was snoring and must have been sleeping on his good ear, because he didn't wake up. I put a jacket over my pajamas and we headed to my car.

"I jumped ship. I wanted to see you one more time in case I die unexpectedly. If I disappear I want you to know the admiral had me killed."

I drove fast, no state troopers around, just angels carrying us at the speed of light. In less than an hour we were at the Brooklyn harbor where the oil tanker was stationed. Steve told me not to stop the car in such an unsafe area. I slowed the car down just enough so he could jump out without hurting himself while holding onto his sea bag, and I kept driving until I got back to New Jersey safe and sound.

Winter of 1982

I started a creative writing class at Brookdale College to help me translate Mama's lyrical poem "And the Black Panther Cried," into a play. Ms. Own was a very young teacher, but was very resourceful at showing us how to describe our surroundings. On the first day of school, she took the whole class on a silent trip through the college's basement. We were to be quiet and use all our senses. When we got back to class we were asked to write what we had heard, felt, and smelled during our walk down the steps to the college's badly-lit and humid basement and also as we crossed the sun-lit campus parking lot to return to our classroom. I had a lot to write about.

Barbara called. "I'm sorry Ronnie I can't be involved with the next theatre production." I was very sad, but I understood. She was too busy getting ready to graduate from high school. Luckily Bernie and Florence, a retired couple from our neighborhood in Kona Park, found out I was looking for a director for next year's show, *And the Black Panther Cried*, and they volunteered to direct the play. In their younger days, they had been involved in theatre and the performing arts. Cathy DiPasquale, who was in *The Time Machine*, offered to be the choreographer, as long as she played Kazminofia, the main character in *And the Black Panther Cried*.

I had all the help I needed. My only concern now was where our next production would be performed.

After waiting a month for a reply from Brookdale Community College, I was denied the use of their theatre because of the word "Black" in the title. They were afraid of repercussions from the white community even though I explained to them the play had nothing to do with the Black Panthers. They said they couldn't take a chance.

I spent a lot of time at the writing lab with Josh, my English tutor. I knew I was his worst nightmare because I loved to write and when I gave him my assignment for him to read, it was four to five pages. Several times he lost his patience.

"You need to let go of your Portuguese grammar. Now go back and rewrite everything." In Portuguese it would be the table blue but in English it was reversed to the blue table and the wife's man was the man's wife. It was not easy to let go of something ingrained in my brain since childhood. But I had my mind made up and I was not going to give up even after Josh lost his cool several times. To make up for his suffering, I bought him a box of chocolates just so that he would stop hating me. I could not give up. I had to make sense of what I wrote if Mama's poem was going to turn into a script I would be proud of.

Everybody in the cast felt we should have a better name than The Broadville Players. Bernie and Florence suggested The Simy Theatre Company after my mother's name since she was the one who had written "And the Black Panther Cried."

"The name Simy is very unique, and as such it gives us a strong professional name," said Florence.

"With a distinctive name like that," said Bernie. "People will remember us."

The Simy Theatre Company had been born. Mama was going to be very happy with the good news. But I still did not have a place to put on the play.

I finished translating Mama's poem into English. I added a lot more characters to the plot and made sure the dialogue was easy for the audience to understand so they could get personally involved with each character and the story line.

All my cast members were white. I went to Freehold High School to pass the word around that I was looking for talented black high school students. I needed a stage full of African natives—acting, dancing, and singing—because the second part of the show took place in Africa where the black panthers lived.

I started writing the lyrics to Mama's music. In the past,

Mama had written a lot of concert pieces and complete ensembles, and I intended to use her music for the show. It would be a musical drama. I wanted to give Mama full credit not only for her epic poem but also for her music. The show was my gift to her. I felt that if I showed her how much I loved her, she would love me too. I wanted her to be proud of me.

My extra free time was taken up with college in the morning twice a week and teaching guitar, banjo, and bass the rest of the day at the music school. At night and on weekends I practiced my writing assignments for the writing class. I only went home to sleep, and I kept the bedroom window open even though Al complained about it.

Brookdale College sent me a letter stating, "If you remove the word "Black" out of the title, you can produce the play in our theatre, next year."

The cast and crew did not want to wait a whole year. Upon realizing the word "Black" was going to close all doors to us, I took the word out of the title.

Freehold High School agreed to let us use their auditorium for *And the Panther Cried* in the spring. The play was about love, music, and Africa.

I ran a poster contest in the *Asbury Park Press*, and that brought even more attention in the news to our next production.

I was getting better and better at getting free publicity in the newspapers. The idea was to offer something new and exciting; then they were more than happy to print and send us a reporter for an interview.

The poster art competition for the playbill's cover provided me with a large selection of art work by local artists. I chose the black and white illustration of a little girl holding on to her dear friend, a black panther, by Melina Kemp, a young artist from Marlboro.

I offered Melina the use of the school lobby to exhibit and sell some of her other fine artwork, and she got a lot of media coverage, including her picture in the *Asbury Park Press*.

~ *Chapter Twelve* ~

MUSIC BUSINESS

1982

Spring of 1982

With Ralph and Steve in the service, I didn't find any good reason to celebrate my birthday. I asked Steve the piano player to be in charge of the musicians in the pit. It was a lot more appropriate for me to remain backstage helping with the props and pulling on the rope of the hefty curtains to open and close them between scenes, while dwelling on my loneliness.

The cast was comprised of fifty performers. Except for Cathy the choreographer who played the main character, most of the cast members had been in a couple of my previous productions, except for the black members of the cast where this was their first time on stage. I was secure and proud of my script. Taking the writing class at Brookdale College had enlightened me on how to write with more confidence.

At the end of the play, the audience was moved by the dramatic action of the baby being taken into the wild by the black panther and the hunters going after the animal to kill her. But the animal had no intention of killing the child; she had lost her little one after birth and all she wanted was to be the baby's mommy. The reason for the title *And the Panther Cried* was well understood by the end of the performance.

After the show, I received a present from the cast—a ceramic black panther with a little white tear. There was no cast party. My house was too small and no one else offered their place for the gathering.

I sent Mama a playbill of the show signed by the cast, the musicians, and the crew. I also sent her a large metal trophy engraved with the inscription: "This Academy Award is presented to Simy, for her original musical And the Panther Cried, USA 1982."

Mama had heard about the Hollywood Academy Awards presented to the American movie stars on television and I was hoping that since it was coming from America, she would believe she gotten the real thing. It was a lie but it did not hurt anyone. My only purpose was to bring her joy and a feeling of personal achievement.

A politician from the town of Howell called. She was the mayor's right hand and wanted to discuss a private matter. I had seen the Howell sign, south of us, just before reaching Lakewood. I had looked for the town once during one of my expeditions into the countryside. There was no town. Most likely it had been a cowboy town that disappeared as the highway went through it.

I invited her to our house. I served homemade butter cookies and tea and did my best not to show how nervous I felt meeting a government person for the first time in my life. "I have been keeping track of your activities through the news," she said. "I'm very impressed with the volunteer work you provide to the young people in your community. My intentions are to start a Cultural Arts Committee in Howell, because the young people in Howell are in dire need of someone like you. My son is a teenager and a very talented musician he will appreciate anything you can do to promote his talent."

"If your son is talented I can always put him in one of my shows, but I really don't know anything about committees." I had no desire to be in the government.

"I have devised the Cultural Arts Committee with you in mind so you can have the township sponsoring whatever you want to do in our community. You don't worry about anything, you just go to the meetings and tell them what you want to do and that's it."

Sounded easy enough, I accepted her offer. She promised to call as soon as she got the group started which may take a few months. I told Al about it and he said, "She's probably after the mayor's job."

After doing a small variety show at a senior center in Freehold with Julie and Bob, two of my younger guitar students, I came up with a routine that worked great for children's birthday parties.

I created my own persona by hiding behind a painted clown's face and used a glittery cape to make myself look like I could fly away while I danced and sang, "I want to live forever. I want to learn how to fly…high!"

The parents paid me $50 to entertain their kids for forty-five minutes. I used a paper towel roll to make the announcements for the acts. For each humorous act, I pulled off a piece of paper towel with a comical, silly drawing already done. I showed it around like a playing card, and then I made it into an airplane and threw it toward the kids sitting on the floor around me. They loved the artwork because it was like what a child would draw. I sang but I did not talk; I was too aware of my foreign accent. At each party I inflated balloons which Julie and Bob passed around. Then they played the bongo drums along with the birthday child, and the other children sang along while I played the guitar.

Each time I did a birthday party I let myself do whatever

came naturally. My favorite activity, besides dancing with the kids, was to roll on the floor acting childishly and have everyone doing the same with me while trying to hold onto their balloons with their bare feet. Julie and Bob got paid five dollars each for being my assistants, and since they were only eight years old, they felt very special. Their parents were also very proud of them for being employed.

I knew I was allergic to our new home. It made me sad that Al made fun of me, even though he heard me sneezing and coughing and my eyes looked like glazed cherries whenever I was home.

I decided to take matters into my own hands and went to the health department in Freehold and described what my health was like since I had moved into the modular home. They gave me a lot of information. "Modular home manufacturers use formaldehyde to treat the carpets and walls and something like 0.10 parts per million is okay to use, it's the standard safety level recommended but if it's more than the legal dosage allowed, the vapors of this chemical can be very harmful to humans, principally if it gets hot inside the house."

They gave me a list of the types of reactions it caused, some of them, burning sensation in the eyes, nose and throat, losing my voice, nose bleeds, coughing, sneezing, vertigo, nausea, skin rash and headaches, matched my symptoms. The list also mentioned other serious illnesses, like tightness of the chest, bronchitis, fatigue, and cancer including leukemia, lung cancer, heart disease and coma. I was horrified to learn that formaldehyde was the chemical used for embalming the dead. They sold me a testing kit to measure the levels of formaldehyde in our house. I put it in our bedroom and I was told to take the kit back in two weeks to be checked out.

It was the formaldehyde! The test showed a high level of

poison in the air inside our bedroom. To be exact .75, a lot higher than the acceptable range limit for humans to breathe. The fumes were being released from the paneled walls and carpeted floor. I showed the results to Al and told him we needed leave as soon as possible.

"Good luck selling a modular home," he said.

Papa would have been proud of my German side. I drew a map of our neighborhood. The name of the street, the name of the persons living in each home, their age, and their health status was to be entered in my logbook. I began keeping track of the local community obituary, which showed how many people passed away each month at Kona Park.

There were 40 modular homes in Kona Park and I was hoping to get enough people involved so we could hire a lawyer to go after the modular home manufacturer. I was not well received. Some of them closed the door in my face and refused to talk. Others listened and I was able to share my map and charts with them, but once they saw my drawings I was told to stop butting into everybody's life. A few were honest and bluntly told me there was no way they were going to help make the whole thing public; if people knew about it, they would not be able to sell their house and they would be stuck there forever.

No one wanted to be part of my proceedings to get out of Kona Park; even Bernie and Florence preferred not to get involved. I sat in their living room and showed them all the proof I had, but it made no difference.

"Honey, at our age we have no place else to go" said Bernie, "This is our home now."

It was lunchtime, and because I didn't want to hurt Florence's feelings, I ate the egg sandwich she made. I didn't tell her she had forgotten to take some of the eggshells out.

Summer of 1982

A morning appointment was set up with Mr. Price, the owner of Kona Park. I asked Al to come with me as a witness after he promised not to say anything at the meeting.

I told Mr. Price about my health problems since I had moved into his community. I needed him to buy our modular home back from us, and I wanted the same price we had paid for.

"There's nothing I can do for you. You need to sell it yourself just like everybody else."

I wasn't going to give up that easy. I remained focused, "I can't sell my house with a clear conscience, knowing it's full of deadly gases." I took some papers from my attaché case and laid them on his desk. "Let me show you this drawing I made of our community with the addresses and the numbers of people who are dying each month on every street."

While he was looking, I eagerly and confidently presented the information I had collected from the health department. "These are the safety numbers for using formaldehyde inside a home, as required by law, and these numbers are the results I found in my bedroom according to the test kit I got from the health department. And this is the list of illnesses. You'll notice death is one of the side effects." I pointed at the list. "According to the health department, formaldehyde fumes get worse in the summer from the heat."

To make my point, I began putting the papers away, and said, "I guess I'll have to take all this information to the *Asbury Park Press*. Everyone in New Jersey needs to know what happens to them if they choose to retire here."

He asked me to sit down and then asked how much I had paid for the house. "I'll give you a check for the full amount right now if you don't go any further with this matter. Is it a deal?"

No one in the Park supported my efforts. I was on my own. I shook his hand. He asked for all my research papers in exchange for the check. I gave him all my detective paperwork.

I had grabbed the bull by the horns, as Aunt Heydee would say. Al was impressed and so was I. We were given one month to move out.

The children's birthday parties had gotten out of hand. I could not handle so many parties every week. I raised the price to $100 but I was still getting gigs on weekends.

I told the last person who called that I was no longer available. The mother said her little boy had been at one of the birthday parties and was going to be heartbroken if I didn't show up. I couldn't say no.

When the next person called, I was ready. "At present I charge $200 for a birthday party."

"Oh my goodness! Do you know someone else who's less expensive?"

I encouraged her to look in the Yellow Pages. What had possessed me to do children's birthday parties to begin with was beyond me.

Steve came home for good after being discharged from the Navy. His dream of becoming a nurse had turned into a nightmare once he lost his head over the admiral's wife.

He moved in with us and to my dismay, he bought another motorcycle.

I found a reasonably priced two-bedroom apartment at the Windmill Club Apartments in Howell. But we were surrounded by lots of tall trees and thick bushes, making the interior dark and gloomy. I missed the sunshine coming through the large windows of our ranch house at Kona Park. If it weren't for the formaldehyde I would have never moved.

I started thinking about the money we had made from the sale of our modular home and how we should invest it. If we did not do anything wise with it, I knew it would all be gone before we could even blink an eye.

I surprised Al with my idea during a television commercial break. "Our little music store on weekends at the flea market is doing well, so why not open a music center, a real business? There are already several music stores in Freehold but none in Howell. We won't have to worry about competition."

He felt $18,000 was a joke to build a store and fill it with instruments, plus pay for rent, utilities, and so on. However, I was getting better and better at convincing him to do things that made sense to me, and I dragged him to Brookdale College to talk to a retired businessman who gave us lots of good free advice on how to start a business. The advisor said basically the same thing as Al; it would take a miracle to make it work with only $18,000. But I believed in miracles, and the only way they worked out was if you reached for them. I began looking for a store to rent, and within a week I found the perfect place for our Howell Music Center on Route 9.

Our music store would need my undivided attention if we were going to make it. I gave a month's notice to Mr. Crocker and the principal at the high school, where I taught adults. I would still be teaching but at my music center.

Receiving so many goodbye presents from my students was very moving to me. It was a nice feeling to know I would be missed. My favorite gift was from one of the adult classes at Freehold High School, a beautifully framed cartoon showing me with a big smile holding a guitar. Underneath it said, "Ronnie, the Music Maker."

Autumn of 1982

After teaching for so many years, I had a large following of dedicated students and it wasn't easy to find someone to replace me at the music school. Every new potential teacher was looked upon as the devil itself. It was as if I had died and a mean stepmother was taking my place. Some of the kids cried, others told me they were going to quit and never again touch their instruments, and others, like Mark and Tom who were older and should have been more reasonable, used sabotage. Both asked me if they could bring soda and cookies and have a little goodbye party. Marcy, the new teacher, was to be the guest of honor. I was very moved when I came into the classroom and they had everything already set up on a crate with chairs around it. I got my camera to take a picture of the happy, yet sad, gathering.

Mark said, "Let's celebrate this occasion as I offer a welcome glass of cherry soda to Marcy, our new guitar teacher." He held the bottle up and poured the soda onto her lap. "This is the way we feel about the new teacher."

Marcy left the room crying.

"Please don't leave us." Mark put his arms around me along with the other kids.

I hugged everybody and walked away, feeling like I had left my children behind.

Mr. Crocker and I said goodbye as friends and I reassured him that I had no intention of taking any of my students with me. He said, "I'm very sorry to see you leave, but I understand." We hugged. "I'm going to keep the clay head you sculpted a few years back, on top of my desk as a reminder of our friendship." He seemed to be experiencing a soft moment. When he wanted to, he could be a nice person.

Braving A New World

A business van was a necessity for delivering pianos, so I sold my Ford Mustang and put the money toward buying a used white van. I thought it would be a good idea to use it also as an advertisement tool. I drew the layout and gave it to Bob Miller, a graphic designer who offered to come to our parking lot and paint the van on both sides for $200 including the paint. Bob put the logo "Ronnie the Music Maker" on both sides of the van with our store's phone number, and he painted in large black letters, "For All Your Musical Needs Call Howell Music Center."

The van looked awesome!

Al and Steve were busy building teaching rooms in the back of our store, one for drums, two for guitar, and one for piano lessons. Steve accidentally smashed his left thumb with his own hammer and he cursed really bad words. I had never broken or smashed any part of my body, but if I did, I would curse too. I had to take him to the hospital to make sure it was not broken.

The cash register and inventory we had at the flea market had to stay there for the weekends. Looking through the newspaper, I found a couple of used glass counters and a cash register, and in three weeks we were open for business with one piano, a couple of inexpensive guitars, and accessories like guitar strings, picks, kazoos, and so on.

Steve was offered a partnership in the business. He and Al were still not getting along but I was hoping that maybe by working together, as the years went by, they would learn to love and respect each other. The telephone rang in our music store. In the past I always picked up the receiver with my right hand and put it against my right ear, but since I had to write down messages from customers I had to listen with my left ear while I wrote with my right hand. I told the customer on the other end to call back because we had a bad connection. But it wasn't a bad connection—I was deaf in my left ear!

What an amazing, wonderful revelation. It brought light on the subject that I was deaf, not stupid. Wow! Now I could understand why I did so poorly while attending school as a child; I couldn't hear well. I also understood why I always asked people to repeat what they said when I was in a crowded room or just shook my head and said yes, such as on the day in New York when Papa asked me how much the museum tickets were. I also became aware I had been using the vibration, as well as the sound, when tuning a musical instrument. I was special. I had been special all my life. Understanding my handicap was an eye opener. I made an appointment to get tested for a hearing aid. I couldn't wait to wear one just like in the television series, "The Bionic Woman."

Steve was still drinking. I made a deal with him. If he committed himself into a rehab center I would pay for the whole thing, but if he continued to refuse, he would have to look for another job and another place to live. Al said, "Are you out of your mind? A place like that will cost us a fortune and it's going to be a waste of our money."

"I don't care. I have to do something to save our son." The days of not fighting for my children's welfare were gone. I owed Steve that much.

Dr. DeCicco died from cancer. He was only 56. They say sadness can cause cancer. I believe that was exactly what happened to him. Being a compassionate doctor consumed him too much. He felt sorry for everyone he could not help. I remembered him crying when he couldn't help Nelly when she was sick with the flu after having a flu shot.

I was going to miss him. Goodbye, Dr. DeCicco.

While in rehab, Steve and I talked on the phone daily. He told me about some of the patients, but the one he was most impressed with was a man who used to be a big executive type, but due to his cocaine addiction, he had lost all his millions, as well as his wife and children.

We had several music teachers working for us and I no longer felt the desire to teach. I had plenty to do managing our music store and taking fun classes at the community college, but I needed a diversion. My childhood dream of becoming a journalist came to mind. Living in America, the land of opportunity, meant nothing was impossible to achieve.

I took a deep breath, put on my best smile, and walked into The Booster News with a positive mindset, an attitude of belonging, and the feeling that they needed me more than anything else in their lives. I was the personification of Clark Kent when I met with Mr. and Mrs. Crawson, the editors in chief. They told me they were a small town local newspaper, and they could use a few good writers, but they didn't have the budget for it. I couldn't help thinking, today the local *Booster News*, tomorrow *The Asbury Park Press*. One could not go any higher in journalism than writing for *The Asbury Park Press*, in New Jersey. I would just have to take more writing classes at Brookdale College, and a class in journalism would probably be a really good idea.

I told them, "I don't need money. I just want to write about all the exciting things happening in Howell."

They laughed. As a matter-of-fact, everyone in the pressroom thought it was hilarious. *Good, this is very good*, I thought. *I'm already bringing them some joy even if they are laughing at my expense.*

"What kind of experience do you have?" said Mr. Crawson.

"My Aunt Ligia is a famous journalist in Portugal. She writes for the *Diário de Notícias*, the number one newspaper in Lisbon, Portugal, and as her niece, I'm following in her footsteps. I have also written a couple of plays, and have taken a creative writing class at Brookdale College. Isn't that enough?"

Mrs. Crawson winked at me, then turned to her husband and said, "She surely is very secure about her qualifications. George, we really have nothing to lose by hiring her." Then she said, "Dear, how often will you be writing an article for us?"

"How often do you publish the newspaper?"

"Once a week."

"Okay! I'll have an article ready for printing every week. How would you like a headline like, 'Did you know?'" I was a lot more prepared than they expected.

They offered to have an ID badge made by the end of the week. It was to be used to get me into places like township meetings and other political gatherings. Ah, life could be so exciting!

After one month in the rehab hospital, Steve returned home. He swore that he no longer had any desire to drink and was cured. I was glad to have him back.

Winter ending 1982

We were closed for a couple of days on account of the worst snowstorm ever to hit New Jersey. I loved driving in the snow; my van was invincible with snow tires. I got in my car and drove with my camera on hand in case I saw something interesting for the newspaper. I snapped a picture of a man braving the storm to walk along Route 9. All I could see was his gray shadow walking through a blistering snowstorm.

I gave the photo to *The Booster News*, but they didn't print it. They did publish my very first article on December 24th.

Braving A New World

Action Report by Ronnie Esagui

Did you know?

The merchandise sold at Collingswood Auction & Flea Market did not come from the black-market, nor was it stolen from someone's warehouse?

These and other thoughts go through many people's minds when they see the great quality of merchandise sold at such low prices in the Collingswood Auction. But the public has obviously been misinformed.

It all started in 1957 when a man by the name of Clifford Schneider made an extension of his Keyport market at Collingswood, which was previously a farm.

Most of the merchants at Collingswood have their main stores elsewhere, using Collingswood as an extension of their regular business. Because they buy in large quantities from their manufacturers, they are able to sell their merchandise at a lower cost to their customers. Collingswood is actually a "super" shopping center, because they have everything under one roof, from nuts to musical instruments to baby clothes, etc. The Auction has become a landmark in the shore area for its flea market, bargains, collector items, and garage sales.

Lillian, from Lil's Fabric Center, has been there faithfully for the last 24 years. She knows her customers and advises them like a friend.

The Bread Box is the delight of everyone hungry for some healthy homemade breads and cakes.

Karen, at The Greenery, doesn't just sell you a plant; she will wrap it for you with tender care, and give you extra instructions.

Al at Ronnie's Music Den—well he is my husband, so I can tell you the very truth—he is the greatest! Musically speaking, of course!

If you are lucky enough to stop at India and Giftware, say hello to Mrs. Stofer. She shops in New York, to bring you the latest styles.

Ruth Franklin at Egg Roll King cooks Chinese food right before your eyes. The food is fit for a king, which must be the reason for the name.

The whole atmosphere at the Auction is geared for a family outing. The miniature car races...the pet shop...the delicious subs...the egg man...the banana man....

Collingswood is a place to meet your friends, a place to browse and buy, or just pass an evening away in a world where people smile back, because the sugar from your fresh hot Zeppole gives you a mustache. •••

Winter of 1983

As promised, I kept my weekly column going. It was easy—once people knew I wrote for a newspaper, they were eager to get their names in print. I carried a tape recorder with me; that way I always had the correct data just in case my bad hearing was playing its usual trick. Mrs. Marziotti, one of our customers at Ronnie's Music Den, told me her husband, Frank Marziotti, was one of the three surviving members from Bruce Springsteen's very first band, "The Castilles."

I could not believe my luck when she said most likely, her husband would be willing to be interviewed. Later that day, her husband called and invited me over to their house in Farmingdale. I was on Frank's doorstep the next morning. Frank not only answered all my questions, but he was also proud to let me take pictures of him holding a couple of old pictures showing "The Castilles" posing on top of a roof.

Three days went by when I got an unbelievable call at the Howell Music Center from Bruce Springsteen's manager! He said, "You can print Mr. Marziotti's interview but if you dare to print in your newspaper Bruce Springsteen pictures when he was a lad, we are going to sue you." Now that was the most exciting phone call I ever had in my life.

I saved the pictures in my photo album as a souvenir, and gave Frank Marziotti's interview and his picture holding a small picture of "The Castilles," to *The Booster News*. It wasn't my fault if Frank held one of the pictures in his hands, when I flashed my camera.

I was very proud of my final product. It went like this:

Action Report by Ronnie Esagui

Did you know?

Frank Marziotti, one of the three survivors from Bruce Springsteen's very first original band, The Castilles, lives right in Farmingdale?

Frank, how did you get to meet Bruce?

F: That story goes back to 1962 when I had a gas station down on Route 33. One day Tex—Bruce's manager —was going by my gas station and he heard me playing the guitar. He was so impressed that he asked me to help him with a young group of musicians, The Castilles. That's how I met Bruce. I played bass and lead, Bruce played lead, George Theiss did the rhythm. By the way, I heard George has his own band and from what I heard, he is just fantastic.

What happened to the other two members in the band?

F: One died in Vietnam…the other from hepatitis.

What was Bruce like, in those days?

F: He was very skinny, with pimples all over his face. He looked like a little insecure kid, but he was just the opposite. Bruce would come up to me and say, "Is this what you taught me?" To my amazement, he would play it right out and quite well. He had that drive to lead, to succeed in this world. I have to give him all the credit.

Frank, tell me about The Castilles and their music?

F: That brings back some memories. We started with a 50-watt, four channel Premiere amp. We would all hook up to it, even the microphone. One time I was playing in a bar with The Rolling Mountain Boys, and a sailor fell on the amp and it blew up. Tex went out and had it fixed. That amp went through a lot.

Anyway, I had started as an advisor to the band; it was never my intention to play with them. They were a lot younger than I was. Even in the book *Born to Run* I am referred to as "the older fellow," but he calls me by name too. At that time, I was also playing country western with The Daily Brothers and bluegrass with The Rolling Mountain Boys. The Castilles played rock, sort of following The Rolling Stones style. That wasn't my kind of music.

One night, we were playing at the Teen Davue, when a teenybopper, about way high, came up to me, really innocent, she says, "Are you Bruce's daddy?" Well, that just blew my mind. That night, I quit.

After you quit, what did you do?

F: My father was very sick, so I sold the gas station and moved closer to him. I started a part time job, which paid out so well that I still work for that company. Then, about 1974, the tip of my finger on the left hand got amputated in a paper fold machine. As you can imagine, that really messed up my guitar playing. I still play the bass and lead, but I seldom play rhythm because of my finger. My favorite music now is gospel music.

When was the last time you saw or heard from Bruce?

F: Last summer he came by our house. Knowing it was my daughter Wendy's birthday; Tex brought him over to surprise us. He took some pictures of Wendy and Bruce together. Bruce went crazy when he saw the old Premiere amp and his own guitar over there, against the wall. You see, when I left the group in 1966, they still had problems with their equipment, so we learned to carry spares. Bruce had asked me at that time to trade my bass for one of his guitars, so I did. Just about three months ago I returned it to Bruce, through Tex, and I got a big thank you. I'm just happy that I had a part in it. I feel I did good for somebody, somewhere along the line.

Frank, would you play for us at Freehold Township High School and at Howell High this spring for benefit performances toward their Athletic Clubs?

F: I would be delighted. •••

The hearing doctor said I had nerve damage in the left ear and surgery may or may not help. I felt I was better off using a hearing aid and seeing if that helped.
    I told the doctor about my ears hurting when I flew, and I had been playing my electric guitar in loud bands for many years, and also as a kid I had every childhood disease known to mankind. When I asked him if any of those things could have caused my hearing loss, he said probably all of them. I lost some of my hearing as a sick child, some playing loud music as an adult, and then I finished it off by flying. But he was also not certain if it wasn't from

something else.
I will never know the answer for sure.

I got a letter from Mama. "Veronica, you're not going to believe this. I was invited to speak at the University of Coimbra about my books, the music I have written, and the paintings I have done in the last few years. But the best news I have to share with you is that your mama is now featured in *The Dictionary of Famous Women in the World*. I put the dictionary in the mail and you should be receiving it in about a week."

Having her name in such a book along with Mother Theresa and the Queen of England was a great honor, and if anyone deserved to be recognized for her accomplishments, Mama definitely did. I felt very proud of her.

Steve and I worked well together. He had a natural knack for selling musical instruments, and we were becoming well-known in the community. Each day was busier than the day before. But when working with Al, it was another story. He could not help being negative and we did our best to keep him busy doing anything besides taking care of customers. Al would rather talk about dirty politicians with their hands in people's pockets and other downbeat things which caused customers to forget why they came in to buy a musical instrument.

We did a lot better when Al was not in the Howell Music Center. Thank God for weekends, where Al was still happily working at Ronnie's Music Den in the Collingswood Market.

Our teaching staff was comprised of two guitar teachers, a bass teacher, two piano teachers, one sax and flute teacher, a drummer, and, a newly hired clarinet teacher who liked to brag about having graduated from Juilliard School, New York.

I put together a plastic board hanging on the wall behind

the counter. It was magnetic, and I drew the days of the week on it. When someone called for a music lesson, all we had to do was set up the magnet with the new student's name under the teacher's schedule. It worked magnificently.

While looking in the Yellow Pages, I came across an interesting profession—chimney sweep. Pete the chimney sweep was delighted to be featured in my column and we made a date to meet at his house.

It was just like I had imagined, his house was covered with moss and surrounded by a jungle of trees. When I met Pete, his only visible facial features were his black jade eyes. The dark curly hair came down to his husky shoulders and covered his bushy eyebrows and the dark thick beard, if white, would have made Santa jealous. His wife, a young girl in her mid-twenties, stepped out onto the small porch, wearing a starched white apron over her long plaid country dress and they held hands when they spoke. They had been married for six months. When I asked him for a picture on top of his roof, he disappeared and within a few minutes, he came out of his house dressed in the traditional all-black garb including his black top hat. Before leaving, I snapped a picture of him standing on the roof of his house next to his chimney.

Action Report by Ronnie Esagui

Did you know?

Chimney sweeps are hated in Portugal? I know that many people couldn't care less about this subject, but how would you feel if one evening as you were sitting with your family eating lunch, someone came screaming at your door, "The chimney man is here!"

As you open your mouth to say, "What the..." a cloud

of black filth comes pouring down the chimney spreading crusty soot all over the furnishings. That's the way they do it over there.

But this is not the case with Pete, the chimney sweep from Howell. As his wife puts it, "Pete takes so much care and pride in his job that I confidently tell all the customers they can have a white velvet couch by the fireplace because they won't even know he was there."

Pete started this business after reading an article on "How To Be a Chimney Sweep."

Children love Pete. When they ask him, "Do you think that Santa really comes down the chimney?"

Pete replies, "I don't know." But then he reaches behind the damper to clean the smoke shelf, and to the children's amazement… "What's this?" he asks after he finds a little piece of red felt. "Could it be that Santa ripped his suit on the way down?"

It's part of his job to find birds, squirrels, and raccoons nesting in the chimney. Pete loves animals and he doesn't smoke them out or burn them like many people do. He takes them to Allaire State Park.

"My job is a lot of fun," says Pete. "Once, I found a big raccoon inside someone's chimney. He was just lying on his back and playing with a plastic ball. The homeowners called me in because this creature's family was living inside their chimney and playing on their roof at night. Putting a screen over the chimney is nothing to a raccoon; he'll chew a hole in it and get right down to the warmth of his new home. I have flue caps guaranteed against intruders. There's also a problem with dead birds and squirrels inside the chimney. A natural thing happens, maggots eat the bodies, and then the maggots form into cocoons. Then, in the spring, the dampness and the heat hatch these cocoons into very large flies. Also, many people make the mistake of loading up their fireplace with too much wood, and, by running it cold, it causes creosote buildup on the walls. That's why there are so many chimney fires."

I was happy to meet Pete and his wife for obvious reasons. Since childhood, I have thought that chimney sweeps lived inside chimneys just waiting for the right moment to strike whole families with soot.

Even though I don't have a fireplace, if I ever have one, I know just what to do. I'll call Pete, the chimney man!•••

Mr. Robertson, our clarinet teacher, had a mean streak to his nature. He walked into our store as if everybody should bow to his greatness and seemed to enjoy insulting his students. The other teachers complained to me that they could hear him yelling at his private students. I tried reasoning with him. "If you are not so harsh with your students," I said. "You will get better results."

"Are you telling me how to do my job?"

"I'm just suggesting that you get more bees with honey than vinegar." I tried to smile. Confrontation was my worst enemy.

"Don't patronize me." He pointed a finger at me. "I'm the teacher and I make the decisions about my students, not you."

"Yeah, but I'm your boss." I crossed my arms and stared straight at him. "You're no longer welcome at our Music Center."

"You can't fire me, I'm a Juilliard graduate and my qualifications make me a professional and..."

"Your qualifications should be about inspiring your students to be the best they can be, according to their abilities. You have no right to make anyone feel inferior to you. Who cares what school you graduated from? You don't belong in our Music Center. Please leave."

"You can't fire me, missy."

"Very well, I'll call my husband and my son right now and we'll see about that." I began dialing the phone on the counter.

"Oh yeah, now I'm really scared, I'd better leave." On his way out he turned toward me and pointed his finger at me again. "Remember this, you woman! Someday you're going to call and beg me to come back to teach but I'm not coming back! I'm the one that's leaving. I quit! Goodbye!" He banged the front door on the way out.

What a creep!

For Valentine's Day week I wrote:

Action Report by Ronnie Esagui

Did you know?

Saint Valentine's Day derives from the ancient Roman feast of Lupercalia, for which young Roman men and maidens drew partners for the coming year by lottery. This day is also associated with the legend that birds choose their mates on this date!

With this in mind, I started interviewing would-be lovers with the question: "What are you doing on Valentine's Day?"

My first interviewee was a young man walking out of a supermarket. "Excuse me sir. I'm from the *Howell Booster News*. Would you mind answering a few questions?"

"Go ahead, ask!"

"Will you be sending flowers to your girlfriend on Valentine's Day?"

"I don't have a girlfriend and as far as I'm concerned, Valentine's Day sucks wind!"

I decided to go someplace else and look for a couple instead. I went to Burger King; it seemed to be a family type setting. In the parking lot a couple with three kids were getting out of their car. I waited eagerly and then said to them, "Hi, I'm from…"

"We're not interested!"

Maybe it was my approach. I was not in the right place at the right time, so I picked the lobby of the hotel in downtown Freehold. The next couple was going to get the full treatment. I attached my newspaper identification badge to my lapel and the flashing camera was ready for action. A couple entered the lobby, the camera's flash was bright and I greeted them with a smile.

"What's that? Why did you take our picture?" screamed the old man with the young beautiful girl. "You have no right! Give me that film! I'm here on business with my…. I mean my…friend."

After I opened my camera to give the gentleman the roll of film, which he quickly snatched out of my hand, I quietly left the lobby.

When I got nervous, I ate. So I went directly to the restaurant across the street and ordered a large portion of French fries and a corned beef sandwich. And that's when I realized that you get what you pay for. The service was good and the waitress got her tip. I looked around…A couple was sitting at a table with their child. Busy eating hamburgers, they were the perfect family picture. I wasn't going to take any chances, and as I approached them I was careful to say something nice. "You have such a beautiful child. What's her name?"

"It's not a she, it's a he, and his name is Francis," said the mother, and she turned her back to me.

"Well, at that age you really can't tell, right?" Not allowing her time to answer me, I added quickly, "I'm a reporter for the *Howell Booster News* and would like to give you five dollars for being so nice and answering a few questions."

"Sure, have a seat. Are you going to take our pictures?" She smiled as she put her son on her lap.

"Well," I said, a bit embarrassed, "I already used the whole roll of film for another interview. What will you both be doing on Valentine's Day?"

"When is Valentine's Day?" asked her husband.

"You see how he is?" yelled his wife, pulling the child away from her and sitting him back on the seat. "We've been married for six years and I have to remind him of our anniversary every year. Tom only knows his birthday!"

"What do you mean by that?" asked her husband. "I'm tired of your constant nagging. It's nobody's business, our private life, anyway."

I got up and handed Tom the five dollars but his wife grabbed the money before it reached him.

That same evening, in my desperation, I turned to my son Steve and said, "Do you know anybody who's actually celebrating Valentine's Day?"

"Yes, of course. You and Dad," he replied.

"What do you mean?"

"I'm taking you both out for dinner. Happy Valentine's Day, Mom!" •••

When it came to visibility, our Music Center was barely seen by the traffic going south on Route 9 and the vehicles driving north missed us completely. Steve loved my idea of moving our business to the corner of the mall and as such, would be facing the road. Al hated changes of any kind, but no longer put much of a fight. He would say, "Once you have your mind made up, I already know there's nothing I can do to stop you, so go ahead."

Al's conversation with customers was mainly about what he read or heard on the news and he took a certain pleasure in further enhancing how the world was nothing but a miserable place to live among thieves and people without honor. But there was one person who was more negative than him—Mike, the owner of the pet store in our strip mall. Steve and I watched a woman leaving Mike's shop crying, while trying to console her sobbing seven-year-old son who held a small fish bowl with a dead fish.

Steve asked them what happened and she said, "The store owner accused me of killing the healthy fish he sold us two days ago, and then he threw us out of his store."

One morning Mike found the glass windows in his shop had been smashed in during the night with stones. He came by and asked, "Why would anyone be that malicious and break my windows? Now you know why I don't like people, principally snotty kids. This is it! I've had it with the human race. I'm closing my shop as soon as my lease is over at the end of this year."

"What are you going to do when you close your store?"

"Go back to my farm."

I was extremely disappointed with my hearing aid. Anything touching the hearing aid made it buzz. I could not be hugged. I could not bring the telephone handle to my left ear. In a busy room the hearing aid was also a problem. It worked as an amplifier, and did not provide the direction from which the person was talking to me. I had to pivot on my feet like a lighthouse to detect who was speaking.

I blamed myself for the predicament I was in. I had wished to be like The Bionic Woman and had gotten my wish, except the darn hearing aid was not working as well as I thought it would. On top of that, I was allergic to the plastic mold and it made my ear itch like crazy so my ear canal would get hot, red, and sore by the end of the day.

I used the hearing aid every day for two whole weeks before I put it away in my jewelry box.

Ralph called. He was out of the Air Force, but had decided to remain in Phoenix, Arizona, and attend one of their colleges. In Phoenix he had good friends and he loved the weather. I was disappointed knowing that he would not be home soon. But little by little, I was learning to let go and accept my sons as adults and as such they were entitled to make their own decisions.

I finally received an official letter from the Howell Township appointing me to the newly formed Cultural Arts Committee. That meant once a month I would have to attend a committee meeting. I told Steve, "I'm worried. I don't know anything about committees or politics."

"Don't worry Mom," he said. "Remember what you always said to me, 'What's the worst that can happen?'"

He was right; I had forgotten.

The guitar teacher and piano teacher requested we soundproof the drum room on account that it was difficult to teach with the sound of drums coming through the adjacent walls. The cost of soundproofing the walls was not in our budget. I had heard about egg cartons being very effective for insulating walls, so I bought dozens and dozens of unused egg cartons from the egg man in Collingswood and Steve helped me to staple the cartons to the walls. The drum room looked startlingly unique.

Drummers were coming in to look at the egg carton walls and wanted to rent the room for practice. Others signed up for lessons. It was amazing what word-of-mouth about something unusual but practical could do as advertising. Steve got rid of his dearly beloved motorcycle. He had been on his motorcycle waiting for the light to turn green when he heard the sound of brakes squeaking and felt the heat coming from the car's engine behind his back. Right then and there he had a vision of the car behind him driving right through him. That was enough visualization for him to put his bike up for sale and start looking for a hefty car.

I was absorbed with promoting the Howell Music Center, writing weekly for the newspaper, taking classes at Brookdale College, and preparing for my next theatre production.

The Cultural Arts Committee's once-a-month meeting

turned out to be a real dud. The members were a bunch of snobbish, middle-aged women. Their interests were far from cultural activities. Their only goal in life was to do a strawberry festival once a year. Everything I brought up got voted down or moved to the next meeting.

Ralph returned home. Apparently life in Arizona had been fine while in the military but as a civilian, it had much to be desired. I did not ask for details. I was just happy to see him again. I felt alive having my two sons back. They were my very best friends; I could talk to them about anything and they knew they could do the same. We were a family again.

I put an ad in the newspaper; "Looking for artists to donate their artwork for the cover of our next playbill, *A Taste of Broadville III*." I figure getting free art had worked great for other shows, why not continue? I only got one response to the ad. Tracey, an art teacher in Howell, called to ask if I would like to look at some of her students' paintings.
    She walked into our store carrying a bunch of canvases under both arms. I was impressed with Tracey's devotion to her students and we became instant friends. I had hit the jackpot!
    Since the Cultural Arts Committee was not cooperating with my cultural endeavors, I decided to continue my musical productions on my own. I held auditions at the Howell Music Center and got the cast for "A Taste of Broadville III."
    The musical production got set up for May 12th and 13th at Freehold High School and May 19th and 20th at Howell High School.

I thought that Ralph would be happy working with us but when I asked him, he said, "Mom, I'm not a salesman. I'd rather work in electronics, which is something I enjoy."

He applied for work at a television repair shop in Howell and got hired. Al said, "I don't want both of them living with us. Ralph has a job, let him get his own apartment."

Al got his wish. Within a month Ralph was more than happy to move out on his own and Steve and his newest girlfriend got their own apartment.

~ *Chapter Thirteen* ~

THE JOURNALIST

1983-1984

Spring of 1983

A woman came into our Music Center and we talked for a while. Her name was Sandy and she lived up the street from the Music Center and had been meaning to come in and check us out for quite some time. Then she looked at me as if she had discovered we were long lost sisters and said, "You're a dream maker. I recognize you because I'm one too."

I thought she was a bit peculiar and I had guessed it correctly. She insisted on bringing me lunch every day because she felt I worked too hard and she wanted to make sure I had enough nourishment. I did not know how to tell her to stop without offending her and tried to convince her to open an Italian restaurant. She made the most amazing spaghetti with meatballs.

Sandy wanted to help me with the next variety show since she had backstage experience. She had worked in Hollywood, California, with some famous actresses and told me confidential stuff about one famous movie star whom I used to regard as a nice person. I was disappointed to know that Sandy quit because this actress was very demanding and hard to work with.

A severely-aged young man (that was the best way I could describe someone who you know is young but looks very old, like when you see a baby with an old person's face and yet you know it's a baby) walked into our music center and said, "Oh wow, Ronnie, what are you doing here?"
"Have we met before?"
It was Richard! He used to be my guitar student and had played keyboard with Ralph and Steve, in our backyard, when they were in their early teens. We had lost contact through the years. He looked ghastly and was practically bald. Losing most of your hair at twenty-three had to be devastating!
In the summer of 1980 he had woken up one morning in the hospital after suffering a heart attack. He was taking heart medication which was affecting his memory, but he had no other choice if he was going to live.
Richard had come in looking for a job as a piano teacher. I hired him without hesitation.

Writing every week for the newspaper opened my eyes to life beyond my own world. After I interviewed a truck driver, I became aware of truck drivers and the perils they faced with ordinary or careless drivers like me.

Action Report by Ronnie Esagui

Did you know?

"Most four wheelers, as we truck drivers refer to cars, don't realize that a truck can't just stop," said Paul Van Derveer. "Everything works by air and not by a hydraulic system like a car has. Most of these trucks are running 80,000 pounds down the road compared to a 4,000 pound car. People don't know that we have blowouts; sometimes we're running with re-capped tires, a tire gets worn-out, and as it gets hot it starts to fall apart. I mean, you got rubber flying everywhere. These lumps of rubber can hit a car and scare you into an accident. You see, people like to drive side-by-side with the trucks. I shouldn't say this, but I tell you, there are a lot of people out there driving that are sick...they like to play games...they jump in front of the truck and put on their brakes, then they take off, because they know you can't catch up with them. They don't care, they cuss you out, and they have no respect, giving you all kinds of gestures with their fingers. I don't know if they are trying to commit suicide or what. On top of it, they are driving sub-compact cars. The wind from these trucks is enough to move other trucks to the side, so you can imagine what it does to a car or a bike. A large majority of people today are not honest, and they will not admit if it was their fault. After a while you get to the point that you say, 'I am not going to hurt myself or anyone else,' but if the driver in front of me causes a problem, well...I wouldn't hurt a bug, but I got a family."

Paul drives an 18-wheeler 1979 dump trailer. If you happen to see him or any of his fellow truck drivers down the road, please get out of their way! •••

Producing *A Taste of Broadville III* at two high schools was a lot of work! The music ensemble went fine at Howell High School, but at Freehold High School, I made the mistake of adding six student violinists. Their violin teacher didn't show up for the show. I cringed in the pit as I heard the violins playing out of tune. During intermission I felt it was better if I didn't show my face and remained in the pit.

A woman came over to me and said, "Magnificent, just absolutely magnificent! The sound of the violins in the background brought tears to my eyes. Very impressive what you have accomplished with these kids!

Congratulations to your group of young musicians."

I figured she was tone deaf but I thanked her for the compliment and then mingled joyfully into the crowd.

We had the cast party at our apartment, and everything went rather well until the next morning when I found my favorite plant, which Ralph had given me a month before, had no leaves left except for one.

It was a marijuana plant! I was against smoking marijuana just like I was against smoking tobacco, but I did not share with Al that I had been lovingly nurturing a marijuana plant inside our living room. I carefully placed the leaf in my photo album to be able to look at its beautiful leaf design at my leisure. It had made a striking houseplant. *A Taste of Broadville III* did very well financially, but I missed the old days. These were not my students, they were kids that auditioned. I did not have a close relationship with them as I used to have with my students. I did not feel energized afterward and I blamed the Cultural Arts Committee for not being involved.

Summer of 1983

Besides writing for *The Booster News* about community events and some of the people I met with interesting lives, sometimes I enjoyed writing about topics that might bring a smile to the reader. I knew it was working because I began receiving phone calls from locals telling me how much they enjoyed my column. Enjoying the freedom to write whatever I wanted, I started exploring some of my past experiences while adding a little of my own Portuguese drama to spice it up just a little. I wrote the next article while reminiscing over the summer of 1973 when my kids were nine and ten years old. I had told the story several times but I had never written about it.

Braving A New World

Action Report by Ronnie Esagui

Did you know?

Summer camp can be an exuberating experience for both parents and children?

According to our vacation plans of two weeks, it was agreed that both our kids would have to go to summer camp, while Al and I went on vacation. Our plans didn't include the children. They would be away from us for the first time, and it took a bit of work to convince them that they were better off without us. After all, they wouldn't really enjoy going to Bermuda, stuck inside a small boat with water all around for miles and miles. In camp they would be with other children, and the food seemed colorful in the brochures we had received; their favorite meals, hotdogs and hamburgers, looked very appetizing. There was also a beautiful lake for fishing and swimming, and archery, and even bike riding available. It was left to their imagination the fun they were going to have while we, the parents, were doomed to a ship drifting toward some lonely island.

After packing the recommended camp list of ten towels, four bed sheets and pillowcases, twelve pairs of underwear, and so much more, I felt like I was marrying them off. As we drove them to camp we happily sang our favorite song, "Ninety-nine bottles of beer on the wall…"

Getting to Pennsylvania was easy; the problem was finding the camp. After an hour and a half of back-and-forth, we realized we were in the camp! The camp's activity director took both children by the hand as we waved goodbye with guilt written all over our faces. We rapidly drove off.

As soon as we got to the New York harbor, we mailed them a postcard; "We miss you. We wish you were here.

Love, Mom and Dad. Kisses and hugs xoxoxo."

Like two lovebirds free from responsibility or any of life's problems, we boarded the cruise ship holding hands and hopping and skipping in unison.

"Just married?" asked the ship's attendant.

"Yes, we're on our honeymoon!"

"Well, let me make a note of that," said the eager-to-please ship attendant.

As we entered our private cabin, Noo, our cabin boy, brought us a bottle of champagne and a basket of fresh fruit with compliments from the captain.

There was an early bird smorgasbord for breakfast, then regular breakfast, lunch, and then lunch brunch, early dinner and late dinner, and—for those still starving—midnight smorgasbord madness. After three days, Al and I looked like we were pregnant. The movies were the latest; the stage shows were direct from Las Vegas. There was a casino on board, and I even enjoyed shooting at flying dishes. The weather was beautiful and so was the fearful Bermuda Triangle; perfect with the sun painting the clear blue ocean with silver waves. The islands like emeralds of green lush vegetation sparkled in the distance waving their palm trees to the soft breeze.

Reality hit us when once again we were driving up and down the hills of Pennsylvania trying to find the summer camp where we had abandoned our children. They weren't in their cabin. The place looked deserted. "The poor things" had been there for two whole weeks, all alone in that forsaken place. They were probably skin and bones, refusing any form of nutrition and crying themselves to sleep. How could we have been so cruel, so selfish to just abandon them in that place?

Someone told us that they were out in the field. We ran into the field through the deep mud that covered our feet and it seemed to get worse as it started to rain. My children! My babies, unprotected from the elements and out in a field of mud!

We heard the sound of motorized bikes. Two dirt bikes appeared in the distance, and there was a mean, rough look about them.

Al said, "It's the Hell's Angels!"

As the dirt bikes got closer, we could see their muddy clothes, and as they took their helmets off they screamed, "Hi Mom and Dad. Do you think you could leave us here for the summer?" •••

A day did not go by at the Music Center without having to listen to Rosa, one of our voice teachers, telling me how much she was in love with Stewart, our piano teacher. She was married and had three small children, and he was also married and had two children of his own. Then she began calling me, in the middle of the night no less, "Ronnie, you're the only friend I have that I can talk to. I love Stewart." She was crying. "Tell me what to do."

I couldn't help feeling a twinge of resentment for being awakened twice that week. I wanted to tell her to grow up and get with it, but instead I said, "You need to think about your children and his too. Is it worth to break down two families?"

"I would gladly give up my family to be with him."

What a selfish person. What did she want me to do give her my blessing? I pondered why people thought I had the answers to everything. There were lots of things beyond my control. My brother José was a good example. I had racked my brain trying to figure a way to help him and our parents out of the situation they were in, but there was no simple answer. I was even willing to have my parents come live with us, but José would have to be put into a home for schizophrenics. I did not know much about mental illness but I knew enough about it from watching scary movies and I would be afraid to have him living with us.

It was not my brother's fault for being the way he was. If anything, I blamed the doctors in our family for drugging José for a whole year when he had typhus. Also, the experimental drugs they had him on when he was younger to see if they could control his asthma must have messed up his mind. He was a perfectly normal mischievous youngster until they started medicating him.

What medical doctors were allowed to do, freak me out! In my opinion they were nothing but legalized drug pushers. My mother was a good example of drug abuse, or I should say, of using prescription drugs for every pain or ailment under the sun. One pill for the heart, another for the liver, another for the nerves, another for the headaches, another for fatigue, another to sleep, another to wake up. I could help most people I knew, except my own family.

What a pleasant surprise! With the month of July soaring into the 90s, *The Booster News* printed my winter snowstorm picture on the front page. It was a full-page spread with the headline "Think Cool." They not only gave me credit for taking the picture, but they also mentioned I was the owner of Howell Music Center.

I received a telephone call from Mrs. Gans, a happy reader who said, "I always look forward to reading your column while drinking my morning coffee." She invited me to her house for lunch and to meet two of her girlfriends. I couldn't say no.

There I was having a tuna sandwich at Mrs. Gans's house when she took a deep breath and said to her two girlfriends and me, "I wish our daughters could have the opportunity to model. They're so beautiful! But, unless we know someone in the field, we can only dream about."

I hated hearing people making wishes and daydreaming about what they wanted to do but did not do anything about it.

"So, why don't you get your girls into a fashion show yourselves?" I said.

"You have got to be kidding. We don't even know where to start. Would you be willing to help us?" asked Mrs. Caputo.

I put on my never-give-up thinking cap and let my thoughts be heard. "Sounds to me like an easy thing to do. Make it a benefit for the Township First Aid Squad. If you donate all proceeds to them I'm sure they will be more than happy to let you use their spacious building just for a couple of hours the day of the event."

"What about the clothes?" asked Mrs. Iomio.

"I'll go to a few good clothing stores and I'm sure that when I tell them there will be free publicity in the newspapers, they'll donate their best clothes to be shown. So, let's go for it!" I took a deep breath and kept on going. "Now, the question is, can the girls get a few male classmates from high school to model along with them?"

Patti Gans, Alyssa Caputo, and Christina Iomio swore that finding male volunteers to model the tuxedos was going to be a breeze. My idea was to have the couples dressed as brides and grooms at the end of the show.

It was going to be the best fashion show Howell had ever seen. Mrs. Gans and her girlfriends were very excited about it and so were their daughters Patti, Alyssa and Christina.

If I was going to be successful at bringing cultural events to Howell, I needed someone voting for me. I needed a friend on the Cultural Arts Committee. The women in the committee were fixated on putting on another spring strawberry festival! Whenever I brought up a cultural project they complained it was too much work. I asked my new friend Tracey, the art teacher from Howell, whether she would accept a position with the Howell Cultural Arts

Committee, if I could get her in.

I called Marcy, my contact person at the township and she agreed to add Tracey as a member of the Cultural Arts Committee.

Autumn of 1983

Tracey attended her first Cultural Arts Meeting and sat quietly next to me as I brought up the idea of doing musicals at the Preventorium Road Auditorium.

Betty, one of the members who smelled like she had dived into a pool of cheap perfume said in her scratchy, deep voice, "Honey, that place has been abandoned for years. It's nothing but a large storage building."

"I've looked," I said. "And it has a really nice-size stage; it just needs to be cleaned up. And the room, oh my goodness, it can fit about two hundred chairs. Just imagine what kind of productions we could do with all that space."

Betty whispered something to Laura, obviously her close friend because she did not mind the stink. Laura laughed, her yellow stained overbite teeth became more visual when she put both hands on the table, bent forward toward me and said, "You always come up with extreme ideas. Let's think of something more reasonable." And they all went back to talking among themselves.

I was embarrassed to speak my mind. Tracey didn't say much, but she was busy sketching rapidly on her notepaper hidden on her lap under the table. She drew a little mouse looking up at a bunch of growling fat-cats. She scribbled "Ronnie" under the mouse and "The Committee" under the cats.

Tracey was right; I was a scared, little mouse. But even though my voice did not carry my words, I was determined not to give up. I would keep repeating my requests over and over again at each meeting and sooner or later they would have to listen. As my mother said to me so many times while I was growing up, "Verónica, you are a hardheaded German just like your father." True, but I also possessed the Brazilian positive attitude of Aunt Heydee and Mama which made me believe that nothing was impossible.

I was busy at the Howell Music Center dusting some of the guitars hanging on the wall, when I happened to look through the glass windows and saw the latest most incredible thing: Breakdancing! Right there in front of our door, three boys between the ages of fourteen and sixteen were trying to outdo each other on the sidewalk. They were better than the breakdancers I had seen on television! A crowd gathered, applauding each move. When the boys stopped, I was stoked and asked them where else they danced. Marlon, their leader, said, "Any sidewalk we can find." My mind was racing; I asked them if they would like to dance on national television and also compete in Howell with other breakdancers from other towns. They were ecstatic.

The Cultural Arts Committee members would most likely look at breakdancing as a trashy kind of entertainment and vote not to be involved. Meanwhile, I began calling television stations. I did not intend to stop until I found one station willing to have them as guest dancers.

I really needed one more friend in the Cultural Arts Committee. The more friends I had, the more votes I would get. I was not savvy about politics but I was starting to learn the ropes. My friend Francis would be perfect as a committee member. I had met Francis as a client at our store and we had become friends. She had three children, and was very interested in music and the arts. Francis was black, so she was also a minority like me; trying to be heard and understood. She was always in a constant battle against ignorance and prejudice.

I called Marcy once again and told her about my dilemma with the Cultural Arts Committee. "How can I bring culture to the town if the committee is anti-cultural?" I also told her about Francis, and how much of an asset she would be to our community.

Marcy said, "I'm very sorry about what you're going through. I started this committee with you in mind. You don't have to worry anymore; from now on, whatever you want, the committee will go along with it and when it comes to Francis, give her a call and let her know she's in."

I got a national television station in Philadelphia interested in showing my breakdancers on their station. The date was set for the end of December. The boys were euphoric when I called them to give them the good news.

We got together and came up with a good name for them—The Floor Lords.

The Fashion Show brought in $550 from the tickets sold. The models had their day in the spotlight, including Jill Kennedy who used to be one of my guitar students in Freehold. I had not forgotten how Jill always wanted to be a model. My friend Tracey brought in Miss Monmouth County and Miss Senior Citizen of New Jersey as guests of honor.

I was addicted to making people happy. When someone told me something awful happened to them, I looked for the positive side of the story, and when I was done lifting their mood, they were laughing and wondering why they had gotten upset in the first place. I loved changing emotional darkness into shiny happiness. If everybody were to do that for each other, the world would be a better place to live and there would be peace on earth.

Winter ending 1983

It happened! I took The Floor Lords to Philadelphia where they performed their dancing routine live on television. Getting them there safely wasn't easy. It was snowing heavily both ways, and the roads were icy and slippery (it always seemed to snow in Pennsylvania). I got lost trying to find the television station and then trying to get out of Philadelphia. Still, we got there with one hour left to relax!

The Floor Lords' parents never called to ask any questions. I should not have been surprised. It was no different from when I used to live in Freehold where the children in the neighborhood spent a lot of time at our house but I never met their parents. I had been lucky as a mother, Ralph and Steve saw me as their friend and we always shared our life experiences with one another even if sometimes I did not agree with their choices.

Winter of 1984

I was alone at the Howell Music Center, sitting on the bench close to the front door and tuning an acoustic guitar, when an average-looking man in his mid-forties looked through the glass window and then came in. I got up and said, "May I help you?"

"No, I'm not looking for anything in particular. I'm more interested in talking to you." He sat on the bench.

I put the guitar up on the wall.

"What kind of music do you like?" he asked as he remained seated.

"Rock," I answered.

"Sit next to me. You work every day?"

I sat next to him. "Yes." I said. I was alone in the store and was afraid to show any fear. Perhaps he would think there were other people just not up front.

"Are you happy?" he asked.

"Yes."

"I notice you have a slight accent. Where are you from?"

"Portugal."

"How old are you?"

"Forty."

"You have nice shoes. Do you have a fetish for shoes?"

"What's that?"

"Obviously you must be very naïve if you don't know what I'm saying."

He picked a couple of loose hairs off my sweatshirt and said smiling, "Now you look better." He stood. I remained seated. He put his hand on the front door, and before leaving turned to me and said, "You're very sweet."

My heart was pounding hard and my hands were shaking. It had been an overall freaky feeling that scared the heck out of me. Steve walked in and I told him what happened. He said, "You're a beautiful lady Mom, he was attracted to you."

I would rather have been invisible.

The Committee gave me the go-ahead to start working on the breakdance competition. I got the Howell High School location for a minimum cost since all ticket proceeds would be donated to the school's music department.

I sent invitations to several high schools and the response was incredible. The Floor Lords would be competing against The Beat Boyz from Red Bank Catholic High School, the NO-ON-Rockers from Shore Regional High School, Girl Jessie from Holmdel High School, Fresh Force Rockers from Keyport High School, Fabulous Floor Rockers from Freehold Borough High School, and In-ZX Breakers from Long Branch High School.

A disc jockey called "Unique Malik," offered his services for the breakdance competition.

It did not take me too long to find five judges: Andrew Profaci, instructor at Arthur Murray's Studios and Studio

54, New York City; Bruno Gallucio, Chairman of the Howell recreation department; Bob Maus, general manager for Ocean County Center for the Arts; Angela Coenblith, instructor at Lakewood School of Dancing and Theatre Arts; and Art Beins, chief instructor at U.S. Black Cat Kenpo, Karate Academy in Howell.

It was going to be the best breakdancing competition of the century and in Howell, of all the places in the world!

Spring of 1984

May 18, 1984 was a day to be remembered in the history of the Howell Township. The talent observed was beyond anyone's imagination. I wondered where those kids would be going from there, and what would become of them after the competition. They were street smart and tough, yet each one of them had that special look when one knows they were the chosen one; the elite. They were the cream of the crop, and they danced with complete confidence as if they had been born to do it. They gave their very best and they had no doubt in their hearts, there had to be a talent scout in the midst of that auditorium which was filled to capacity.

There was nothing wrong in dreaming. Someone was going to put them up on a pedestal along with all the great stars who had graced the stage throughout the centuries. But I was the only talent scout I knew of and I could only offer them one night of stardom. There was nothing else afterward. I was glad I was not one of the judges. I would have sent each group home with a trophy.

The Floor Lords were the winners by applause, and the judges were in agreement; they were truly the Floor Lords of breakdancing!

Summer of 1984

The year's musical production was *That's Entertainment*. I

wrote the comedy skits between each musical act, and then I held auditions. I did not turn anyone away. I directed and choreographed most of the scenes, as well as designed the program and the posters which I had printed along with the tickets. I ran around placing the advertising posters at different stores. The rehearsals were done in our Music Center. But I did not work myself to death. I paid attention to Francis's advice, "Veronica, you need to learn to delegate."

I took her advice to heart. I visited a couple of dance schools; the dancing teachers were more than happy to offer their top dancing students to perform in our show. It saved a lot of rehearsal time since four of the musical numbers were basically prepackaged and ready to go on opening night.

This was also the first time I had help from some of the Committee members. Besides my two friends, Francis and Tracey, helping out with the front-house concession, Cathy and Barbara, two new committee members, and even Marcy helped backstage and at concessions.

Steve was more than happy to participate as a performer. His rock band "Black and White" was composed of Bob Byrn on lead guitar, Marc Larson on drums and me on keyboard. Since I had taught music for so many years and played several string instruments, improvising on the keyboard was a breeze. Steve sang two of his original songs and I let him borrow my electric guitar, the one Mr. Crocker had given me many years ago.

We closed *That's Entertainment* rocking the Howell High School auditorium to the beat of "Black and White," original music.

I was alone at the Music Center, had dusted all the instruments, ordered some music sheets and books from our order book, and then began to wonder if the alarm button under our register worked. What if the alarm had gotten disconnected by accident and a highway robber were to come in, point a gun to my head, and ask me to open the register. I would most likely press the little red button, but what if it did not work. I wondered once again.

Impulsively I pressed the red button. It felt like five long minutes had passed by. I pressed it again; maybe I had not pressed it hard enough the first time. Suddenly, a bunch of police cars showed up all at the same time and surrounded the store with weapons drawn and facing me.

Boy were they upset when I told them there was no robbery! I was only trying to see if the alarm was working. Cops definitely lacked a sense of humor.

My poor van took its last breath as I drove it into the parking lot of a van dealership. It was my Old Faithful until the end, waiting until I had put enough money together to buy a replacement.

Steve and I spent a lot of time playing guitar and singing together. Our old gig of disco dancing never came to light because we simply stopped practicing. But we did follow-up with going to the White Elephant Bar and Grill in Lakewood and playing a few tunes on Friday nights. I did it only for him. I still loved playing guitar and keyboard, but not in public. I never cared for playing in public. I tried to convince him that he did not need me to play along, which was the truth. He played the guitar with a lot of sentiment and sang with the same passion and intensity. He could easily do a one-man show.

One night at about 1:30 a.m., we received a call from the police department. Someone had broken into the Howell Music Center. A cop was waiting for us when we got there.

We were missing three guitars by the front window, and the glass door had been smashed in. There was broken glass all over. The cop said he was driving by and saw the broken glass door. He called the chief at headquarters. So while Al talked to the cop, Steve and I started looking for clues.

I told Steve every detective book I had ever read, criminals always left evidences behind. Al thought we were nuts because Steve and I were inspecting the sidewalk and the parking lot very carefully. Steve found an empty cup of tomato soup from Dunkin' Donuts in the parking space in front of our store.

"Funny," I told Steve, "that's where the cop parked.

Cops and Dunkin' Donuts. Very interesting!" Steve and I were thinking like detectives. I recalled using a broom to clean the sidewalk and the parking lot in front of our music center the night before. When we closed at nine in the evening, the sidewalk and the parking lot were spotlessly clean. I did that twice a week because when people opened their car doors they accidentally dropped their trash out.

The next morning Steve and I went to R & J Pizzeria, which was next door to our Music Center, to talk to Cesar. His father and mother were the pizzeria owners and Cesar worked with them. Cesar was the same age as Steve and they were good friends.

R & J was the only establishment in our mall that remained open after everybody else had closed for the evening. After hours there was no other traffic in our parking lot except for pizza patrons.

"Nope," they said, they'd had no traffic at all the night of the robbery. As a matter of fact, it was so quiet, they closed early; at 11:30 p.m. to be exact.

Steve and I came to the conclusion that the break-in had to have happened after 11:30!

We went to the only Dunkin' Donuts in our neighborhood, which was one traffic light down from us. The night employee was very helpful. She told us she remembered the night of the break-in clearly; the cute gas station attendant across the highway had bought two cups

Braving A New World

of tomato soup at 11:00 p.m., and at about 1:00 a.m. a cop bought a cup of tomato soup and a doughnut.

Steve and I went to the gas station and spoke to the manager. He had worked late that night to catch up on some paperwork. Mark the gas attendant and he had worked the nightshift together. Neither had left the gas station except for Mark who had gone across the street to pick up two cups of soup at Dunkin' Donuts.

Steve and I went to the police department and spoke to the chief of police. We were not accusing the cop of being the robber, but we wanted further investigation. The chief told us the department had the rookie cop under observation for some time because some of the robberies he called in didn't jive with the time reported. He would be investigating further, and appreciated if we stayed quiet about the whole thing until he knew for sure.

I got a call from Marcy; she had put in a request to the mayor and they had sent a working crew to the Preventorium Road Auditorium and gotten rid of all the junk they had in storage for so many years. The place was now mine to do as I liked. The Cultural Arts Committee approved my project for November, *A Streetcar Named Desire*. I needed to find a bona fide director for my next ambitious production. I would also need someone to set up stage lights and run them during the shows at what we now called the Civic Center.

Through one of her friends at St. Veronica's Church, Francis found someone to do the lights for us, and even though he came highly recommended, she felt we should meet with him and see if he could handle such a big project.

The chief of police called us at the music center and asked Steve and me to come to his station. The rookie cop had confessed after being caught doing other robberies. The chief thanked us for bringing him to his attention and asked us not to share this unpleasant incident with anyone else. The police department was proud of their men and this guy had been caught in time. The Tomato Soup Case was closed, but the items stolen were never returned.

When it came to prejudice I could not point my finger at all the other members of the Cultural Committee, but one of them asked me not to tell Francis about her backyard barbeque party to which I was invited. Her husband was a professional golfer and his very southern white family would be very upset if she were to invite a black person into their house. What would they say if they found out I was a Jew? Crucify me?

The day of the party I excused myself by calling in with the flu.

Autumn of 1984

As a new promotional idea I put together two oversized printed pages to look like a newspaper. To make the first page enticing, I featured the artist of the month as Simon Le Bon of Duran Duran and wrote a short bio under his picture. The *Music News Gazette* was sent out to all Howell residents.

The phones at the music center would not stop ringing. We got swarmed by teenagers looking for Simon Le Bon, as if he had nothing better to do than to spend a day at the Howell Music Center in New Jersey!

We got a lot of publicity and the coupons printed in the back of the *Gazette* brought in a bunch of customers with one thing on their mind: looking for Simon. I never meant to fool anyone. They had read what they wanted to believe and it was very annoying. They called to ask, "What time is Simon going to be there?" "How many days will he be at your music store?" "When do you expect Simon to be there today?" "Is Simon with his band?" and on and on it went.

I would keep writing once a week for *The Booster News* without the responsibilities that came along with printing my own newspaper. There would be no more *Gazette,* once had been more than enough.

Shortly after I passed the word to my customers that I was looking for a director for *A Streetcar Named Desire*, one customer gave me a lead. She suggested I talk to Andy, who worked as a shoe salesman in the mall near our music center, and he used to be a theatre director in South Africa where he was born. I decided to visit Andy. The worst that could happen would be for him to say, "No, I don't direct without getting paid," or "No, I don't have the time for this childish community project which is below my professional ability."

He was busy with some clients and asked me to wait a few minutes. As I sat there watching him selling children's shoes, I learned the true meaning of the phrase, "Kiss ass." I couldn't believe my eyes; it was just too much for me to watch a grown man on his knees acting like a desperate salesperson.

He put on a dramatic facial look and raised the pitch of his voice, "Your child is the most beautiful child I have ever seen in my whole life. With such precious little feet (and he would kiss the child's feet), only these shoes can guarantee your child's feet will grow normally and be healthy." And he went on and on. Nobody left without buying their child the shoes he felt they desperately needed.

When he finally got some free time, I introduced myself and he kissed my hand as passionately as he had kissed the children's feet and their mothers' hands. He immediately accepted my proposal and said with what I perceived as tears of joy, "I swear on my honor as a theatre director." He laid his right hand spread open, over his heart. "*A Streetcar Named Desire* will be ready to open by the scheduled date of November."

When I got to work I told Steve and Al, "I got a director for the next show, but if you want to see the most pathetic example of a man, go into the shoe store in the mall next to us and watch what this guy does to sell a pair of shoes. He must be working solely on commission."

"So why are you working with him?" Al said.

"I have never worked with a professional director before. Maybe they are all groveling types like him. Besides, he is the only one I can get for free."

Francis and I met with our future lighting technician at the Civic Center. His name was Michael. He was in his early twenties, probably twenty-one. He was very tall and skinny, with dark curly brown hair, and a warm, kind look in his eyes. His clothes, including his leather jacket, were badly worn-out and too big for him. He put out his cigarette when he entered the building and excused himself for his appearance, explaining that he worked nights and was on his way home to get some sleep.

Michael knew everything about electrical circuits and lights. He had been a vital part of the Belmar Theatre management before it closed down due to insufficient funds. Besides acting and building sets, he ran their stage lighting. I imagined him as a young Don Quixote de la Mancha. He also reminded me of João, my very first pretend boyfriend when I was a young girl, although João and I hardly ever spoke to each other because we were both too shy.

I didn't say much at the meeting with Francis and Michael. I thought I would relax and listen instead. I kept busy entertaining Francis's little baby. If it had been me hiring him, since I did not know much about stage lights, I would have simply asked, "Can you set the lights up and run them?" and if he said yes, I would just hire him.

Michael agreed to help us in a volunteer manner since

the committee did not pay any salaries. Francis was concerned that without getting paid he would not want to take on the job. He said, "That's okay, I don't do theatre for the money. Theatre runs in my blood." Talk about passion!

We held two days of open auditions for *A Streetcar Named Desire* at the Civic Center. Andy and I spent a whole afternoon going over their applications and how they read for the roles. We put together what we believed to be the best cast and my job was to call them the next day for rehearsal dates.

Meanwhile, the word went out like wild fire about our intended production and the need for technical support. I really don't know how he heard about us, but Bill Goods, a retired professional lighting designer, volunteered his expertise with setting up the lights. It was not easy to mount the lights on the super high ceiling of the Civic Center. Michael welcomed Bill with open arms and the two met to draw the plans and how to make it work.

I was at the Civic Center one day seeing how the lights were working out and said to Michael, "After this production, I would love to do a Broadway musical. Do you have a suggestion?"

"Godspell," he responded without giving it a second thought. "If you decide to do it, count on me to help you. I have done it twice and it's definitely the most, awe-inspiring musical, loved by everyone who sees it."

I brought Michael's recommendation to the Cultural Arts Committee. It hit them like a ton of bricks. "We need to think about that." They responded as if in unison. "It's a religious show with a bunch of hippies and we don't know if it's such a good idea for a place like Howell." Said the one with the colored red hair, I could never remember her name.

"Why, what's wrong with Howell?" I grinded my teeth, knowing exactly what she meant.

"It's not what's wrong with Howell." Laura said as if reprimanding a small child. "A show about hippies, drugs and loud music is not right for Howell, that's what. That type of show can only attract trash to our community."

Tracy stared at me with a mischievous smile as if saying here we go again and Francis shrugged her shoulders. When I got home, I called Marcy.

Stanley, in *A Streetcar Named Desire,* had to break a beer bottle before attacking Blanche, but having broken glass flying all over the stage was not conducive to safety. Michael told me about a company in New York where they sold beer bottles made of sugar.

Marcy had more political power than I had given her credit for. The Cultural Arts Committee came up with the thirty dollars to pay for the bottles, which were five dollars each, *and* they gave me their okay to start planning for *Godspell.*

Tracey was a good friend, but she loved to gossip. "Veronica, have you noticed that Andy is gay?"

"Who cares?"

"You should care. He's the director, and he's working with male actors. Imagine if the Cultural Arts Committee were to find out."

"If they don't like it, it's too bad. Live and let live is my motto."

Michael and I had a long discussion about Andy. He agreed with me. Andy's sexual preference was none of our business.

During Sunday's rehearsal Andy got up from his chair and threw the script into the air. He screamed from the top of his lungs "Laura! You are Blanche Dubois! Not the little rat, introverted Laura. You're about to get raped! Where's your natural instinct? Fight woman, fight with all you've got!" He turned to me and said, "I made a big error in casting her for the part. This is the last time she pisses me off. But I'll take care of it, don't you worry." He yelled out to the cast, "Everybody off the stage. We start again in ten minutes."

I saw Laura crying on the side and stayed away from her.

Ten minutes later Andy announced, "I want Blanche and Stanley back on stage, same scene. Stanley, I want you to grab the beer bottle; you are going to rape Blanche. Blanche, when he comes toward you, I want you to back away from him and into the chair behind you. Sit hard on it."

When Laura went to sit down she got up screaming at the top of her lungs. Andy had put a needle in her chair.

"That's the emotion of terror I want when Stanley comes after you!"

She cursed at him and cried and everyone was upset concerning his method of directing. I was astonished she did not quit right then and there.

My first professional production was a success. The newspaper reviewer bragged about the play and everybody's acting, and in the end, we all forgot about the needle-in-the chair incident. Andy had done an outstanding job and I asked him if he wanted to direct the next production. He said, "I'm so very sorry. I feel terrible having to decline such a magnificent opportunity, but I need to concentrate on editing and "cleaning" the script I've written about the apartheid system in Africa. It's my dream to someday direct my own play." He kissed my hands in his usual dramatic manner and added, "It would be a great honor for me if when I finish updating my script, you read it and give me your honest opinion." He then hugged me and whispered in my ear, "I don't have any experience directing musicals. You're better off with someone who knows what they are doing."

A week later, Mr. Storken, a musical director from Red Bank with a long history of musicals under his belt, applied for the volunteer position of directing *Godspell*.

After auditions, I met with Mr. Storken and the cast to discuss the costumes. With what they already had in their closets, getting the costumes together became a fun project. Thrift shops were dusty and smelly but I found some cool clothes. I washed them and brought them to one of the meetings, and everyone found a piece they liked.

Rachel, one of the actresses in *Godspell*, offered to help me sew patches of cutout flowers to three skirts. Rachel was nineteen, with long blonde hair and blue eyes. She was perfect for the part she played in *Godspell*. We sat on the floor in one of the teaching rooms at the music center, and while sewing, we talked about dating, love, and marriage. She said, "I don't care if I'm in bed with a man or a woman, I just want to be held."

I kept looking down as I stitched the pink flower to the hem of the dress. "My best lover was bisexual," she said. "He took his time hugging and holding me; he really knew how to make love."

I wondered why a bisexual man made a better lover than a regular guy, but I did not ask because I did not want her to think I was ignorant about stuff like that at my age.

"I was seven years old when my grandfather introduced me to sex," she said. "He always hugged me before we did it."

She spoke matter-of-factly and I kept nodding my head as if it all sounded normal. She was beautiful on the outside but so messed up inside.

Papa used to say, "Women who cheat or can't get satisfaction from anyone have lost their soul, and the only time they have a sense of security is in the comfort of someone else's arms. They are the saddest, loneliest people on earth." I could not imagine anyone having sex just to get a hug. I felt sorry for Rachel.

Michael had to leave unexpectedly for Texas. His brother Robert, had been seriously hurt in a motorcycle accident. Michael left with the *Godspell* script in hand, promising to call as things developed. He was studying to play the part of Jesus. *Godspell*, was to be performed November 30 and December 17.

Besides Michael having to leave all of a sudden, Mr. Storken our musical director fell down a staircase and was in the hospital with a broken leg and a head concussion. One of the actresses got mononucleosis, and Judas had to quit because of college finals. We had two and a half weeks until opening night with no director nor any news from Michael. We could do without a director, but without Jesus and Judas we had no show.

I was about to give up when Joe Polinski, a schoolteacher at the Griebling School, called. "I heard from one of my students that you are producing *Godspell* but have been plagued by several problems. I've directed *Godspell* in Summer Stock Theatre and also played Jesus several times." Joe had just become our savior, no pun intended! Then, another miracle happened; Diana Di Stefano joined us. Yes, she was blind, but it did not stop her from skiing and roller skating, and most important of all, she could sing and dance up a storm. Diana was engaged to Mike, who came along as her partner to be in our show and was more than willing to play Judas. She only had one practical request. I was to apply long strips of coarse tape, three feet from the stage's edge. Her naked feet would warn her not to go any further.

Woody Pizzi, a high school student came highly recommended by Mike, to play the role of John the Baptist.

Joe Polinski would be directing our play and playing the part of Jesus, but if Michael came back from Texas in time for the show he was willing to give the part of Jesus back to Michael.

The newspapers gave us full coverage after I wrote to them about Diana. Hopefully, other people with handicaps would be inspired by her fortitude.

Michael made it back two days before opening night. The doctors in Texas told him his brother was no longer in danger and was going to be fine. He did not say much more than that. I had a feeling he was hurt for having been replaced as Jesus. I told him, "You never called us from California. I had to make a decision very quickly when Joe called. I could not take a chance that you might not show up in time."

"Bill called me and he is not available to run the lights for this show. As much as I wanted to play Jesus, I've decided to run the lights for *Godspell* instead."

The show was a great hit and we were sold out each night.

At closing night emotions were running high on stage and afterward we all went out to celebrate at the Howell Diner. Everyone who signed my playbill stated they loved me. Michael wrote, "All good thoughts are yours," and drew an ankh, the Egyptian symbol for life, next to his signature. I felt disappointed that he did not write the word love like everybody else.

Winter ending 1984

Andy came by my music store one morning and handed me a thick yellow envelope. "This is the script I told you about. I'm putting it in your hands. I have poured my soul into every line and I want you to read it. I know you are going to love it. You are the only one I trust to produce it. I only ask one favor, let me direct it."

I pulled my hands away from him. "Andy, if it's that good, I'll produce it. You don't have to kiss my hands. Just give me a few days to read it, okay?"

I did not have much experience with reading scripts, except for the ones I had written, but I could see he had touched every form of human quality and weakness, and it dealt with the apartheid system, which to me represented a very serious subject.

Of course when I brought it up to the committee I was not surprised when my request went over like a death sentence.

"We don't want a riot. We don't want this kind of show. We don't want publicity where blacks are involved." We don't...and we don't.

The Cultural Arts Committee was nothing but a group of narrow minded Republican older women, or as my friend Tracey said, "These women were put into the committee as a payoff to their husbands, who helped put the Mayor into power. They know nothing about culture if anything they lack any kind of finesse."

Winter of 1985

I gave Andy's script to Francis hoping she would get as excited about it as I was. Francis called me two days later. "I read the script and it's good, very good. But I have mixed feelings about Andy. I don't trust him. Don't ask me why; I really don't know why I feel this way. I need a few more days to think it through before I vote."

When Andy called, I told him I was waiting for Francis to give me the okay to produce it. Without her blessing I would not be able to get enough votes from the committee to do it and I was afraid Marcy would not back me up either.

For the holidays, the township invited the Cultural Arts Committee members and Andy to a dinner party. It was my first experience with Pasta e Fagioli. I had a small bowl just in case I did not care for it, and then shamelessly devoured two heaping servings. I asked Sally, who was a committee member and the creator of the heavenly dish, for the recipe. She said, "My Pasta e Fagioli is a family recipe and I don't share it with anyone."

Andy came over to the table where Francis and I were seated, got on his knees, grabbed her hands, and kissed them while crying copiously. She looked at me with pleading eyes and I got up to rescue her. I had never told her about Andy's fixation for kissing women's hands and babies' feet. "Andy, if you excuse us, Francis and I need to use the bathroom."

He remained on his knees. "Give me just two minutes to talk to this beautiful lady, who I admire greatly. I have to tell her something very, very important that she must know in order to understand why my play must be produced for the whole world to see." He put his head close to hers and whispered to her as he cried with little sobs in between. Tracey and I and two other women seated at the same table watched. His hands flew over his head, then he sobbed louder, then he kissed her cheeks like the French did, twice on each side, and then he pointed to his testicles, and we looked at each other wondering what kind of story he was sharing with Francis. We knew it was over when he put his head on her lap like a child. (Was he waiting for her to pat his head?) Francis looked at us as if asking, now what? Then he got up and very tenderly kissed the top of her head, as if it were a raw egg, and he made a graceful ballerina turn and walked away without looking back.

We all clapped except Francis. "What an act!" she said. "I'm not going to fall for it. He told me that because he was against the apartheid system in South Africa he had been jailed and tortured with an electric device attached to his penis. He had been shocked several times in that way, as punishment for associating with black people and if needed, he was willing to show me his scars. After months of torture he had escaped miraculously from his cruel jailers. Can you believe it?"

"Andy is definitely melodramatic," I said. "But what if it's true? What if he is telling the truth. Besides, you told me last night, his script is very good, so why not go for it?" After we talked for a while, she agreed that maybe I was right. My next mission was to call Marcy the next day to pull the strings on the committee puppets.

I got a letter of recognition from the Jackson Mayor's Commission for the Handicapped stating they had done well monetarily when we put on *Godspell* to help them raise funds for their cause. I put it in my photo album with the other paper awards.

Over the weekend, Michael invited me to take a ride with him to see the inside of the Belmar Theatre, which was scheduled to be torn down the next month. He used his pocket knife to break the rusted security latch from the back metal door and we sneaked inside the dark building yanking the door behind us. He used a large flashlight to light our way across the musty smelly, torn-apart theatre, going carefully up the steps to the second floor where we took out time rummaging through what used to be the dressing rooms. Michael had lived with a girlfriend in one of those back rooms for a few months.

It felt like I was walking through a sinking ship. Michael had been the essence of that ship, and once it was gone, so would his past life. He had been the manager, the stagehand, the electrician, and the gofer. He substituted as an actor when the occasion arose, and even played Dracula among many other characters. He *was* the Belmar Theatre.

My wish to find a theatre of my own where I could do whatever I wanted without going through a committee grew bigger and bigger in my heart.

Francis shared with me her dream of opening a children's museum in Howell. I did not have the courage to tell her there were too many politics to overcome, not only in the committee, but also with the township. I gave her some hope by including in the 1985 Calendar of Events, the opening of a Children's Museum.

The committee voted to sponsor Andy's play. I was not surprised. I called Marcy to thank her.

After two weekends of grueling auditions, Andy found his cast. Tracey became our prop mistress. The title befitted her. She was the greatest when it came to finding or making the oddest props. She was my fun friend. Francis was my emotional-strength friend and Michael was a combination of both. I felt like I could count on him for anything.

I did my usual dealing with public relations, handling the advertising, and designing the playbills. The Cultural Committee members were like ghosts. We would never see them except for a few who would show up for opening nights, but considering the subject matter of the next play, I didn't count on it. They were busy arranging to have a bunch of cops standing by the Civic Center in case there was a riot on opening night.

When I used to do theatre with young people, there was always a discreet romance going on, but with adults, it was a lot more visual. Two of the girls in the cast openly kissed each other on the mouth, and when we went out to the local diner after rehearsals, they shared their mozzarella sticks until their lips got close enough to stick their tongues into each other's mouths. They proudly announced that they were lesbians, but they also liked men and they bragged about sharing their boyfriends with each other.

One evening, a man showed up at the Civic Center during rehearsal and introduced himself as Maureen's husband. Maureen was our stage manager and set designer.

"When I come home, she's not home. I hardly see her anymore. What's going on in here? Is she seeing someone else? Our marriage is falling apart."

"I don't know what to say." I excused myself and went to sit next to Andy. I could not tell him that Maureen was not only working backstage, but I had seen her several times alone with Richard, sitting cozily in his car. Most likely they had become friends, but it looked like they liked each other more than just working together.

A week did not go by without receiving a call from a church asking us to perform *Godspell*. It was a bit ironic since when I first brought up the musical for the Cultural Arts Committee's approval, they felt it might be a little too much for our religious community. We did one performance at the Griebling School to help them raise money for their school, and another performance at one of the churches in Howell, and another at a church in Freehold.

In the beginning, everyone enjoyed the idea of being a traveling theatre company, but we were getting tired of it. When the cast agreed to stop performing, I could not have been happier.

I had three priorities in my life: my family, the Music Center, and finding myself a theatre. I put taking any further classes at Brookdale College on hold for now.

Francis was busy getting ready for her personal project, the Festival of Choirs, in the first week of February, and it took priority in her schedule over Andy's play, which was slated for the first week of March. He finally came up with a name for his play, *Sabona* which meant "hello" in the Zulu language. I liked it.

Working with Michael gave me a nurturing, peaceful feeling. He never yelled or lost his patience. He listened and never criticized me; if anything, he held the same beliefs. I looked forward to talking to him and hearing what he had to say about his past theatre experiences, music, and the way he perceived the world. I spent a lot of time helping Michael with stage work and the lights. I admired his background in theatre. "When it comes to properly rolling and tying electrical cables, there's only one way to do it." He proceeded to show me.

"Looks easy." And I took over at rolling the next cable. "You learn fast," he said. "I think I'll keep you as my assistant." I liked receiving his compliments.

Meanwhile, I was busy going from one school to another trying to make a connection with the band instructors in Howell, Jackson, and Lakewood. The band teachers told me the kids were already renting their band instruments from a company in North Jersey and they had no need for our services.

It took me a week to type up a two-page proposal which included a mission statement, the reason why they should be working with us, and a list of all the services we offered. I called the schools back and made appointments to meet the band teachers once again.

I was ready when I walked into the first band room. Just in case the band teacher would throw my proposal in the trash, before I handed it to him, I read it out loud. "By working with us, you will be supporting a local business. We are conveniently located in Howell and we are open on weekends, so if necessary, a parent can drive by and drop off or pick up their child's instrument. When you call us, I will personally deliver and pick up any instrument that needs repair, and in its place, give you a brand new one; the students don't have to wait for their band instrument to return a week later from North Jersey. All our instruments are well-known brand names and available new or used if parents want to buy instead of rent. And most importantly, we at Howell Music Center promise to provide good service and customer satisfaction with every single instrument."

"I don't deal with a woman," he said disdainfully. "You know nothing about the needs of a band teacher."

"I'm a woman, but my son and my husband are men, so you don't have to talk to me, how about that?"

"That's right, I don't have to talk to you. Goodbye."

I left the school demoralized but by the time I got to work I was too angry to give up the fight.

The next band teacher was more forward about the "real" reason he didn't want to work with us. "Are you prepared to give me free reeds and accessories so I can sell them to my students and make extra money? What about books and other items like binders, music stands, and occasional musical instruments? The band company in North Jersey provides all of that to me at no charge. Are you going to do the same?"

"We are a small shop and can't afford to give you gifts."

"My point," he said as he opened the door of his music room and added, "goodbye."

I left the school shaking a bit, but not defeated.

When I told Al what happened he said, "Screw it, we don't need them anyway." But I talked to Steve and he agreed with me; we definitely needed them!

I called the New Jersey State Board of Education. I told Mrs. Simpson what was going on in the school system and parents should be made aware that their kids were not given the freedom of choice as to where to rent their band instruments because some teachers were getting special treats from the only company they did business with.

Mrs. Simpson told me she was going to get in touch with each school district and would be calling me as soon as she got to the bottom of what was going on. "If what you are telling me is true, we will put a stop to it."

The Festival of Choirs at St. Veronica's Church was performed most regally. Francis had designed the playbill in the handwritten format style of medieval times. She was very creative. We got along like sisters and confided in each other about our personal issues and had long discussions about life.

Tracey was also a good friend, but our relationship had more to do with fun and joking. Her sense of humor and creativity through me for a loop one morning when she invited me for lunch at her house and afterward asked me to follow her to the cellar to see some of her latest creations made of wooden pieces she had found while walking in the woods, in back of her house. She stripped the red velvet cloth covering her pool table. "Voila," she laughed heartily. "Pardon my French. But do they look real or what?"

I stared in disbelief at the anatomical pieces. "Yes, it's amazing how real they look. You really are an artist."

"Thank you, thank you." She picked up one piece and held it up admiring her own creation. "All it needed was two shelled peanuts on each side." We laughed in unison.

~ Chapter Fourteen ~

THE PRODUCER

1985-1988

Spring of 1985

My memories of young Shana went back to when she was twelve years old and I used to teach her to play acoustic guitar. I remember one day asking why she had missed a month of guitar lessons and she said, "If I tell you where I've been you won't like me anymore."

Out of respect for her, I stopped asking where she had been, when she would disappear for a few weeks and then return again. When she stopped coming for lessons, I assumed she had lost the desire to play guitar. Five years went by. Steve went to a private party in Marlboro and met Shana for the first time. They fell in love and he brought her home. I learned that Shana had started doing drugs at a very young age. Her adopted parents kept putting her into rehab centers but once she got out, she went back to doing the same. Finally they gave up and threw her out of their home. She had no place to stay so I offered our house. Al was against having Shana live with us, but I swore to him that it would be temporary. "Look, she's still a child, only seventeen. Steve is going to help her to kick the drug addiction and since they are in love with each other she will most likely be cured by her own choice. That's what love does to people." I said convincingly

Over the three weeks that Shana lived with us, Steve got her to stop doing drugs. He was able to bring her self-esteem up and even gave her self-confidence to look for a job. He bought her a spring dress with a matching jacket, shoes, and purse so that she could look professional when she went to apply for employment. I remember how lovely she looked. She smiled a lot more as Steve convinced her that she was not only beautiful, but also smart. She was ready to face life with its ups and downs. Things were going well, and Steve and Shana were very happy. He asked me if I was okay with them getting married. I gave him my blessing.

But nothing lasts forever. The cops came by our house in the middle of the night and took Shana back to her parents who had changed their mind about her not living with them. She was only seventeen and as such, they had the last word on where she could live. I cried with Steve when the cops took Shana away from us.

Opening night of *Sabona* was a hit! The actors were made for the parts. Some of the audience cried as they got emotionally involved in the dramatic plot. The cops stood outside waiting in vain for the riot to happen. It was three nights of good quality theatre with a heartfelt standing ovation and most importantly, it made people think about others less fortunate than themselves.

Performing *Sabona* took our cast to places like the Naval Air Engineering Center in Lakehurst in celebration of Black History Month. We were also invited to compete in the Festival of American Community Theatres. There were four theatre groups from New Jersey, including us, that would compete against all the other states. To me, the idea of being chosen to perform against so many other theatres was in itself an honor.

Braving A New World

The Board of Education called. I was to get ready to deliver band instruments to the schools in Jackson, Lakewood, and Howell that September. The teachers would be giving the students two forms to take home; ours and the one from the other company. It was up to the parents to choose which they wanted to use.

I knew parents would rather deal with us. As far as I was concerned, we had won!

Richard was doing a great job teaching piano and the students loved him, but he looked very fragile. I worried he might drop dead while teaching. The idea made me very sad. I always thought that only old people had problems with their hearts, but I was wrong.

I got a very disturbing call one morning. I was sure it was from the band instrument rental company in North Jersey.

A man's voice said, "Are you Ronnie Esagui?"

"Yes, I am."

"If you deliver band instruments to the schools in September, watch out for a bomb underneath your van. We're going to get you."

I did not tell Al about it; he would have freaked out. I talked to Ralph and Steve instead, and we came to the conclusion that the phone call was intended only to scare me. Come September, Steve and I would share the load of delivering the band instruments to all the schools. We would provide such excellent service that the teachers would soon start to appreciate us and be glad they were working with us. But we were no fools, New Jersey was Mafia owned and in September before getting into our vans we would be looking under the hood and listening for ticking sounds.

Steve was impressive with his selling abilities.

"Mom, do you see that guy walking out there, in the

street? Watch me bring him in to buy an instrument."

About half an hour later, Steve walked back into the store with the passerby who bought one of our new upright pianos. The man gave me a charge card and said, "I can't wait to have the piano home and start taking piano lessons here."

Mr. Dietrich, the violin teacher at our music center, had told me several times how much he would love to give a lecture about music and computers, so I figured it would be nice to have him lecture at the Civic Center. After going through the usual begging at the Cultural Arts Committee meeting and calling Marcy, I got their acceptance vote. I made a lot of flyers announcing "Music in the Computer Age" and sent the information to all the newspapers and the radio stations. We were sold out.

Mr. Dietrich, took all morning setting up the stage with six electronic keyboards of all sizes and two computers.

There were electrical wires all over, and it looked very impressive. The audience, including myself, was anxious to hear him play.

Mr. Dietrich stood on the stage and began lecturing. His heavy foreign accent, which on a day-to-day basis was acceptable for teaching private students, had become a compilation of enigmas. He talked and talked and talked and everyone tried to stay awake while hoping he would stop talking and play us a tune. But he never did. Francis, Tracey, and I almost dozed off to sleep, and I was sure that most of the people in the audience were also trying to stay awake. One and a half hours later Mr. Dietrich said, "Tanki ol far kamin," and after giving a polite bow, he walked away from the stage. There was a moment of silence from the audience and everyone looked at each other like, *What the heck was that all about?* Then everybody stood up clapping heartily as if they had just found out everything they wanted to know about music and computers. I clapped too.

We were all walking out of the Civic Center when I heard someone commenting, "The man is a genius. He's beyond our capability to understand."

Between working at the music center, writing for the newspaper and producing my next community activity for the Cultural Arts Committee, March was a busy month for me. We closed the month with a musical performance by the young virtuoso composer Jesse Clark.

Jesse was a local boy who almost lost his life after being in a car wreck. Even though he did not have the use of his legs, his musical brain was constantly working at full speed on some unique, electronic musical composition. The day he auditioned for me, I imagined his music along with modern dancing on the stage. I told Michael about the idea and he immediately suggested we have a light show to complement the music and the dancers. I had never met anyone like Michael; he always expanded on my ideas and was ready to help.

I called Kathy, the choreographer for *And the Panther Cried*, and asked her if she wanted to be part of the show. Kathy got all excited about it and offered to put a professional group of dancers together.

The night before the light show, the fire department almost busted us. The Civic Center could not handle the electrical overload of lights hanging from the ceiling and the walls. When the fire department called the Civic Center to find out what was going on, Michael knew we were in trouble. We heard the sirens coming our way up the hill and we all took part in helping to hide some of the stage lights. When the firemen showed up, we acted like a bunch of innocent actors and Michael did all the talking.

The combination of the light show, the music, and the dancers made a perfect trio of entertainment. It was a very exciting and unusual production and everybody loved it.

Kathy was so happy with the turnout she decided to start her own dance company. She named it The Blue Unicorn Dance Company.

In April, the New Jersey Youth Orchestra performed at the Howell Civic Center. Francis was the only one from the Cultural Arts Committee who showed up in time to help me bring out the one hundred and fifty metal chairs from storage situated on the opposite side of the parking lot. With two chairs under each arm we walk up and down the steep pathway, but we had the room ready for an audience by the time they began to arrive. The committee had neglected to inform the township to provide us with any type of help. The orchestra was sublime, a masterpiece of sound coming from a bunch of very professional young players. Sitting next to me Francis clasped her hands in despair. "Where is the township pride? Look at these walls, they're dirty and dilapidated. They should be ashamed of this place. And where are the Cultural Arts Committee members? How come they're not here to support this group of talented children who have volunteered to play for our community?" Obviously, the committee members couldn't care less.

Francis and I decided to do something about the Civic Center's drabness. We got some complimentary paint from the township and over the weekend painted the walls ourselves with the help of our families, Michael, and a few stagehands and actors. The new creamy colored walls made the place a lot more inviting.

The mayor mailed Francis and me certificate awards for outstanding civic contribution in renovating the recreation building.

We were doing well at the Howell Music Center and Ronnie's Music Den. We paid our bills and I was able to save a good percentage of our income each month, but that money belonged to the music center, not to my personal theatrical endeavors.

I saw a building on Hwy 9 that would make a perfect theatre, but Ed, who was Tracey's husband and knew all about construction, told me the building foundation was messed up and to fix that and the broken-down chimney would cost a fortune.

Every day as I drove around, I looked carefully to my right and then to my left making sure I did not miss any possibilities. I was confident that sooner or later I would bump into a dwelling, begging to be transformed into the theatre of my dreams.

We had an art show in May which covered every wall at the Civic Center with all types of artwork and media from artists of all ages and backgrounds. We offered ribbons for first, second, and third place, which made it even more exciting for the artists.

Another weekend we had a Country Music Jamboree at the Civic Center which brought lots of country folks from towns I had never heard of. The musicians asked me if it was possible to have a Music Jamboree every month. I told them it was up to the Cultural Arts Committee. I didn't tell the musicians what the committee thought of country music.

I was driving on Route 9 when the Kobe Japanese Restaurant caught my attention. I had never been in it but I had always admired the massive white building with its simple architectural design. I went into the restaurant and asked to speak to the owner. Katie, a Japanese lady dressed in a Japanese kimono, graciously bowed to me and introduced herself as the manager. "I'm looking for a place to start a dinner theatre, do you have space available?" Isaid confidently. She smiled, bowed again and said, "Follow me upstairs, please." Before my eyes there it was—a room big enough to fit about one hundred people. I immediately imagined the stage built on the opposite side of the bar, and small, cozy round tables all around the stage with an enthusiastic, applauding audience. Katie was just as thrilled as I was, and told me she was going to talk to her boss, Mr. Ounuma.

I had barely made it back to our music center when I got a call from Mr. Ounuma. He wanted to meet as soon as possible. I drove right back to his restaurant.

"I have a theatre! I have a dinner theatre! My wish came true!" The first person I called was Francis to give her the good news and to ask her if she would like to be my partner. She thanked me for thinking of her, but she had her hands full taking care of her family, and she was putting all her energy into finding a permanent building in Newark where she and her husband could help children with AIDS.

I called Tracey and Michael and asked them to meet me that evening at the Lakewood Diner. I had to control myself from telling them the news on the phone. I simply said, "I have super great news to share with you." Then I sat down and wrote a nice letter of resignation to the Cultural Arts Committee.

Just like I thought, Michael and Tracey were thrilled with the news. Michael offered to set up the stage lights and build the stage and sets. Tracey said she would take care of the props since that was her strong point.

"Okay, that's good," I said. "I'll do everything else."

"Everything else has a name," Michael said. "It's called production. Are you sure about that? It's going to be a lot of work for you."

"I'm very sure. With you and Tracey as my partners, I know we can create the best and most successful theatre in New Jersey."

We shook hands.

Braving A New World

When I got home I shared the news with Al. "You're making a big mistake in making Tracey your partner," Al said. "What does she know about theatre anyway? You'll be cutting down on your earnings. Why don't you get the props yourself?"

I saw it differently. Making money was not the answer to everything in life. I liked her as my friend; she was creative and had a good positive attitude. I needed to have that by my side.

Summer of 1985

"My name is Roberta Stack and I'm a new Cultural Arts Committee member. They asked me to call you. We're in a serious predicament trying to find entertainers for the Fourth of July township celebration in the park. Is there a chance you can help us by providing a full day of entertainment?"

"Do you have an outside stage and a sound system?"

"I'll call you right back."

She called an hour later. "We can get a stage, but can you supply us with the sound system?"

"If you have someone to come to our store and pick it up you can rent it from us." The freebee days were over.

"Okay, I can do that," then she changed her voice to a softer almost whispering tone. "I understand you did a lot for the committee when you were a member. I'm sorry it didn't work out."

"Thanks. It sounds like they have you doing all the work for them now. I wish you my best and don't worry; I'll get you gals all the entertainment you'll need."

In three days I had four rock bands ready to perform, a few solo acts, and dancers galore. I purposely put Eric, a solo electric guitar player and one of our most devoted customers, at the very end of the day. Eric wasn't going to be easily accepted by the Howell residents. Eric was a seventeen-year-old rebel. He was about 5' 7" and sweated a lot, possibly because he was out of shape, but that wasn't really the problem. The problem was the combination of both his disheveled looks dramatically mixed with his type of music.

Eric's favorite solo, "The Star Spangled Banner," was not only loud enough the people in China could have sung along, but he also added the unique sound of his own homemade distortion pedals to his performance. With a Jimmy Hendrix hallucinogenic look on his face accented by his long and unruly, curly and fiery-red hair, Eric prompted any people who were still at the park later in the evening to put away their picnic baskets and rapidly leave with their children.

Eric came into the music center the next morning and he had a lot to say. "I'll never ever give the township people the pleasure of hearing me play the guitar. They're nothing but a bunch of stuck-up, miserable bastards who have no appreciation for real music."

He shook my hand. "Thank you for letting me play yesterday. By the way, I got a real kick out of watching their faces as they left the park." He laughed in his usual thunderous, disconcerting way. He then abruptly stopped laughing and turning to me with a very serious look on his face whispered, "Ronnie, Jesus is watching us. He's sitting over there." He pointed to the corner of the ceiling behind him.

I looked up but all I could see was the white ceiling. I was thinking of what to say next without upsetting him. He was looking at me as if he could read my mind and it scared the heck out of me.

He got closer to the glass counter which I was happy to be standing behind, and whispered again, "Don't tell me you see Jesus sitting up there on a chair. Don't tell me you can also see him, because I'm the only one who can."

Just then the phone rang. It was Al. "Hi Ronnie, I need you to bring home a dozen drum sticks and a box of guitar picks I'm running low at Ronnie's Music Den."

"Okay, no problem I'll do that." He hanged up but I remained on the phone acting as if it was one of my friends. "So tell me, how is your brother?" I kept talking and talking while praying Eric would leave since I was not feeling too secure being alone with him. Thank God a customer came in with his young son and Eric finally waved goodbye and left.

I was not a mental health expert but I had a strong feeling that Eric suffered from the same ailment as my brother José, who had been diagnosed with schizophrenia.

A few days later I received a call from another committee member, not telling me how wonderful the entertainment had been throughout the day, but to express how appalled they were at the worthless, drugged-out musician who closed the night with such an offensive way of playing our most patriotic song.

I said, "Yes, a real surprise for me too. He reminded me of Jimmy Hendrix, don't you agree?"

I got another certificate of appreciation from the mayor of Howell. I put it with my collection of certificates. Most likely the last one I would receive. Once I quit the Cultural Arts Committee, so did Francis and Tracey.

It was not easy to convince Al to have lunch at the Kobe Japanese Restaurant, but he did it for me. It was definitely outside of the ordinary food we were used to eating. I was turned off by the little square pieces of what looked like fat in the tasty miso soup, but I enjoyed the teriyaki steak and rice. When the waitress came to take away the soup bowls, I asked her why they put little squares of fat in the soup and she laughed. "Not fat, it's called tofu, very healthy protein." Al barely ate anything and said once was enough for him.

I went back for lunch several times by myself. Since I would be working at Kobe in the very near future, I wanted to learn more about the people who ran the restaurant, their food, and their culture.

Having a music store came in very handy when someone was looking for other musicians to play in a group. For the last two years, I had been allowing young rock bands to use our sidewalk for their performances. On Sundays the parking lot became a large auditorium of cars and lawn chairs as people spent the afternoon with us. The merchants were happy because it brought people from other towns to our mall and businesses did well, principally the pizzeria next to us. Even though I was still writing my weekly column and mentioned the bands playing, it was nice when, a reporter from The Asbury Park Press would get interested and come by to take pictures and publish a small story about one of the groups.

Michael put out a lot of his money to buy the lumber to build the stage and the sets. I promised to pay him back from the theatre profits. He worked as a night watchman, and slept at odd hours during the day. Because of his job, the building of the stage and the set was going very slowly. I did not have the courage to say, "Hurry up, we need to get going!" Instead I felt guilty he was missing sleep and spent his waking hours building the stage and the walls. I didn't know there was so much to do to make a professional theatre a reality. I would have never been able to embark on such a venture without him. Michael had learned from his father everything there was to know about carpentry. "My father left my mother and the family once he ran out of things to fix around the house." His joking tone of voice had a hint of irony when he added, "He was so happy to leave us he didn't bother to take his tools with him."

Braving A New World

Michael and Madeleine, his mom, were heavy smokers. He was tall and slim and she was short and overweight but not obese. She was a pleasant lady who had a rough, but infectious laugh. When she laughed, it made me laugh too. I liked her. When I went to their house, which was becoming a regular daily trip, to help Michael cut the wood in his cellar to build our stage floor, I always found Madeleine sitting by the window at the kitchen table reading the newspaper, drinking coffee, and smoking. Their house was very old and smelled of mold, cigarettes and pets possibly from all the dogs and cats that had the run of the place. I had to watch my step not to trip over one of them. But I did not mind, I just wanted to be with Michael. We were the best of friends; we thought alike, and I was happy when I worked with him. I learned to use a drill, a jigsaw power tool, and after one month helping to build set pieces and door frames and windows, I felt like I was a natural with any carpentry tool.

Michael never gossiped. He never asked me for any money to cover his cost of lumber or his hours of labor. He never got angry or used bad words when I messed up something. He had a good sense of humor and was also very perceptive about life. Most of all, he liked the same music I did—rock and roll.

I had a bad experience after having lunch at the Kobe restaurant one day. Once again I learned the meaning of food poisoning after I had a bowl of miso soup and a salad. Ralph told me most likely the salad had been exposed to salmonella. Whatever it was, I almost died. It wasn't just a simple stomachache. It was diarrhea and vomit at the same time. Thank God I was home, or more precisely, in my bathroom, when I dropped on the floor unable to move, breathe, or talk. I tried my best to think positive thoughts while waiting to recover, and it took a long time for my system to return to normal. I fully understood why some people died from what sickened me. It was even worse than the first time I had experienced food poisoning. It had happened at one of Mr. Crocker's get-togethers with his staff at a hotel in Freehold. I had eaten two mushroom appetizers and drank some club soda. Halfway home, I had to stop the car on Route 9 and get down on the grass to puke. I believe the club soda is what saved my life, it acted as a bubbling explosive to make the two poisoned mushrooms shoot out like a scalding volcano.

Over the weekend I helped Michael carry the extremely heavy stage floor pieces to the Kobe Japanese Restaurant, and upstairs to our dinner theatre, the Simy Dinner Theatre Company. With all the heavy lifting I was scared my back was going to give out, but it did not. Maybe my back was cured or my tight jeans were working well as a back support.
    Michael made plans to come during the week and attach the stage pieces. He would have to crawl underneath the stage and connect the 4'x8feet plywood sheets so there were no gaps in between. Someone could trip or fall if the stage floor was not smooth.
    Every once in a while Mr. Ounuma came upstairs to watch us put the stage together. He would smile, bow his head and leave. "Theatre looking good," he said one day. "Perhaps also talk show like on American television, with famous movie stars?"
    Michael advised me to paint the stage ceiling black to give it depth. I asked Mr. Ounuma and he said, "Do whatever necessary to make it a grand theatre."
    Over the weekend I bought two gallons of flat black paint and started painting the ceiling over the stage area. Five gallons of black paint later, Mr. Ounuma came upstairs to see what I was doing and instead of screaming at me because I was covering his beautiful white ceiling with black paint, he held his hands behind his back and pacing

Braving A New World

calmly, he shook his head approvingly. He smiled, bowed and said, "Looking very good." Then he walked away.

I was impressed with his undemanding attitude. The ceiling looked horrible and it was sucking up gallon after gallon of black paint. In desperation, I called Michael and he came in with a bunch of spray cans. Between the two of us, we finished painting the ceiling after using six gallons of black paint and can after can of black spray-paint.

That week, The Simy Dinner Theatre Company's permanent metal sign went up on the left side of the Kobe building, facing Route 9. It could not be missed; bold black letters on a white background. It was big and beautiful. Mr. Ounuma was just as excited and I was thrilled when he offered me the space below his large restaurant sign, facing both the north and south bound lanes on Route 9. There was plenty of space on both sides of the restaurant sign to advertise the name of the play and the dates. He gave me a bag of black magnet letters but I would have to buy more because some letters, like vowels, were needed more than the others.

Tracey called and invited me to lunch. "We made a big mistake in making Michael our partner," she said. "He has not contributed any money, like you and I have done. In my opinion we should just pay him by the hour to build the stage and put up the lights. That way we can make more money after each show."

I was upset with her greediness, and tried to reason with her instead. "It's true that you and I put $500 each toward the initial expenses of starting this business, but he is putting in a lot more than both of us together. He has been purchasing lumber to build the stage and the sets and is spending his free time doing all the construction at no charge to us. Without Michael, there is no stage, no sets, no lighting, and no theatre. When the three of us got together at the Lakewood Diner, a contract was initiated between us, we shook hands and said we were equal partners."

"It's not a written contract. My son-in-law is a lawyer and he told me Michael is not entitled to anything."

"So you are not entitled to anything either, right?" She didn't answer me. I went on, "In my country, a handshake is a legal bond between partners. And I would like to keep it that way. Besides, do you have any idea how much he has spent already building the stage and sets? Do you realize how much it would cost us to get a professional carpenter? He is going to run the lights during the shows; do you realize how much it would cost us if we were to pay someone to do it?" I guess I spoke with a lot of passion because she said, "Well, you are the producer so you make the final decision."

The Simy Theatre was going to be a professional theatre. People were going to pay a good price to see the shows and they expected the best and that was what I was going to provide. I would surround myself with the best people to make it happen, and Michael was one of them.

Michael brought six large stage lights into the Kobe he had inherited from the Belmar Theatre. But we still needed a dozen smaller ones for the first row close to the front of the stage, and six more of the larger lamps in back of them. He gave me a list of what I needed to buy.

I made a few phone calls and finally found a company specializing in stage lights. They made me an offer I could not resist. If I paid everything off in six months, they would not charge me interest.

I put an ad in the Asbury Park Press, "Looking for professional directors and actors to audition for "The Simy Dinner Theatre Company." The auditions at the Simy Theatre turned out even better than I had expected. Actors, actresses, and directors answered the ad. I talked to each one individually and took their resume. Out of respect for

Andy, since we had worked together in two theatre productions, I called him about the dinner theatre getting started and then informed him we each had to go our own way. I did not feel it was necessary to mention I had based my decision on his inappropriate behavior in our apartment during the last cast party for his play, when I wasn't present. I was at the party, but I didn't go into the bedroom where Andy was having a private gathering with Steve and other boys. Steve and one of his friends trusted me enough to share what happened. I was relieved when Andy said he understood and if I ever changed my mind he would be glad to work with me again.

I invited all the people who had come to audition back for a meeting at the Kobe. We all sat on the newly-built stage. "As you know the theatre is in its infancy," I spoke as if addressing my own family. "I have to be honest with you, until I pay off the lights and the expenses encountered to build the stage, I have no money to pay anyone. Your understanding and support is what will make or break the start of this theatre." Except for their glare, there was no response. I went on, "I promise on my honor that once everything is paid for 50 percent of the monies earned will be divided equally among the actors no matter how small or large are their roles. Directors will get paid a set fee, and so will the stage crew. Is this reasonable to everyone?"

One actor said, "It's more than I expected. The other theatres didn't pay anything." The others nodded their heads in agreement.

We talked about the first show and I paid a lot of attention to what they were saying. They may have been thinking, "Oh, she's a theatre producer, so she must know what she wants and what she's doing," but they would have been wrong. I was a novice producer in dire need of learning what to do next, but of course I didn't say that. By the end of the meeting, one director had volunteered to direct the first show, which was voted by the majority to be *Plaza Suite* by Neil Simon.

Our theatre productions would run for one month, Friday and Saturday nights, with a matinee on Saturdays and Sundays. Mr. Ounuma would collect the money he made from the dinners served by the restaurant, and I would make the money from the theatre tickets. It was a win-win situation.

Horror of horrors! Three weeks before opening night I had to fire Tony, the director. The cast was up in arms concerning the show's direction and wanted him out of the picture. Firing someone had to be the worst thing anyone could ask me to do. Tracey said, "I'm only the assistant producer and as such it's not my job to fire anyone."

I called Michael. "Tracey is right," he said. "Ronnie, you are the producer, it's your job to do the dirty work."

So I called Tony, and asked him to meet me at the Howell Music Center. I took his arm lovingly and walked him outside. "Tony, I'm very concerned about your heart. The excitement of directing is in my opinion too much for you. I have to ask you to resign from directing." (It helps when firing someone very old to blame it on their heart. I could not say, "I have a mutiny on my hands and the cast wants you out of their lives, because you can't direct.")

Tony replied, "Yes, my heart is not as good as it used to be, but that's not going to stop me from directing."

I panicked. "Oh yes it will. You get excited with the actors when they don't listen to you. You scream at them and your blood pressure goes up, and then what? I'll have a dead director on my hands."

He would not listen and kept arguing with me. Finally I took a deep breath of courage and said, "Please don't make it worse for me than it already is, but, you're no longer the director for the show."

"You're firing me?"

"I think so." I mumbled, then more firmly, "Yes."

He walked away.

Barbara Shiavone, the main character in the play came to the rescue. She had directed *Plaza Suite* some years ago with another theatre and was willing to direct our production. I counted my blessings.

Michael called. "It's a real joke if not mind boggling that you are producing dinner theatre and have never been to one." I could hear him snickering. "I highly recommend that you and Tracey come Saturday night to the Foodtown Restaurant in Asbury Park. I'm doing lights and sounds for their dinner theatre production at the restaurant and I can get you both in for free.

The food was mediocre, but the play had everyone laughing heartily. We barely saw Michael who was busy operating the sound and light board in the back of the room. I was impressed with his work; everything seemed to go smoothly and on cue. Before we left I congratulated Michael on a job well done and then added, "Well, now I know what a dinner theatre is like. People have dinner and then watch a play. Thanks for the invitation, I appreciate it."

Tracey and I were walking in the parking lot and as we were about to get into my van, we noticed a bunch of thick electrical cables lying on the ground next to it. Except for a couple of cars, the parking lot was basically empty.

"This is so odd," I said to Tracey. "Could it be a gift from the Gods, since we need cables for our theatre? What fool would leave this much electrical cable just lying on the ground?"

"Ronnie, every time you wish for something, there it is. Someone left them for us is the only answer. It's incredible, that's all I can say."

Feeling a bit like Bonnie and Clyde, it was decided we were taking the cables with us. We were laughing uncontrollably as I started the engine and Tracey began gathering the heavy cables and putting them in the back of the van.

"Hurry up, Tracey. If the cops catch us doing this we're both going to jail." I was laughing with tears in my eyes, watching her put the cables into the van as quickly as she could manage.

"Don't worry Ronnie, my son-in-law is a darn good lawyer; he'll get us both out." She was laughing her head off, too.

I drove the van out of the parking lot like a bat out of hell as she said, "Well, at least we didn't get mugged."

Asbury Park was no longer a safe place to visit. There was too much crime going on, especially in empty parking lots!

I was proud of myself when I took Michael to my van to surprise him with my newfound treasure.

"Those are my cables!" he exclaimed.

"What do you mean they're your cables? Tracey and I found them in the parking lot outside the restaurant in Asbury Park."

"I went crazy looking for them after the show. I forgot I had taken them out of my car. Thank God you took them and not someone else."

Tracey and I had done well after all.

On opening night I did the backstage work. I was the stage manager and Michael ran the lights. Tracy sat up front with her husband and Al. The reviewer for the *Asbury Park Press* was also seated in the first row of round tables. We had a full house. During the second act, the lights on the stage went out unexpectedly. Quick as lightning, Michael ran into the dressing room and fixed the circuit breaker. The stage lights went back on to find the actors—God bless their artistic souls—frozen in time and then instantaneously returning to life as if nothing had happened. Applause from the audience was their sign of appreciation, and the show went on without any further disconcerting events.

"It's live theatre and anything can happen," said Michael afterward, "but at least we can brag that we have the most professional cast one can wish for."

I believed him. Michael had done a lot of theatre and he knew when something was outstanding.

We all read the *Asbury Park Press* review of our show over and over again, including Mr. Ounuma who translated the review in Japanese to his wife. He made extra copies for everyone in the production. We were introduced to the readers as the best new theatre around. A merited mention of Michael's prompt action getting the lights on, and the actors not losing their stage presence and remaining in character during the blackout was announced loud and clear for everyone to read. The *Asbury Park Press* reviewer called *Plaza Suite* "a shining production."

Autumn of 1985

Getting up at five in the morning in order to get the band instruments to the schools was not as bad as I had imagined it would be. Steve and I shared the delivery load. After two weeks of delivery, I would be free to sleep in late again. I needed ten hours of sleep; otherwise my brain did not work at full capacity.

I got an odd feeling one day when opening the mail, for along with Mama's usual letter; she had enclosed a couple of poems I had written when I was a teenager. At that time she was testing me to see if I had any poetic talent. She must have thought they were worthwhile to have kept them all those years. But why didn't she ever share those proud feelings with me? Why did she always push me away? Someday I would get the courage to ask her why she never showed me any love when I was growing up. She had written, "Here are some remarkable poems you wrote when you were a teenager. You might like to read them now that you're older."

Why? What was I supposed to do with them 25 years later?

The Howell Music Center and the Simy Theatre needed my undivided attention so I stopped writing my weekly column for *The Booster News*.

I kept my reporter ID badge in my wallet along with my driver's license. When the highway patrolmen stopped me for speeding and saw the badge, which looked like a police badge, they assumed I had something to do with the police department. I always got an "Okay, I'm going to let you go this time, but you better drive at the speed limit from now on."

Michael nicknamed me, "Roadrunner."

Our second production, *Eat Your Heart Out*, was cancelled three weeks prior to opening night. The main actor, who had been complaining of constant headaches, had to be admitted to the hospital with a brain tumor. After the initial shock, I called Barbara Schiavone. She told me how to get hold of Bill Daniels, who in her opinion, was the best actor and director she had ever worked with.

Bill was very happy to get involved with our theatre. He had done *Mass Appeal* some years back, and felt it would be the best choice since we did not have much time to get another show together. In return for helping us out, Bill only had one request—he would like to direct the comedy *Murder at the Howard Johnson's*. We shook hands on it.

Al told me that if he were rich, he would get a chauffeur to drive him around. I would buy a big truck and drive it myself. Al would like a big house with servants. I would rather have an apartment. What would I do with a big house? I only needed one bedroom! He bought his clothes new but they got trashed quickly. I liked mine used. They had their own personality and lasted longer. Even though I washed them, he was worried I would catch some kind of skin disease so I stopped telling him where I bought my wardrobe. He loved Enrico Caruso, an old opera singer. I loved rock and roll. He preferred to spend the day watching television. I preferred to go to art galleries, attend a concert, and visit a museum. He did not like to have friends. I did. He liked to talk about depressing subjects. I liked to talk about positive, inspiring stories. I enjoyed making people happy and being surrounded by happy faces. Sometimes I would say silly stuff on purpose to make people laugh.

"Ronnie, you're always so happy," people would say.

"They" thought I was happy, but I fooled everyone. When you smile, people smile back. Nobody wants to know about your problems. Crying and suffering is for the weak they lack inner strength to solve their own problems. When I described something bad that happened, I liked to describe it as a joke unless it was so atrocious I was better off not mentioning it at all. After all, life was a joke and should be looked at like a circus with the clowns acting out their silliness. I considered myself a pretty good clown. Go ahead clown, tell me how funny life is. It's a joke!

Al had gotten a raw deal when he married me. He would have been better off marrying a normal, mature person.

It wasn't easy to get *Mass Appeal* ready on such short notice. For Bill and Steve, the other actor who had already performed in the show, it was only a matter of reviewing the script. But for Michael, Tracey, and me it was no picnic. Michael had to build and put up a whole new set in one week. And then it came to Tracey and me to paint it and get everything in place within twenty-four hours because Michael needed to get some sleep.

Mr. Ounuma was great to work with but we were forbidden to use the air conditioner unless it was show time. So there we were, Tracey and I painting the set and sweating our balls off—as some men have the custom of saying—when Tracey turned to me and said, "You know what Ronnie, we're the only two people up here. I don't know about you, but I don't sweat. I'm afraid I'm going to pass out any minute unless I take my clothes off."

"I don't sweat either. That's the reason I don't go to the beach in the middle of the day when it's too hot. I always wait until the sun goes down; otherwise I'll have a stroke. When I was a young mother and too hardheaded to admit how sensitive I was to the heat, I used to go to the beach and lay down in the sand trying to get a tan like everybody else. After half an hour my head would start to throb and I would be feeling weak, as if I were going to faint. I would have to get my mother-in-law and the kids into the car and quickly drive home. Once I got home, I had to lie down with ice on my head. It took me years of suffering to finally accept my weakness and sensitivity to heat. Tracey, I'm taking my clothes off, too." It was in my Portuguese blood that whenever I wanted to say something it went on into a long story.

We got down to our bras and underwear and we were laughing and joking when Tracey said in a mischief tone, "What do we do if Mr. Ounuma suddenly appears?" We were laughing as she went on, "He would probably faint from seeing two beautiful women half naked, painting the stage!"

Suddenly we heard someone coming up from the back stairs leading down to the kitchen. We ran to the double doors and blocked them with our bodies, holding our breath.

"This is it Ronnie. We're going to get raped!" She was not kidding.

Someone tried pushing the door to open it but we were holding it back with our bodies.

"Hello... I'm the night watchman!" It was Bruce's tenor voice on the other side of the doors. "Is anybody up here?"

I yelled back, "Yes, we're the stage people and we are painting and... you can't come in."

"Why not? Open up" He tapped on the door.

I yelled out, "It's very hot up here and... we're not decent."

Tracey shouted, "Go away, we are in our underwear."

After a few moments of silence he said, "Oh, okay, Mr. Ounuma told me you might be up here painting. Just turn off all the lights before you leave the building."

We didn't move an inch until we heard his footsteps going back down the old creepy wooden steps to the kitchen below, clunk, clunk, clunk.

On opening night the set was still drying. *Mass Appeal*, starring Bill Daniels and Steve Steiner, was not well attended because people thought it was a religious play. One evening a couple showed up to see the show but when they took a look inside the theatre and saw the cross on the stage they turned to leave. Thank God I was upstairs and asked them why they were not staying. The husband said, "We're not Catholic." I asked them to stay, and if they didn't like it I would refund their tickets in full. They loved the show and said they were going to tell all their friends about it.

Getting great reviews still didn't bring in the crowds like *Plaza Suite*, however even though it wasn't a great financial success, just having a show was in itself a miracle and kept us afloat. We had accomplished the impossible in exactly one week.

The play basically went without any theatrical abnormalities except for one of the nights when Steve forgot to zip up his pants before he entered the stage. Bill happened to catch Steve's white underwear sticking out of his pants and gave him a subtle look toward the crotch. Steve looked down and realized why the audience was laughing instead of being moved by his insightful speech. He turned ever-so-nonchalantly with his back to the audience, but everybody was aware of "the closing of the zipper." That was the funniest part of the show that evening.

The play's title of *Mass Appeal* may not have been a great draw for large crowds, but *No Sex Please, We Are British* more than made up for it with a full house every night. Like everybody says, put the word sex into the title and watch the sex-starved crowds show up.

If we continued to do well financially, it was just a matter of getting another crowd pleaser and I could pay off the lighting system and then start paying the cast and crew.

Winter ending 1985

For Christmas I hid all the money I owed Michael for stage supplies inside a hubcap I had found on the road. I wrapped it with Christmas wrapping paper and added a bow. I took the present to his house and gave it to Madeleine to put under their tree. I wished I could have seen his face. I added $500 extra to help cover the hours he had worked without charging us for it.

Winter of 1986

Nanette, a reviewer for a local newspaper, and I became friends after she came to Kobe to interview me. Nanette was in her mid-sixties. She was a petite woman, barely five feet tall. She wore her blonde hair in a short pixie style that favored her high cheekbones and large green eyes. Her face reminded me of a Persian cat. She must have been a real knockout when she was younger since she was still very beautiful. But she suffered from low self-esteem and did not see herself the way I did. All her clothes were of different shades of purple, the only color she wore along with a collection of gaudy purple-stone rings which adorned all her fingers. Even her eyeglasses had a purple tint with a dark purple rim.

Papa used to say, "When a mature woman puts on something purple, she is looking for her last passionate love affair." Maybe he was right, but Nanette was also looking for attention. She told me several times how much she loved it when people referred to her as, "The Purple Lady."

Nanette had gone through a bitter divorce ten years prior and she lived alone with her furry white Siamese cat in a huge neglected house. She did not have any friends, and she liked it that way. "You're my only true friend; everyone else is a phony." She sounded a lot like Al when it came to trusting anyone. Both her son and daughter were married and lived in Virginia. Since her divorce, she had cut all ties with them by calling them despicable people. But Nanette loved our theatre and every month came to opening night and wrote a review. She was also a food critic and a lot of times she invited me out for lunch. She reviewed their food and service and she did not hold anything back.

Nanette turned out to be a good friend. She was bright, energetic, and a great person to talk to. One day I told her, "You would make a great television show host because you are especially good at asking questions and listening."

"How did you know that's my dream to do someday?" she asked surprised.

Most of the time I drove our van and Al and Steve did the muscle work of moving the pianos. But whenever possible, we hired two guys willing to do the backbreaking work for $25 each. John was a fairly average looking guy, but Tony, his partner, weight at least 300 pounds of solid bulging muscles. He was big, very big, and his head alone must have been close to 50 pounds. His black beard and greasy long dark hair, tied back into a ponytail, made him look like something between a bandit and Bluto, the nasty cartoon character from *Popeye the Sailorman*. The only difference was that Tony had the personality of a pussycat and little John was the one with an impatient, crabby attitude. Walking down a dark alley with Tony was most likely better than carrying a gun.

One afternoon we went to deliver a baby grand piano to a Mrs. Thompson in Spring Lake. My job was to drive and oversee the delivery.

On the way to the customer's home, Tony told me Susan, his girlfriend of three years, had left him. He made a few jokes about her new boyfriend and described him as a loser and a pin-head.

The huge house and the matching stairway leading to the music room next to the library on the second floor, reminded me of the set for *Gone With The Wind*. John looked up and crossed his arms. "Shit! Are they out of their minds? Why didn't they put the fucking music room downstairs? We can't do it. Forget it!"

"It's a piece of cake. Of course we can do it." Tony patted John on the shoulder. "C'mon, you take the top and I'll hold the piano from the bottom."

I stood at the top of the steps with Mrs. Thompson watching them carry the piano and forced myself to smile at her. "Don't worry," I said. "They're professional piano movers."

They were about halfway up when Tony stopped and began crying out loudly, "I miss my woman! Why did she leave me? Why?"

John yelled, "Come on man, this is heavy! Don't you dare let go."

"No, I can't go on," said Tony, sobbing uncontrollably.

"I give up on this shit and life!"

"Come on Tony, don't screw with me now. I can't do it by myself, man!"

It was my turn to panic and instead of staying safely at the top of the steps; I squeezed myself between the piano and the wall and got behind Tony.

I tried to speak softly while maintaining a certain dignity as I suddenly realized I had made a big mistake by getting behind him; I imagined both the piano and Tony rolling down the steps and crashing on top of whatever was left of me once we all hit the bottom. "Tony, if you let go of the piano I'm going to die with you. It's only a couple more steps to go. Here, let me give you a hand. I'll help you, okay?" I put my hands flat on his large bottom in an effort to push him up the rest of the way. Although I was pushing I doubted I was actually moving him at all.

His tears turned into laughter and we got to the top of the steps safe and sound.

Barbara Schiavone was an amazing director. The critics described the production of *The Owl and the Pussycat* as a rare gem. Tracey complained a lot about Barbara's despondency concerning the props being there on time and being exactly what she demanded. If an actor did not fit Barbara's expectations, she had no problem replacing them. Barbara was a perfectionist and she prided herself in creating unforgettable masterpieces. I felt very lucky to have a director of such a high caliber and gave her complete freedom to do as she pleased.

One night, before falling asleep, I began to think how wonderful it would be if I could travel to a different planet, and suddenly there I was, going through the insides of a world made of crystals of all sizes. The sky was on the inside of the planet, and the rays of light bouncing from the different shapes of the crystallized walls produced colors I had never seen. The best part of the dream was that I knew I was dreaming "Wow! This is a reality dream! Nobody is going to believe where I've been. Wow! I'm flying, but I can't fall because I'm dreaming."

Michael said he was jealous. He hardly ever dreamed and wished he could have dreams like mine.

Ralph sold me his old computer for a few bucks. I needed it to make a mailing list for the theatre patrons. He connected everything for me so the labels could get printed. I eagerly typed in the names day after day, and was entering label number 220 when Al came into the bedroom and turned the light switch off. "You don't need the light on in this room," he said. "Just open the curtains."

Bang, I had lost everything I had typed in! The computer was connected to the switch! Weeks and weeks of typing had vanished forever, not to mention enduring weeks and weeks of looking at a green screen that made me nauseous and gave me a pounding headache. I cried and cursed and cried again. It was devastating and horrendously horrible to lose all my data.

I received a surprise letter from Mr. Joe Szostak, my old music teacher at Brookdale Community College.

He wrote, "Dear Ronnie, whether you realize it or not, I have often singled you out as one of our department's pride and joy. Your music career and success has been a medal on our chest. I have a favor to ask you. Would you contribute your success story by helping to publicize the Music-Dance Program at Brookdale?"

I called him. "How did you find me?"

"I have been following your achievements through the news," he said.

"They're not achievements; they're hobbies that have turned out to be successful."

"Are you trying to diminish what you have done?"

Braving A New World

"No."

"Then come to the college and be an inspiration to others. We need you."

I went to Brookdale College and they took my picture for their newspaper advertisement. I walked around the campus reminiscing over the old days. I missed the learning environment, but did not know what classes to take at that point in my life.

Ralph came over during the week and showed me how to save my work in the computer at the end of each page. We also decided to play a prank on Steve. Ralph set up the computer with automatic answers to questions we knew Steve would ask. Ralph typed in Steve's name and how old he was and that he had a girlfriend named Bobbie Sue.

When Steve came home, Ralph called him over to see my new computer. "Hey Steve, did you see Mom's new computer? Did you know computers are able to see and think on their own?"

"No way, I don't believe it!"

"Alright, if you don't believe it, go ahead and ask the computer a question."

Of course Steve fell for it hook, line, and sinker.

"Okay," he asked defiantly, "computer, what's my name?"

Ralph and I looked at each other, trying not to laugh. Ralph pressed a button and acted as if he was talking to the computer. "Go ahead computer, tell us what my brother's name is."

Across the screen came the words, "Hi, nice to meet you, Steve Esagui. How are you?"

Steve's eyes opened wide. "Okay, okay, but I bet the computer doesn't know how old I am."

Once again Ralph pressed the magic key and automatically brought up a sentence on the screen that stated, "Steve, you and I both know your age. You are 21 years old!"

It was just too much for Ralph and me to hold a straight face. Steve caught on to our game and we all laughed heartily. We always had so much fun when we were together.

I held a meeting with our music teachers at the Howell Music Center to discuss a students' recital, but I wanted something unique and inspiring. What could be more inspiring to students than seeing their teachers play first? We would have an intermission and then the students would play. They all agreed to do it and I thought it would be even more special if we could have the recital at the Kobe. The teachers and students could use the stage and feel like real performers. Mr. Ounuma said we could use the theatre for the recital and there would be no charge.

Even though I no longer taught guitar, bass, or banjo, I offered to play one of my old favorite tunes on the banjo. I was doing fine announcing each performer, and then Bill, the sax teacher, decided to get in on the fun and said, "Ladies and gentleman, I would like to present to you Mrs. Ronnie Esagui. She is the owner of the Howell Music Center as you all know, and she has done a wonderful job putting this recital together."

Everybody applauded and I was feeling good about the whole thing when his big blubber-mouth went on, "Yes, let's have another good round of applause for this little lady. She is very nervous but she's going to play for you a very nice tune on her five-string banjo."

I felt very relaxed and competent and wondered what he was talking about.

But Bill was not finished. He tapped me on the shoulder and whispered, "Don't worry; you're going to do fine." Of course I was going to do fine; I had played "The Hillbillies" tune hundreds of times with my bluegrass band.

I sat down and began to play when suddenly my fingers started to shake. I could not believe it. *You stupid idiot*, I told myself, *don't let that moron get to you.* But it was too late; no matter how I tried to stay calm, my playing sucked. That incident opened my eyes to the power of suggestion.

With the letter I sent to Mama and Papa each week, I enclosed $50 to help them with bills. Old age was horrible enough when you were sick, but being destitute was a double whammy. Mama said the maids were now charging a pretty penny and the cost of living kept going up and up in Portugal. They no longer had two maids and the one they had didn't work on weekends. My cousins from England were also helping my parents with a monthly check, to cover utilities and food and but nothing was enough to cover the care they needed.

I had just finished tuning an old piano, getting it ready to be delivered that week, when Francis walked into our music store. "My, oh my," she said. "I didn't recognize you. You look like a young girl. For a moment I thought you had a new employee."

I have to admit that I was happy to hear such a nice compliment from a friend. I knew my youthfulness would not last forever and sooner or later I would look my age or even older. Chronologically I was forty-two but in my head I was still fifteen, and until I found a good reason to come out of my ageless seashell, I preferred to remain fifteen until I died. I also believed the reason I looked the way I did was because I had good genes, and I had maintained the same weight ever since I had gotten married. I also believed the clothes I wore made me look younger. When Francis came in, I was in my worn out jeans and Andrea's jean jacket.

Andrea was one of Steve's girlfriends. Steve only went out on a date for one reason—sex. After he wore her jacket for a month, he gave it to me when I said how much I wished I had one just like it.

Andrea's jacket became my lapel pins, brooches and special buttons carrier. My favorites were two Stalin pins given to me by a Russian customer as a thank you, after I sold him a couple of guitar strings and some picks. The jacket was a bit big for me, which was good; it had lots of room to display all my little trophies collected through the years. It also made a great conversation piece.

I had a weakness for used clothes. It started the day I first wore my grandmother Rica's long evening dress made of black lace intertwined with colorful stones and embroidery. The dress had been a present to Grandma Rica from her husband Leão, who bought it in Paris around 1920. Mama inherited it but when I came to America, she gave it to me. The first time I put it on I was only seventeen and I felt it was the closest I could be to Grandma Rica after she had died so many years ago. Her dress hugged me as if it were glad to be alive again.

I enjoyed shopping for clothes at thrift shops. I particularly liked the hippie era as I thought it was a true reflection of my spirit—fighting for my identity. But when I was at the Simy Theatre, I did my best to dress in accordance with the image of a theatre producer.

I finally came up with the perfect word to describe Al's constant nagging. The Portuguese word *fenia* said it all. It meant "nagger," but said in Portuguese, it had a lot more meaning. When Al was in the *fenia* mood, Steve found an excuse to leave the music center, such as having to make a delivery. I just said, "I'll be back later." He never asked where I went; he was good that way. I got in my car and drove around for a while and returned later a lot more relaxed. I spent many days going to New York City, just to walk. I loved New York City and it was only an hour's drive away.

Braving A New World

Spring of 1986

Nanette would not tell me what she was up to for my birthday. It turned out to be a trip to Maine, to a very specific restaurant that had all-you-can-eat crab. I liked crab but I was not as wild about it as she was. I enjoyed the long trip more than anything else. Nanette and I never ran out of conversation.

The restaurant was at Casco Bay and it reminded me of a huge log cabin with its back surrounded by yellow birch and sugar maple trees and its spacious wood deck in front facing the harbor below. Nanette did not care for the way the seagulls were acting above our heads so we moved inside.

After three big crabs, I was done. I remained seated and watched in amusement at how Nanette ate one crab after another with her hands, which was really the only way to fully enjoy them. After the fourth crab, she realized that she'd better pull her sleeves up and take off her huge rings as each finger was dripping in crab juice. She placed the rings inside a bowl next to me and said, "Veronica, please don't let me forget them."

I watched the crab juice dripping from her hands down her forearms and elbows. There were no boundaries to her eating as she took her time sucking on each of her fingers, tasting and enjoying each morsel of crabmeat and its juices to their last drop. She ate what I would call an "ocean of crabs." I was impressed how someone so petite could devour so much food. As she said, "For me, eating is better than having sex."

That would explain why she ate so much. It was a crab orgy! When she finally stopped, I knew she was satisfied.

She enjoyed the attention the restaurant owner gave her when he came to our table to meet the famous "Purple Lady" from New Jersey. I could read his mind when he shook her hand. "Thank God this woman lives in New

Jersey!"

For my birthday, Michael surprised me with a book by Douglas Adams, *The Hitchhiker's Guide to the Galaxy*. He knew how much I loved Douglas Adams' sense of humor. Adams had become one of my very favorite writers after Michael lent me other books by the same author. He was the only writer who was able to keep my attention with wacky science fiction. In my opinion, the reason his books were able to feed my imagination was because Douglas Adams had the perfect recipe for how to scramble together human faults and qualities with impossible possibilities, which was something I personally thrived on.

Tracey invited me for lunch at her house. As I was driving through her neighborhood, I saw a dark-red velour loveseat and a matching full-sized couch sitting on the curb, waiting to be picked up by the garbage man. The couches looked like new. I immediately went for the brakes and started pushing and pulling the furniture into my music van.
 A woman came out of the house waving at me. "Is that you, Ronnie? I can't believe this. What are you doing here?"
 I was surprised too. It was one of our music customers who happened to live there.
 "I have a dinner theatre and these couches will be perfect for one of our shows." Then I dared to ask, "Can you help me to put them into my van?"
 We could only get the loveseat to fit into the van, but she promised to hold the full-sized couch until the next morning. Mrs. Lawson hated to get rid of the couches, but she was redecorating the living room and the red color did not fit into the new décor. When I got to our music center I called Michael. He had broken off with his girlfriend and moved in with some young friends. He was sure he could borrow a truck from one of them. Most likely they would

be happy to have some extra furniture and anytime we needed the couches we could just come and get them.

On Wednesday morning we got a phone call from Cousin Joe. "You all need to come to Long Island at once." He sounded frantic. "Nelly fell down. She's in the hospital and may die at any moment."

Al and I left Steve in charge of the music center. We met Joe and Ginny at the hospital and planned on staying with them for the night. Nelly was connected to machines that kept her heart beating and blood circulating. Her doctor told us she might be bleeding internally as a result of her fall. She was not responding to any stimuli and without the machines she was connected to, she would be dead. Al took the news calmly but Joe was tearful and I got the impression that Joe loved Nelly more than Al. I stared at Nelly lying in bed connected to wires and the idea that she was not allowed to die felt medically sinister and inhuman.

Ginny and I went out to get some sandwiches for lunch the next day and I was taken by surprise when she told me she was planning on having a wake for Nelly if she died.

"You mean laying Nelly in an open coffin for the family to see her for the last time? Ginny, that can't be done. As you know, in the Jewish religion when someone dies, they just get buried. It's not acceptable to display the body to the open public like a show of some kind."

Her eyes opened wide. "What do you mean by that? Nelly is Jewish?"

I was surprised at her foolish question. "Yeah, and so is Joe and Ruth and everybody else in our family! You mean, you didn't know?"

"Joe never told me. His mother, his sister, how can that be?" She was crying copiously now. "All these years, married to a liar! How could he have done this to me? Ruth never said anything either. No one ever told me anything."

I didn't know what to say but to apologize to her for my

own ignorance. I really thought she knew. Personally, I felt that Ginny was making a big deal out of nothing. Except for going wild buying Christmas gifts and chocolate eggs for Easter, neither she nor Joe practiced any type of religion. Being a Catholic or a Christian had to be more than just having fun during those holidays.

When the doctor came into the waiting room to ask Joe and Al if they should keep Nelly on life support, they said yes. I did not agree with their decision and told Al, "If this ever happens to me, I do not want to stay connected to any machines. I want to die in peace."

Ruth would be back Saturday from her vacation in Florida and then they would make a decision as to what to do about their mom. Joe asked Al to stay with him and I drove that same day to New Jersey. After twenty-four years of marriage, it was the first time Al and I were separated. I did not miss Al. If anything, I was experiencing the same feeling of freedom I had when I left Portugal and came to the US.

I spent the weekend at Ronnie's Music Den in Collingswood during the day and my nights at the theatre. Michael ran the lights and I did the stage-managing. After the show on Sunday we went home, each on our merry way.

So, what do I want, I asked myself. *What is it with me? What more can I want?* I knew exactly what I wanted. I wished that Michael and I could hold hands and fly across the endless space, like in the Douglas Adams' book *The Restaurant at the End of the Universe*.

On Monday, Al called me at noon. Nelly had been disconnected that morning and was officially dead. I prayed, "May her soul rest peacefully in Heaven where she will find her husband, her parents, and brothers all waiting for her."

Ralph and Steve came with me to Long Island. I had

never been to a funeral. I did not know what to think of death, but I was willing to wait until I was dead to get all the answers. I only knew my parents were older than Nelly, and sooner or later death would also take them away. I was glad I was not living close to them. I understood that such a feeling was part of my selfishness, but I did not know if I could deal with their deaths. My brother José was thirty-five years old but because of his health, he was no better off than they were. When my parents died, he would not be able to care for himself. My brother Max-Leão felt that José should have been committed a long time ago, but Mama would not allow such a thing. As long as she was alive she would take care of her son.

I heard a story a while back on the radio about a mother caring for her son, and I never forgot it: Once upon a time, a man got married and his wife, who was jealous of his mother, said to him, "If you really love me, kill your mother and bring me her head Then I'll know that you love me more than her."

He went to his mother's house and cut off her head and he hurriedly ran down the street holding his mother's head in his hands. He tumbled over a rock and fell, bruising his knees. His mother used her last breath of air to say, "My son, are you okay?"

Summer of 1986

Al and I found a two-bedroom condo for sale in Lakewood. We had a pretty good down payment but since we couldn't pay in full, we still had to get a mortgage. Paying a monthly fee of close to nothing in principal along with a high interest rate went against my principles, but it was a lot less per month than what we were paying in rent for the apartment in Howell.

It was about three in the afternoon when Steve's ex-girlfriend Joan, walked into our music store wearing a loose black raincoat and super-high heels. Joan was eighteen, and as Aunt Heydee would say, "When you are young, it does not matter what you wear. Youth makes you automatically beautiful."

Joan was tall, blonde, and slim but she was not a beauty queen until she removed her coat and stood wearing nothing but a tiny blue bikini. She said to Steve, "I want you to see what you're missing."

I moved Mrs. Lawson and her two children toward the other side of the store and Steve picked up Joan's raincoat and did his best to cover her while walking her out of our store. It was summertime, but nobody walked around in a bikini unless they were at the beach. It was odd to see what love did to people. If anyone asked me to describe what love was, I would have said love is like a dangerous sickness of the mind if not under control.

Besides giving the cast and crew a free hibachi dinner on our final closing night after the show, Mr. Ounuma was so happy with how our theatre had increased his clientele, that he began adding a free dinner for us after *every* Friday night show. The salad was always served with the most delicious ginger and garlic dressing and the meals were unique and specially made for us. However, on one Friday, the dinner went "beyond" our expectations. The cook prepared, just for us, pork chop pancakes! We did not know what possessed him to create something so dreadful. We ate the rice and the salad, but everyone left their pork chop pancake on their plate.

Of course we did not want to offend the cook and certainly not Mr. Ounuma. So we stacked the pancakes between a couple of plates, and Tracey and the new stage manager followed me discreetly into the back corner of the kitchen. I pulled open one of the large garbage cans and removed the contents from the top. The pancakes were quickly dropped in and covered with all the existing garbage. No one saw us.

When Mr. Ounuma came by our table, he was impressed. "Wow, you all really loved the pork chops, even the bones are gone!"

Tracey came to our rescue with a huge smile. "Oh yes, and we already took a few of the plates to the kitchen, too. You feed us and we clear the table. It's only right." She got up with a few other actors and removed the rest of the dishes from the table. It had been a meal to remember!

While preparing to head home one evening, I was locking the front door to our music center and Steve was getting into his car when I heard the roaring sound of a car engine and the screeching sound of tires. I turned around just in time to see Joan drive straight toward Steve's car and then stop an inch away from hitting it. She came out of her car crying and he got out of his car screaming, "Are you out of your mind?" She tried to hug him. "I love you! If you don't take me back, I swear I'll kill myself."

"That's a good way to show me how much you love me by trying to kill us both." He pushed her away from him and drove off.

Joan was madder than the Mad Hatter in *Alice in Wonderland*.

Autumn of 1986

I asked Steve if he knew the whereabouts of Shana. The last time I had seen her had been about a year before, at the new flea market in Howell. She was not wearing shoes and her clothes looked battered and dirty. Her long tangled hair and her sunken eyes made her look old. She was trying to sell a record player to a passerby and when she saw me she asked me if I would like to buy it from her. I don't believe she recognized me her, blank look lacked any emotion.

"I knew you would be sad so I didn't tell you. Shana died from AIDS a few months ago."

"Oh dear. I should have made an effort to bring her home with me that day at the flea market."

"Mom, when you saw her last year it was already too late to help her. She was deep into drugs, and she had already been diagnosed with the AIDS virus."

I cried for her young soul to rest in peace, something she did not find while she was alive.

Michael Miller, the director for *Ten Little Indians*, requested French doors for the set. When I suggested we use "regular" doors he said, "The French doors are a must. They're a crucial part of the set. Agatha Christie will roll over in her grave if we don't have French doors."

It was just my bad luck that Michael was still living with his friends from whom he rented a room and all his carpenter tools were still at his mother's house.

I went looking for French doors and about passed out when I saw the price tag. I had two weeks left to put the set up but the thought of paying hundreds of dollars for something most likely used once and then put into storage, drove me nuts. I began wishing for a miracle.

The statement in the playbill, "Your discards may be our treasures," prompted a caller to ask if I could use some furniture and other odds and ends. There was a divorce going on and she was selling the house and did not want the furnishings. Of course I was at her house the next day with Michael, and just as we were walking out with her kitchen table and chairs, I looked at her living room doors that opened to the back patio. They were French doors! They were the expensive kind, made of black wrought iron, with golden pleated curtains on the inside.

"We sure could use those French doors for the show that is starting this weekend." I held my breath.

She looked at me, and then looked at the doors, and shrugging her shoulders said, "If you can unscrew them from their hinges, they're yours."

Michael just happened to have a screwdriver in his toolbox.

On Sunday night I drove to Michael's place with Jeffrey and Sam, my stagehands. Michael was wearing pajama bottoms and yawning when he opened the front door. "Sorry to wake you up Michael," I said, "but we need to pick up the love seat, for *Ten Little Indians*. The director expects it tonight for rehearsal."

"That's fine. You guys just go ahead and take it and then close the door behind you. I have an early day tomorrow." He disappeared down the hallway.

When Michael Miller came into the theatre he was thrilled with the French doors, and loved the red velour love seat, but he wanted a bigger one.

I drove right back with Jeffrey and Sam. Michael would not answer the door, and since it was not locked, we took it upon ourselves to go in. His roommates must have been sleeping also or else they were not home. We took the big couch and put the love-seat in its place and wondered why a dog in another part of the house had suddenly stopped barking.

The next day I asked Michael if he heard us when we returned to his place to exchange the couches, and he said all he heard was the annoying barking dog by his bed so he stuffed a golf ball into its mouth.

Winter ending 1986

Just as a new comedy, *Norman, Is That You?* directed by Barbara Schiavone, was about to begin, a young American couple showed up. They had not called for reservations and did not know we were sold out to a private party of fifty

Japanese women.

The couple was very disappointed. It was their wedding anniversary and they had driven all the way from Trenton to have Japanese food and see the play. Mr. Ounuma spoke to the leader of the Japanese women's club who was very gracious and allowed Mr. and Mrs. Smith to come in. I sat them at one of the side tables.

It was a site to behold seeing fifty Japanese women dressed in luxurious, colorful silk kimonos, but what was even more unexpected was that they were all carrying suitcases. Michael said, "Maybe they are going on a trip afterward."

"Yeah," I said not too sure of myself. "Maybe they don't want to take a chance on leaving the suitcases in their cars." We laughed.

At the start of the play the women tried to control their laughter by putting their hands over their mouths, but half an hour later—perhaps they may have had a bit too much plum wine or sake—they were all laughing a lot more freely. It was also interesting to observe the difference in cultural understanding between the women and the young couple. When the American couple laughed at certain punchlines the Japanese women exchanged puzzled looks. The same would happen when the women would laugh or giggle and the line wasn't even funny. Michael and I agreed, their English was most likely very basic. The action is what made them laugh. The Japanese Club leader requested that our intermission, which was normally fifteen-minutes, be extended to thirty minutes. The reason for such an odd request came to light when they took their luggage into the bathroom and changed their kimonos for the second part of the show. Apparently they wanted to show off their two best kimonos to each other. Then the most unexpected thing happened when Frank and the cast came back on stage to take a bow at the end of the show. Those very sweet, polite, shy women jumped on the stage screaming like a group of wild teenagers and grabbed Frank, the main character in the play, who was no spring chicken, and tried to pull off his clothes.

He did have a certain charm for a man in his mid-sixties, with silver hair and a smiling face. But seeing a bunch of drunken, loose women in tight kimonos jumping on the stage trying to rip his clothes off could not even be described. It was as close to a mob scene as I ever wanted to be in. Michael and I leaped on stage to rescue Frank. "It's okay, I don't mind," he said as Michael and I guided the women off the stage. "This was a first for me," he said beaming with delight. "I must say, at my age it was a great feeling to have such adoring female fans wanting every part of me. My wife is not going to believe it." After the play, we went to check on the stage props for the next day. The nude male calendar was gone.

We knew the culprits were not the young American couple. So much for the dignity and proper manners of "nice" ladies who drank too much or simply had a great night out.

It took about $3,000 to put on a theatre production. The royalties were fair, and the props were inexpensive, but twenty-five cents here and three dollars there, and it all added up quickly.

Tracey did an awesome job-hunting for props, and when she did not find them she made them. Her fake food looked good enough to eat. She came into the theatre one evening carrying a platter of fake fried chicken, peas, and mashed potatoes. "You are not going to believe what happened to me when I walked in downstairs." She laughed and we all wanted to hear her story. "Mr. Ounuma took a look at my platter and said, 'Tracey, I'm sorry but you can't come in my restaurant with American food. It's just not appropriate.' He couldn't believe it was fake and had to touch it." She laughed again. "I am the queen of props."

We all applauded.

I was having no luck finding an actor to play the part of a cop breaking down the front door in *Wait Until Dark*. There was no dialogue to memorize and the appearance on stage was too short for any "good actor" to bother with.
    Al offered to play the part. The idea of no words and playing a "cop" was extremely appealing to him. He stopped drinking soda, eating white bread with butter, and consuming his usual gallon of vanilla ice cream before bedtime. In two weeks he lost seven pounds.

Ralph hurt his back lifting a television set at the shop where he worked and went to a chiropractor for the first time. I was shocked. "Why didn't you go to a real doctor?"
    "Mom, chiropractors are doctors. He helped me a lot."
    He explained how the "doctor" had moved his spine into place and he no longer hurt. I cringed at the thought of having my back cracked. I really felt he was better off with medical drugs. He had taken a big chance with his life seeing someone who might have broken his back.

Winter of 1987

Auditions for *Hurray for Hollywood* introduced us to an assortment of comedians, singers, and dancers, and the most cherished of all, Sam, a local comedian that specialized in impersonating female movie stars and comedians. He became the host and principal character in the musical. He did not hide his sexual preference but he did not push it on people. He radiated kindness and his smile was contagious. Everybody loved him, including the audience who always gave him a standing ovation at the end of every performance.

Every morning Steve and I looked for used pianos for sale

in the classified section of the *Asbury Park Press*. Once we found what sounded like a good deal, Steve did all the bargaining and closed the transaction. A lot of the pianos had been abused by the owners and were badly stained from food and drinks. But once we got them in the store, they got tuned, washed with a soft scrub, and the wood was restored with Old English. It took me about a week or two before I had them ready for sale. Used pianos were our bread and butter when it came to making a large profit.

"Sorry Ronnie," said Tracey, "but coming up with a refrigerator for the play *Wait Until Dark* is out of my league. It looks like you'll have to buy one."

I started visualizing a refrigerator. It had to be white, an older model, and small enough to fit effortlessly into the kitchen set...

It was about time we expand our music center. We needed more teaching rooms. Steve agreed. Al did not. Over the years we had been in business I had managed to save $25,000. I had all the money hidden in the bottom of an old toolbox kept in the broom closet, on top of one of the back shelves between cans of paint and other tools. I was sure no robber would ever think of looking for money inside a dilapidated metal toolbox.

Finally Al agreed that it would be to our benefit to move our store to the corner of our mall where the pharmacy was. It was a lot bigger and a lot closer to the highway. No one driving north or south would be able to miss us.

I took a chance and went to visit the pharmacist. "Mr. Johnson, if you ever decide to move out, will you let me know first? I would love to move our music store to this space."

"Funny you should tell me that. It just so happens I'm going to retire in May and I was planning on closing the business. If it's okay with our landlord, the space is yours."

I ran back to our store to give the news to Al and Steve. Then I ran back to measure the pharmacy.

I bought a large sheet of draft paper and began drawing our new music center. A large room would be used for teaching dancing and acting classes, and also for recitals. I also drew the plans for six private teaching rooms and an extra washroom. Our Howell Music Center would not only be a music store but also a real music school. Al and Steve saw my plans and they said it looked pretty good. I rolled the draft paper up, put it under my arm, and took it to the Township Municipal Building so I could have authorization to start building, but they said they couldn't accept it. They wanted an architect to draw up the plans.

After calling around and getting together with a few architects, I came to the conclusion that architects most likely were into buying new and expensive cars, homes, and probably wives, too. The average fee was $200 an hour and a starting minimum of ten hours plus ten percent of the cost of the project, attached to their final bill. But like Aunt Heydee had said so many times, "If you don't give up, it will happen. Also remember the old saying, God only helps those that help themselves."

Using the Yellow Pages carefully so as not to miss anyone on the listing, on my seventh dialing I found an architect in Lakewood for one quarter of what the others wanted—$1,800 and no strings attached.

It happened! I was driving to work one morning when on the side of the curb there it was—a medium-sized, white refrigerator. I immediately went for the brakes, took all the loose parts out of it, and dragging it like a superwoman, I got it into my van. Later that day, Michael came to the theatre and took the motor and the guts out and made it into a perfect lightweight refrigerator. He remarked, "Once again you have outdone yourself."

Spring of 1987

Before I even got engaged to Al, I wondered what it would be like to be able to choose the person you wanted to date, and what was it like to get to know someone, even if you never got married. Working so close with Michael as my associate allowed me to know someone of the opposite sex and yet we were only good friends. In the old days, principally in Portugal, dating was a time to learn about each other and the couple always had a chaperone to make sure there was no kissing or touching Sometimes I wondered if dating was a lot like the relationship Michael and I had but in an old fashion way.

A month had gone by since I had heard from Mr. Robertson, the Lakewood architect. I called him on Friday. "Mr. Robertson, I don't mean to rush you but you promised to have the drawings ready last week and I have not heard from you."
"I have been very busy, but if you come by my office next Friday I'll have them ready for you."
On Friday I went to his office, but his secretary was surprised to see me. "Nope, he's not here. He must have forgotten to tell you that he's out until Monday. Give him a call then, okay?"

Summer of 1987

I called and left messages, but the architect was never available. I began to wonder if he was ever going to finish the project.
I decided to surprise him during my lunch break. His secretary was not in, but he was. When he opened the door he could barely stand. His breath was heavy with the scent of liquor as he apologized for the delay. He promised to have the drawings finished by the end of next week.

I returned to see him exactly seven days later. Mr. Robertson must have drawn the blueprints when he was intoxicated, because he drew the dancing room with a support column smack in the middle of the room. When I told him that having a beam in the middle of the dancing room was not going to be safe for the dancers, he had the gall to say, "Just ask the students to dance around it."

"That's funny," I chuckled trying not to show my apprehension. "How about if I pay you everything I owe you right now and you allow me to make just a few little changes to the drawing. All you have to do is sign it."

He agreed. I gave him his check and took the plans to the engineering department at the Howell Township.

Barbara's husband Larry worked for Bell Labs and he put a good word in for Ralph. Ralph went for an interview and they called him back to return for a second interview. Knowing someone who would give a recommendation was a dream for anyone looking for a job, but the truth is that any recommendation only goes so far if the person does not have the skills or aptitude needed for the job. In Ralph's case, he possessed an engineering mind and was very quick at learning.

I was not surprised when they hired him.

Autumn of 1987

I went to see Dr. Lakvinski for my yearly checkup, and after the exam he said, "Are you having any menopause symptoms?"

"I heard about menopause. What kind of symptoms should I have?"

"Hot flashes, not sleeping well, and mood swings."

"Sometimes I have trouble sleeping and wake up with a sore neck. Is that menopause?"

"It could very well be. You had a partial hysterectomy in

your twenties, so it's probably a good idea to get you started on estrogen."

"But I heard that estrogen can cause cancer."

"Pills may not be a good idea, but there's something new on the market. The estrogen comes in patches now, and you can put them on your abdomen so nobody sees them. The body then absorbs only the estrogen it needs from the patches, so you don't have to worry about taking in more than you need. It's perfectly safe."

It sounded good to me. Besides, I had heard that if a woman had low levels of estrogen she developed a mustache. I decided to follow his advice.

We got a call from the township; their board had approved the plans for building our new store. Upon paying their required fee, we could start construction.

One of the waitresses at the Kobe wanted me to tell a couple of regular patrons at the restaurant the tip they left for her was not enough.

"We have to share tips with the cook and that's a problem when we have a cheap customer," she said. I had never heard of waiters sharing their tips with the cook. It must be a Japanese custom. I told her I sympathized with her dilemma, but in America people left what they wanted as a tip and it was not proper to tell them they were being cheap.

Winter ending 1987

Michael had gone back to live with his mother and that was lucky for us because he once again had all the power tools at his disposal. We needed to extend the stage from wall to wall and Michael came to our rescue. The size of the stage made the theatre look impressive. What a set for *Biloxi Blues*!

Ralph was very happy working at Bell Labs and doing exactly what he loved as an engineer. He was working side by side with physicists and some of them were going as far as asking Ralph to proofread their books that were about to be published.

I Ought to Be in Pictures starring Katie Grau had the audience spellbound for the New Year's show. The patrons got their money's worth. For $100 each, there was a hibachi dinner, followed by our play, and then a DJ kept everybody dancing until midnight when champagne and more food were brought upstairs. Mr. Ounuma went all out with the midnight buffet. It was almost sinful to eat something so exquisitely presented. It was incredible. But I came to the conclusion that from then on, musicals would be the most conducive to a genuine, festive party feeling. I got a hug from Michael at midnight and then he was gone.

Winter of 1988

The new and improved Howell Music Center was starting to take shape. It was a bit bigger than I had imagined. About four times the size of the old one, it meant the cost of running it was going to be four times more. I had dealt with the electricians and carpenters, and when the bids came in as high as $60,000, I settled for the lowest bid and managed to get everything done for exactly what I had saved—$25,000.

Spring of 1988

I never had bags or dark circles under my eyes and then one day, there they were. I looked like a raccoon. Barbara recommended Dr. Skinton, a dermatologist in Freehold whom she said was very good.

The doctor came into the exam room and said, "Hi, Mrs.

Esagui. Are you on estrogen?"

"I use estrogen patches...how did you know that?" I admired his sixth sense.

"It's evident by looking at you," said the dermatologist. "Too much estrogen in your body can do that to the face. You obviously have enough estrogen in your body already and don't need any extra. Stop using the patches and it will go away." He left the room.

As soon as I got home I called Dr. Lakvinski's office. I told his nurse what happened and she said he would call me back. She called an hour later. "The doctor said if you don't like the patches, stop using them."

"It's not that I don't like them. They don't like me. I need to talk to him."

"I already gave you his message." She sounded annoyed.

"I believed him when he told me it was safe to use the patches. I had to pay another doctor $175 to find out that Dr. Lakvinski misinformed me. I want him to reimburse me for that and the cost of the estrogen patches."

"That will never happen." She hung up.

Except for the dermatologist who nailed my problem right then and there, I put Dr. Lakvinski on my list of lousy doctors.

Summer of 1988

The Foreigner was my pride and joy in set design. But I almost got myself killed when I tripped over the trapdoor in the stage floor. I was sweeping the stage and forgot all about it. We've never had a hole on stage until Michael made one just for that production. I fell backward off the stage. I literally did a backward summersault and landed on my feet still holding onto the broom. It was a most amazing experience, because it all happened as if in slow motion and I didn't even get hurt. I have never been able to do anything that even resembled gymnastics, and to fall the way I did, I had to have had an angel helping me out. I had no other explanation for not breaking my neck.

I believe we are all born with an angel on our shoulder. I was definitely born with one, because in spite of all the bad things that could have happened to me throughout my life, I have always escaped safely. Steve was living proof that angels did exist. He had an angel on his shoulder or he would have been killed in the Navy. Steve's angel was also by his side when Steve used to ride his motorcycle. His angel unquestionably took him home safely when he drank too much. Of course I wouldn't tell these things to Al because he would call me mad, or to Ralph because he also had an engineering mind. To them only proven facts counted. I didn't have facts; only feelings. It was the only thing that made any sense to me. I shared these thoughts with Michael. He told me he believed in angels and told me several stories proving that angels did exist.

Michael didn't come into the theatre during the week unless something technical needed to be addressed. He still ran the lights on weekends, but sometimes he asked me to take over the job. I had no problem with that since I had hired a stage manager. During the week, whenever Tracey had the time, she came to Kobe and sat with me to watch the rehearsals. We always had a great time chatting, and afterward we got together with the cast at the diner across the street. Life couldn't be better.

Autumn of 1988

The Indecent Act of Jeff Zelinski was a great show according to the critics and the audience. We did well financially. The word "indecent" brought in large crowds to see what the act was all about.

I am very proud of my set designs for each show. After *Ten Little Indians*, I began building mini-stages inside a shoebox. The directors loved seeing the set, way ahead of time, and make changes if needed.

I finally got up the courage to stop at a plastic surgeon's office in Lakewood. "I would like to have a little button nose and get rid of my chipmunk cheeks." I told Dr. Falkon.

He grabbed my face with one hand and turned it sideways. "Great nose job," he said. "When did you have it done?"

Couldn't he see as a skilled plastic surgeon that my nose was the real thing? Kind of embarrassed to even mention my nose again after such outburst of admiration I dared to say, "Can you lift up my cheeks?"

He picked up my face in his hands as if the rest of my body were not attached and said, "Oh yes, it's an easy procedure. I will be cutting here on the inside of your mouth from both sides to make a tuck, and while you're still under I will cut over here behind the ears and pull the skin up from both sides."

The word "cutting" was too much for me to endure. I paid $150 for the consultation and quickly got out of his office, glad to remain the way God had made me.

Winter ending 1988

Aunt Heydee was going to be eighty-nine years old in May, but she was still wearing super-duper high heels, refused to wear eyeglasses, and would not use a cane for support. She was in the hospital for the first time in her life. She had fallen and broken her hip and was having surgery. Mama assured me that Aunt Heydee would be home soon.

When Al and I were on vacation in Portugal a few years back, we saw Aunt Heydee walking down the street toward us. I asked Al to remain quiet and I bumped into her on purpose but she kept walking as if we were invisible. I turned back laughing, and grabbed her arm. "Aunt Heydee, it's Al and me, can't you see us?"

Squinting her eyes she said, "Sorry, but I broke my glasses."

I felt terrible and told her we would go shopping for new eyeglasses the next day. That same evening we were at my parents' home, and I was walking down the hallway to the bathroom when I noticed Aunt Heydee sitting in the living room watching television and wearing eyeglasses. When I walked up to her, she rapidly took the glasses off.

"Aunt Heydee you do have eyeglasses!"

"I only wear them when I am alone. I didn't want to tell you, but I refuse to wear glasses in public. Glasses are ugly."

"Aren't you taking a chance crossing the streets? As you know, pedestrians have no rights here. You're going to get hit by a car and kill yourself!"

"I keep my hand out when I cross the street so they think I can see them. They have to stop."

Mama called me at the music store with bad news. Aunt Heydee had died. Feeling like a knife had stabbed me in the stomach, my knees went weak and I bent over behind the counter crying. When Steve came up front, I ran to the bathroom so I could cry harder without bothering anyone.

Mama's letter explained everything. Aunt Heydee had been robbed in the street. When they pushed her in order to steal her purse, she had fallen and broken her hip. A few days later after the surgery they sent her home. That night, Mama and Papa heard Aunt Heydee crying in her bedroom.

Papa got up to see if Aunt Heydee needed anything, and she asked him if he could heat some water and put it into a hot water bottle so that she could use it against her sore tummy.

Papa brought her the hot water bottle and she said, "God

bless you, Joachim."

The next morning they found Aunt Heydee dead in bed. She was eighty-eight years old, but as Mama said, with Aunt Heydee's blonde hair loosely falling on her youthful face, she looked more like an angel. One of the men who came to carry her body out of the house said to Mama, "She is so beautiful. She looks like the Virgin."

Mama said, "Yes, she was."

Aunt Heydee, I'm going to miss you! Everything in life that was so beautiful to your eyes you no longer can see it, and it makes me sad, but I'm also glad that even without knowing the love of a man, you still enjoyed life to the fullest. You were always thankful for your freedom, as you told me so many times. Thank you Aunt Heydee for the spirituality you instilled in my heart and for all the good things you created around you to benefit everybody else. You will live forever in my heart and soul.

Aunt Heydee, you always told me the biggest mistake one can make is to keep feelings bottled up inside. You said all that does is cause stomach ulcers, if it doesn't kill you first.

I'm going to take your advice and continue to write my diary, I don't want to develop ulcers. I always feel better after I write but I'll continue to write in Portuguese for my own peace of mind. Thank you, Aunt Heydee, you taught me well and like you I'm free to be who I am. I love you.

ABOUT THE AUTHOR

 Dr. Veronica Esagui is a chiropractic physician and the internationally and critically acclaimed author of *The Scoliosis Self-Help Resource Book*. In addition to maintaining a successful practice in West Linn, Oregon, she hosts *The Author's Forum*, a television talk show featuring authors, publishers, editors, and others involved in the production of books. She is a member of The Northwest Association of Book Publishers, Pacific Northwest Literacy Alliance and the recipient of the NABP Member of the Year Award. She is the Chief Executive Officer of the Northwest Annual Book Festival, The Northwest Writers and Publishers Association, (NWPA) and Papyrus Press LLC, Publishing Company. She is an active member of the Northwest Independent Writers Association (NIWA).

Additional Works by Veronica Esagui

Veronica's Adventures Series:

Book I: *Journey of Innocence* (1944-1962)
Describes in the most candid manner the first eighteen years of Veronica's life growing up in Portugal, until a prearranged marriage with her cousin brings her to the USA in 1962.

Book III: *Awakening the Woman Within* (1988-1994)
Her children are now grown. Her ex-husband is still her friend, but her lovers don't fit the model of the romance novels she read as a young girl.

Book IV: *Angels Among Us* (1994-1996)
Experiencing the darkest days of her life, Veronica is thankful for the angels along her path, some of who were still exorcising their ghostly past as they strived to earn their wings.

Book V: *The Gift* (1996-2003)
A stranger follows Veronica into a supermarket and hands her a small pottery, insisting that the gift is meant only for her. Veronica's rich life experiences as a time traveler have finally taught her to recognize that her quest for happiness has finally been granted.

Mary Celeste – The Solved Mystery of a Ghost Ship
Historical fiction. Mary Celeste was an American Brigantine ship found adrift and deserted off the coast of Azores, on December 4, 1872. The vanishing of Captain Briggs, his wife, child and crew remained a ghostly mystery for over a century and a half until now. (Massachusetts mid 1800's)

The Scoliosis Self-Help Resource Book
(is available in English and Japanese.)
It includes the illustrated step-by-step approach to TESP (The

Esagui Scoliosis Protocol) a very specific group of exercises for the spine. With this book, a person with scoliosis will discover that they may have options other than drugs or surgery.

To learn more about the author and her books, visit her website: www.veronicaesagui.com

www.ingramcontent.com/pod-product-compliance
Lightning Source LLC
Chambersburg PA
CBHW071852290426
44110CB00013B/1111

9780982648490